I0796365

The "Glas House" 1933
Visionary Architecture in Vienna and Exile

The "Glas House" 1933
Visionary Architecture in Vienna and Exile

Edited by
Caroline Wohlgemuth
and Maximilian Eisenköck
with Photographs
by Stefan Oláh

PARK BOOKS

Contents

Caroline Wohlgemuth

Introduction

When Hans Glas built a villa at Wilbrandtgasse 37 in Pötzleinsdorf for the Jewish physician couple Anna and Philipp Rezek in the historically portentous year 1933, the building counted among Vienna's most visionary residences. The architect Hans Glas is nearly unknown today in Austria. Born into a Jewish family in Vienna in 1892, Glas studied architecture at that city's Technische Hochschule and was among Adolf Loos's first students, attending the legendary architect's private "Bauschule" along with Richard Neutra, Rudolf Michael Schindler, Felix Augenfeld, and Ernst Freud, a son of Sigmund Freud. In addition to designing houses in Vienna, Belgrade, Prague, and Olomouc, Glas also planned a housing complex for "Red Vienna" in the Leopoldstadt district that is today listed as a historic monument.

In the 1920s and 1930s, Vienna was reemerging as an inspiring cultural metropolis—including in the areas of architecture and furniture design. It was the age of Stefan Zweig, Franz Werfel, and Joseph Roth, whose novels were read around the globe. Alban Berg and Arnold Schoenberg wrote music history, Max Reinhardt's theater productions were internationally recognized, and the ideas of the Vienna Circle (Wiener Kreis) informed twentieth-century philosophy. Vienna was the home of renowned scientists of the time: Alfred Adler, the founder of Individual Psychology, lived there until 1937; Sigmund Freud and his daughter Anna until 1938. Ludwig Wittgenstein also had his official residence in Vienna until he emigrated to Great Britain in 1939. What made Vienna exceptional in this period were the connections between the individual arts and sciences—such as architecture and music, but also medicine, psychoanalysis, and psychology. The "Glas house," as the grandchildren of the Rezek family still refer to the villa, also tells of these connections.

The Villa Rezek is an important testimony to the Viennese Modernism of the interwar period. The influence of Adolf Loos and Josef Frank on its architecture is unmistakable, as is that of Ludwig Mies van der Rohe. The house represents the quintessence of modern architecture and the philosophy of domestic culture in 1930s Vienna. Not only guests and friends of the family but also many passersby on Wilbrandtgasse marveled at the visionary architecture of the villa, with its modern windows and expansive terraces offering breathtaking views across Vienna. In 1936, the Viennese art historian Max Eisler published an article in the English magazine *The Studio* about the modern terraced house. That same year, articles about the villa appeared in the architecture journals *Österreichische Kunst* and *profil* and even in the Dutch magazine *Het Landhuis*, placing the house in the international spotlight as well. Numerous interior and exterior photographs of the house taken by Franz Gino Mayer, a well-known Viennese photographer at the time, documented the structure.

Sadly, the Rezek family had only a few years to enjoy their modern villa. In spring 1938, Philipp Rezek was forced to flee from the Nazis—first to France and then on to the US. Anna Rezek, along with the couple's two daughters, Esther and Susanne—at the time fifteen and twelve years old, respectively—and her mother-in-law, escaped from Vienna via London to New York City, where they arrived in November 1938. Hans Glas was forced to flee as well: In summer 1938, he emigrated to Calcutta, where he was able to successfully continue his architectural career. The Villa Rezek was Aryanized in 1938.

In addition to all the human tragedies, forced emigrations like these also meant the abrupt end of the golden age of modern architecture in Vienna and the *Wiener Wohnkultur*. With very few exceptions, the exiled artists and architects did not return to Austria after World War II. The loss was irretrievable; it was a fissure in time followed by decades of silence, of repressing and forgetting the past. Anna, Philipp, Esther, and Susanne Rezek never moved back to Vienna, either; nor did Hans Glas. Only following restitution procedures that dragged out over more than four years was the Rezeks' house returned to them in 1953. But a life in Vienna after the Holocaust was out of the question for them, and they sold the villa.

In the course of the restoration of the house and the research work for this book, a photograph was unearthed leading us to the Rezeks' grandchildren, who today live in the US. In 2019, Maximilian Eisenköck discovered on a digital photo platform a picture of the villa taken in 2006, showing several people, including an older woman, standing in front of the house at Wilbrandtgasse 37. The photo is titled "Mom's house in Vienna" and led us to the grandchildren of the original owner. We contacted them in hopes of finding out more about the Villa Rezek, its history, and the fate of its occupants. This first contact was followed by numerous personal conversations and ultimately also visits to Vienna by the children of Esther and Susanne Rezek. The family was gracious enough to generously share with us its family history, the stories their grandparents told about Vienna, and personal photographs. And the background of the mysterious photo was now clarified as well: In 2006, Susanne Rezek had traveled to Vienna with her family, and they gathered in front of the villa on Wilbrandtgasse to see the house of their parents and grandparents. A neighbor approached them and offered his help. When he discovered that they were the family of the original owners of the house, he kissed Susanne Rezek's hand and said, "We are so sorry."

Houses such as the Villa Rezek and the life stories of their former occupants and their descendants shape the memory of a city. Since 2010, the Villa Rezek has been listed as a historic monument. The present book, *The "Glas House" 1933: Visionary Architecture in Vienna and Exile*, offers completely new perspectives on Vienna's architectural history and the story of the residents of the house who were driven out by the Nazis, and of the Loos student Hans Glas. Today, the ideas and design principles of the visionary architect Hans Glas are more relevant than ever. With over 130 historic and current photographs and plans and the distinctive imagery of the Vienna-based photographer Stefan Oláh, the story of the Villa Rezek is brought back to life and thus saved from oblivion.

Caroline Wohlgemuth

The "Glas House": A Modern Terraced House in Vienna

In September 1932, the Jewish physician couple Dr. Anna Rezek and Dr. Philipp Rezek acquired an undeveloped parcel of land from the City of Vienna between Wilbrandtgasse and Peter-Jordan-Straße in Pötzleinsdorf, in the district of Währing. The couple had two daughters, Esther and Susanne, who at the time were nine and six years old, respectively. To plan their new home, the Rezeks commissioned the Viennese architect Hans Glas (1892–1969), who had studied in the architecture school of the Technische Hochschule in Vienna and also attended the private Bauschule (architecture school) of Adolf Loos (1870–1933). For the family of four, Glas designed a single-family home set on a nearly 1,500-square-meter lot. On November 28, 1932, the building permit for the house was issued; in 1933, construction began, and in spring 1934, the young family moved into the four-level terraced house measuring some 550 square meters. The flat-roofed house with an extraordinary view across Vienna, expansive terraces facing south with modern, metal railings painted in white, and distinctive windows that in some cases could be retracted into the floor, counted among the city's most modern villas at that time. As the grandchildren of Anna and Philipp Rezek reported, family and friends referred to the visionary villa as the "Glas house."

"Light, air, and sun": a guiding principle from the medical field adopted for modern architecture

The idea of modern terraced houses was not completely new in Vienna at that time: Already twenty years before, in 1912–13, Adolf Loos had designed the Scheu House for the attorney Dr. Gustav Scheu and his wife, the author and publisher Helene Scheu, at Larochegasse 3, in the thirteenth district—one of the first modern terraced houses in Europe.[1]

In the direct vicinity of the Villa Rezek, at Wilbrandtgasse 3–11, Josef Frank (1885–1967), who then was working in a joint office with Oskar Strnad (1879–1935) and Oskar Wlach (1881–1963), planned a modern villa colony in 1913–14 with four small houses featuring terraces and flat roofs. "Here, all rooms open up via large French doors to the garden, and on the upper levels to large projecting terraces," is how Frank described the advantages of these modern, flat-roofed houses, which were among the first villas he designed in Vienna.[2] In the neighboring district of Döbling, on the Hohe Warte, Arnold Karplus (1877–

1 It was in this house that the daughter of the family, Elisabeth "Lisl" Scheu (1912–2011), later Elizabeth Scheu Close, grew up. In 1930, she began studying architecture at Vienna's Technische Hochschule. In 1932, Lisl Scheu emigrated to the US, completed a master's degree in architecture at MIT in Boston, and became one of America's first successful female architects.

9 The Villa Rezek
at Wilbrandtgasse 37
in Währing; design:
Hans Glas, 1932–33,
photographed ca. 1935.

The south-facing garden side of the Villa Rezek. Here, Hans Glas planned expansive windows and terraces; photographed ca. 1935.

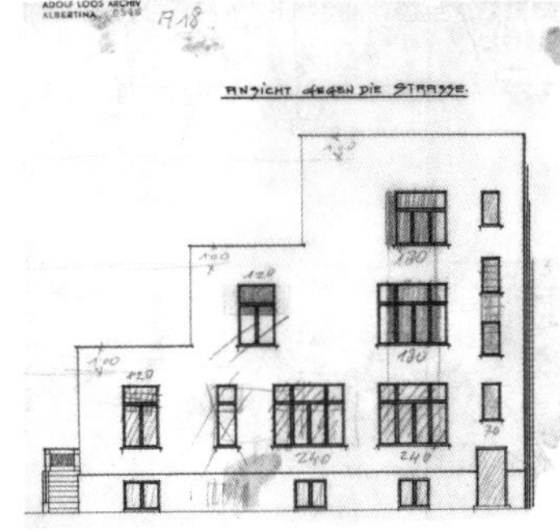

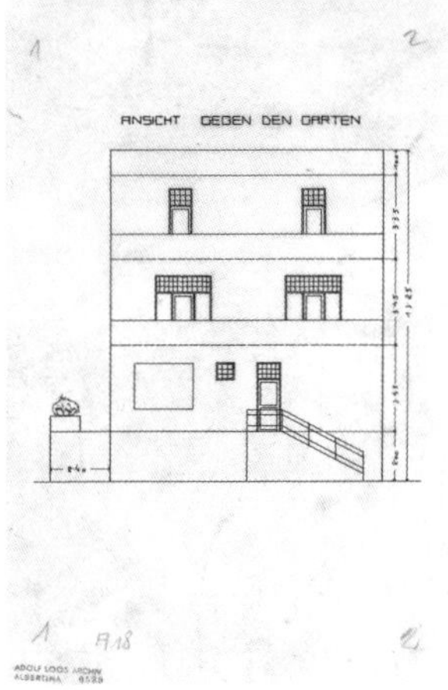

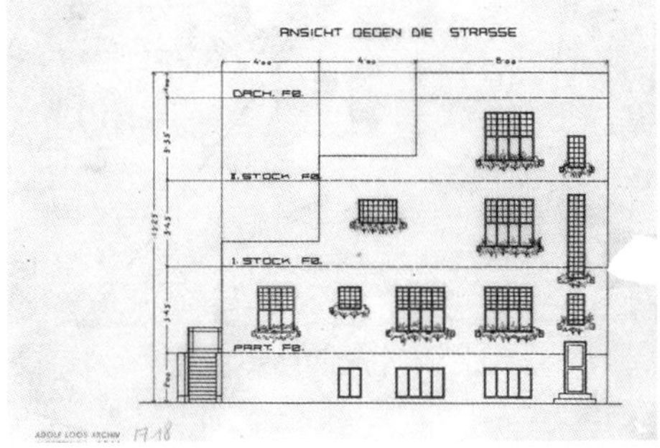

A–D
The Scheu House
at Larochegasse 3
in Hietzing; design:
Adolf Loos, 1912–13,
photographed ca. 1930.

1943) designed a modern, gleaming white terraced house in 1927–28 for the industrialists Otto and Agathe Krasny, with views over Vienna. Josef Frank and Oskar Wlach, who beginning in 1925 operated the home-furnishings shop Haus & Garten together, designed the interior of the Krasny House, the garden, and a tea pavilion.

For the textile businessman Hans Moller (1896–1962) and his wife, Anny Moller-Wottitz (1900–1945), a former Bauhaus student, Adolf Loos planned the Villa Moller at Starkfriedgasse 19, in Pötzleinsdorf, in 1927–28. Here, only some 330 meters away from the Villa Rezek, he continued to develop the idea of the modern terraced house that would provide the occupants with light, air, sun, and open spaces.

In 1929–30, Frank and Wlach were commissioned by the shoe-sole and rubber producer Julius Beer and his wife, Margarethe, to design an approxi-

2 Josef Frank, "Das neuzeitliche Landhaus" (1919), reprinted in Johannes Spalt and Hermann Czech (eds.), *Josef Frank 1885–1967*, exh. cat. (Hochschule für angewandte Kunst in Wien, 1981), 15–17. Frank planned several houses on Wilbrandtgasse in 1913 and 1914, of which two were realized; see also Maria Welzig's essay in this volume.

E–F
The Krasny House at Fürfanggasse 5 on the Hohe Warte in Döbling; design: Arnold Karplus 1927–28; interior furnishings, furniture, and landscape design: Josef Frank and Oskar Wlach for Haus & Garte photographed ca. 1930.

G
The Villa Moller at Starkfriedgasse 19 in Währing; design: Adolf Loos; construction management: Jacques Groag, 1927–28, photographed ca. 1930. View from the house's garden side toward Wilbrandtgasse, ca. 1930. The Villa Rezek had not yet been built at this time.

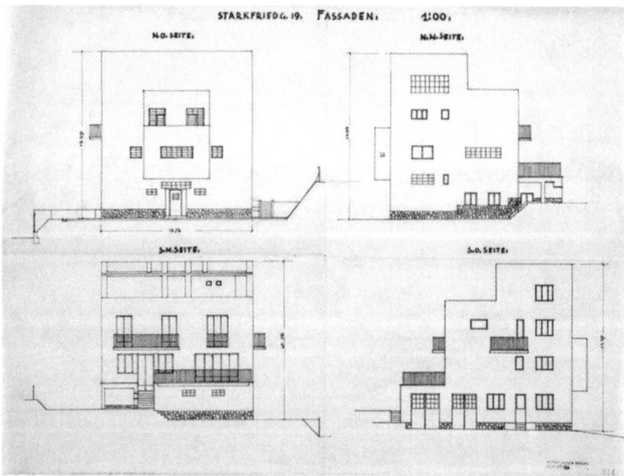

H
Plans for the Villa Moller by Adolf Loos, 1927–28.

I–J
The Villa Beer at Wenzgasse 12 in Hietzin design: Josef Frank and Oskar Wlach for Haus & Garten, 1929–30, photographed ca. 1930.

K
The Werkbundsiedlung housing project in Hietzing, built under the direction of Josef Frank, 1932.

L
House No. 47 of the Werkbundsiedlung at Woinovichgasse 9 in Hietzing; design: Richard Neutra, 1932.

mately 650-square-meter, cubic, four-level villa with a flat roof and spacious terraces at Wenzgasse 12, in the district of Hietzing.

An important expression of modern architecture in 1930s Vienna was the Werkbundsiedlung housing project in Hietzing, which was built under the direction of Josef Frank in 1932. The seventy small, flat-roofed houses with terraces and gardens, which were designed and completely furnished by architects invited by Frank, were to serve as examples of modern and healthy living and of housing developments of the future. This housing project stood for a diversity in dwelling forms with a social commitment and high level of comfort—an important local manifest of modern residential building in Vienna. The economist and philosopher Otto Neurath (1882–1945) wrote of the project that it should show visitors "how people in the near future should be able to live with the greatest happiness."[3] Even in the smallest of dwelling spaces, light, air, sun, and a garden were to provide the occupants with a healthier living atmosphere and a better quality of life.

The demand on the part of the clients and architects of the interwar period for better housing and living conditions was not only a response to the catastrophic circumstances that were endured by workers in major cities in the

3 Otto Neurath, "Die internationale Werkbundsiedlung als Ausstellung," *Die Form*, 1932, reprinted in Iris Meder (ed.), *Josef Frank. Eine Moderne der Unordnung* (Anton Prustet, 2008), 62.

nineteenth century but also to the massive housing shortage that Vienna faced after World War I. In Vienna, tuberculosis—particularly pulmonary tuberculosis, also known as the "Viennese sickness"—was widespread and one of the main causes of sickness and death in that period. Compared with other European cities, Vienna had an especially high rate of tuberculosis at the time. Poor hygienic conditions, cramped and dark apartments, and malnutrition promoted the spread of this dreaded disease. About half of all city hospital beds in those days were occupied by tuberculosis patients.

The guiding principle of modern architecture evolved from medical insights: Fresh air, daylight, and sunlight in living areas were to reduce the susceptibility to tuberculosis and significantly improve the general health of the population. Following the slogan "light, air, and sun," an extensive housing project was initiated in 1919 in so-called Red Vienna, which was ruled by the social democrats, that was aimed at a substantial improvement of the housing and living conditions of the people of the city. By 1934, 382 *Gemeindebauten* (city housing projects) with some 65,000 apartments had been built, planned by no fewer than 199 architects. From 1919 to 1922, most of these housing projects were designed by architects from the Vienna Municipal Building Office, but from 1922 to 1934, the City of Vienna also contracted with many freelance architects, among them Josef Frank, Oskar Wlach, Arnold Karplus, and Hans Glas. After World War I, Adolf Loos was active in nonprofit residential construction as the chief architect of the City of Vienna's housing office.[4]

Healing architecture: hospital buildings as a model for a healthier life

In his 1929 book *Terrassentyp* (Terrace type), the German architect Richard Döcker (1894–1968) also called for daylight, fresh air, and sun as essential for

M–N
The terraced hospital in Waiblingen, Germany; design: Richard Döcker, 1926–28.

4 See https://www.dasrotewien.at/seite/architekten-des-roten-wien--5 (accessed Aug. 7, 2025).

a better and healthier living situation and praised the model of a "terraced hospital" as the "truly healthy building complex."[5] The interior and exterior spaces of a building should flow seamlessly into each other, he wrote, with the living spaces extended into the outdoors. He presented as a model his own building project, the hospital in Waiblingen, Germany, which was constructed from 1926 to 1928 as a terraced structure. Via projecting terraces, all patients' rooms received ample sunlight and daylight and were optimally ventilated by means of large windows and terrace doors. These improved conditions with regard to light and air, maintained Döcker, resulted in quicker recovery times for the patients. For him, this type of construction was a universally valid principle not only for hospitals but for all kinds of buildings.[6] In Vienna, as well, the demand for light, air, and sun was considered in the planning of pulmonary clinics and tuberculosis pavilions for the city's hospitals. Dr. Julius Tandler (1869-1936), physician and beginning in 1920 Vienna city councilman for public welfare and health in Red Vienna, made available considerable financial means to combat tuberculosis.

Planned in 1929–30 by Fritz Judtmann (1899–1968) and Egon Riss (1901–1964), the Lainz tuberculosis pavilion, an elongated structure on the grounds of the Lainz Hospital in the thirteenth district featuring expansive south-facing windows, was a model building for social-democratic health-oriented architecture.[7]

The connection between modern architecture and medicine in the Villa Rezek

The link between modern architecture and medicine is apparent in the Villa Rezek as well: Hans Glas planned the house on Wilbrandtgasse for Anna and Philipp Rezek, two physicians who had studied at the University of Vienna Medical School. The clients' academic training and occupation had a significant influence on what the young family of four desired in a home.[8] Philipp Rezek was an internist and tuberculosis specialist. Hans Glas's elder brother, Richard Glas (1890–1961), was a physician as well: a urologist, he worked as an assistant to Julius Tandler.[9] For the Rezeks, Glas planned a modern house with a stepped profile in a green setting, with spacious flat roofs that could be used as terraces. On a rectangular building area of 15.4 by 13.7 meters, Glas planned four levels on top of each other, with the two top levels recessed on the south and west sides. While the façade facing Wilbrandtgasse has a smooth and reserved feeling, the house's south side opens up toward Peter-Jordan-Straße with ex-

5 Richard Döcker, *Terrassentyp, Krankenhaus, Erholungsheim, Hotel, Bürohaus, Einfamilienhaus, Siedlungshaus, Miethaus und die Stadt* (Akademischer Verlag Fritz Wedekind & Co., 1929), 1f.

6 See ibid., 2.

7 See the essay by Maria Welzig in this volume.

8 See Ulrike Matzer, "Das beauftragende Ehepaar Philipp und Anna Rezek," in *Villa Rezek, Conservation Management Plan* (SIMB-Verlag, 2023), 30–37.

9 See Österreichische Nationalbibliothek (ed.), *Handbuch österreichischer Autorinnen und Autoren jüdischer Herkunft*, vol. 1 (De Gruyter, 2002), 420f.

The garden / south side
of the Villa Rezek,
photographed ca. 1935.

The terrace on the upper level of the Villa Rezek. Hans Glas utilized the "Patentschiebefenster System Nikolaus," which at the time was also often used in hospital construction; photographed ca. 1935.

pansive terraces and large windows to the garden. The window system used here was the "Patentschiebefenster System Nikolaus," a retracting type of window frequently utilized in hospital construction in Vienna. It was used in the tuberculosis pavilion in Lainz as well, but in that case, it was made of three parts that could be raised to allow the patients' beds to be wheeled directly out onto the sundecks.[10]

> "A good architect is also a good psychologist!"
> (Oskar Strnad)

Modern architecture and the philosophy of domestic living in Vienna was substantially influenced not only by medical insights concerning healthier and more hygienic living conditions but also by the teachings of Sigmund Freud (1856–1939). Freud's psychoanalysis and the Individual Psychology founded by Alfred Adler (1870–1937) were frequently discussed in the 1920s and 1930s. There was even a personal connection between Loos's students and Freud: Freud's youngest son, Ernst Freud (1892–1970), was himself an architect and during his studies at the Technische Hochschule attended Adolf Loos's private Bauschule as well, along with Hans Glas and Felix Augenfeld (1893–1984).[11] Around 1926, Augenfeld designed a unique desk chair for Sigmund Freud that was tailored to the sitting habits of the world-famous doctor. Augenfeld, together with Karl Hofmann (1890–1962), also renovated a country home in Lower Austria for Anna Freud (1895–1982), Sigmund Freud's youngest daughter.[12] In his writings, Oskar Strnad, who along with Josef Frank was among the pioneers of the "Neues Wiener Wohnen," stressed that he built houses for the soul—that houses, spaces, and furniture should be made for people:[13] "When the architect designs an apartment," wrote Strnad, "he creates an organic relationship among the things in the space and a conformity of these things with the soul of the people who are to live in this space."[14]

In his 1931 article "Raum und Bewusstsein" (Space and consciousness) about the modern architecture and interior furnishings of the Villa Beer, the German journalist Wilhelm Michel (1877–1942) wrote: "The caesura between the two tendencies was basically brought about by psychoanalysis. Not that interior designers expressly went to psychoanalysis school, but the very 'thought mood' that the new psychological investigations are based on . . . this thought mood also had an accordant effect on the modern design of living spaces."[15]

10 Michael Rainer, "Das Gebäude und sein Zustand," in ibid., 16–29.
11 See also Caroline Wohlgemuth's essay "Hans Glas – The (Un)forgotten Architect" in this volume.
12 See https://www.architektenlexikon.at/de/12.htm (accessed July 27, 2025).
13 See Max Eisler, *Oskar Strnad* (Gerlach und Wiedling, 1936), 11.
14 Oskar Strnad, "Mit Freude Wohnen, 1932," in *Neues Wohnen, Wiener Innenraumgestaltung 1918–1938*, exh. cat. (Austrian Museum of Applied Arts, 1980), 98.
15 Wilhelm Michel, "Raum und Bewusstsein," *Innendekoration* [Darmstadt], October 1931, 378.

The railings of the Villa Rezek's terraces are reminiscent of those of a ship; photographed ca. 1935.

Together with Albert Esch (1883–1954), at the time one of Austria's most renowned landscape architects, Hans Glas designed for Anna and Philipp Rezek a harmonious connection between the villa and the surrounding garden. Not only was the villa conceived as a terraced house; the garden was also laid out in terraces. To the south, the lot on Wilbrandtgasse slopes down steeply, falling some ten vertical meters to the edge of the property on Peter-Jordan-Straße. The main entrance to the Villa Rezek is located on Wilbrandtgasse, while Glas planned a garage on Peter-Jordan-Straße, equipped with a flat roof that could be used as a terrace, as well as a separate entrance to the house's garden. This also meant that the garage was out of sight of the house.

In the design of the Villa Rezek, the garden played just as important a role as the architecture itself—an aspect that was also emphasized in the contemporary discourse. In his 1931 work *Gärten von Albert Esch* (Gardens of Albert Esch), the Viennese author Karl Maria Grimme (1897–1983) urged that the modern house should "open itself not only to the entrance of light, air, and sun but also to the green area outside the house. . . . The new kind of construction is a natural kind of building, related to nature's creation," wrote Grimme in praise of Albert Esch's landscape design.[16]

Hans Glas provided the Villa Rezek with many details that are reminiscent of a ship. The house's south side, in particular, exhibits a Mediterranean flair: The projecting terraces, but above all the terraces' slender metal railings and the outside stairways, call to mind the hull and railings of a ship. Similarities to the Krasny House, which Arnold Karplus planned on the Hohe Warte in Döbling in 1927–28 in collaboration with Frank and Wlach and their home-furnishings shop Haus & Garten, are evident: The south-facing garden sides of both houses, the railings, and the terraces display nautical references. As Esch did with the

Q–R
The south-facing garden side of the Krasny House on the Hohe Warte displays nautical elements; photographed ca. 1930.

16 Karl Maria Grimme, *Gärten von Albert Esch* (Michael Winkler, 1931), 3.
17 Max Eisler, "Werkstätten 'Haus & Garten' in Wien," *Innendekoration*, November 1930, 406.

Villa Rezek, Josef Frank and Oskar Wlach designed the garden of the Krasny House as a terraced garden. "The garden behind the 'K. House on the Hohe Warte': The first step is a terrace, tightly encircled by the curve of a concrete balustrade; the second around the circular edge of a fountain of red granite, covered with the precise pattern of broad paving slabs of white Solenhofer stone, interspersed with strips of grass and flower stands; the third a grassy area with a tree- and rose-lined path and a pavilion in the corner," is how Max Eisler praised the garden design of the Krasny House. "This garden alone is sufficient to recognize what the ultimate objective is here."[17]

Nautical elements were common in the modern architecture of the 1920s and 1930s. Among the most impressive examples are the houses of the Irish designer Eileen Gray on the Côte d'Azur: E-1027, built at the end of the 1920s in Roquebrune-Cap-Martin, and *Tempe à Pailla*, built around 1933 above the French town of Menton. Particularly this transfer of nautical motifs to Pötzleinsdorf in Vienna shows to what degree the image of an ocean steamer had become a symbol for mobility, modernity, and an international sense of life.

In Hans Glas's Villa Rezek, these elements are an expression of an open and forward-looking way of living that transcended geographical borders to align itself with the avant-garde movements of the time. That Le Corbusier (1887–1965) devoted an entire chapter to ocean liners in his pivotal work *Vers une architecture* underscores again what symbolic and artistic significance this machine aesthetic had for the self-conception of modernism.[18] For Le Corbusier, steamships stood for progress, efficiency, and the combination of function and beauty—ideals that are recognizable in the Villa Rezek as well.

In a September 1927 interview titled "Vom neuen Stil," Josef Frank was asked how the "home of our time" should look—"like a sleeping car or a ship?" The architect's answer was: "No. Like a house."[19]

S
The *Tempe à Pailla* house in Menton on the Côte d'Azur; design: Eileen Gray, ca. 1933; photographed ca. 1935.

18 Le Corbusier, *Vers une architecture* (Les Editions G. Cres et Cie, 1923, chapter title: "Les yeux qui ne voient pas – Les paquebots," 73–88; English edition: *Towards a New Architecture*, trans. Frederick Etchells (J. Rodker, 1931), chapter title: "Eyes Which Do Not See: Liners," 85–103.

19 Interview with Josef Frank, "Vom neuen Stil" (1927), reprinted in Johannes Spalt and Hermann Czech (eds.), *Josef Frank 1885–1967*, exh. cat. (Hochschule für angewandte Kunst in Wien, 1981), 180.

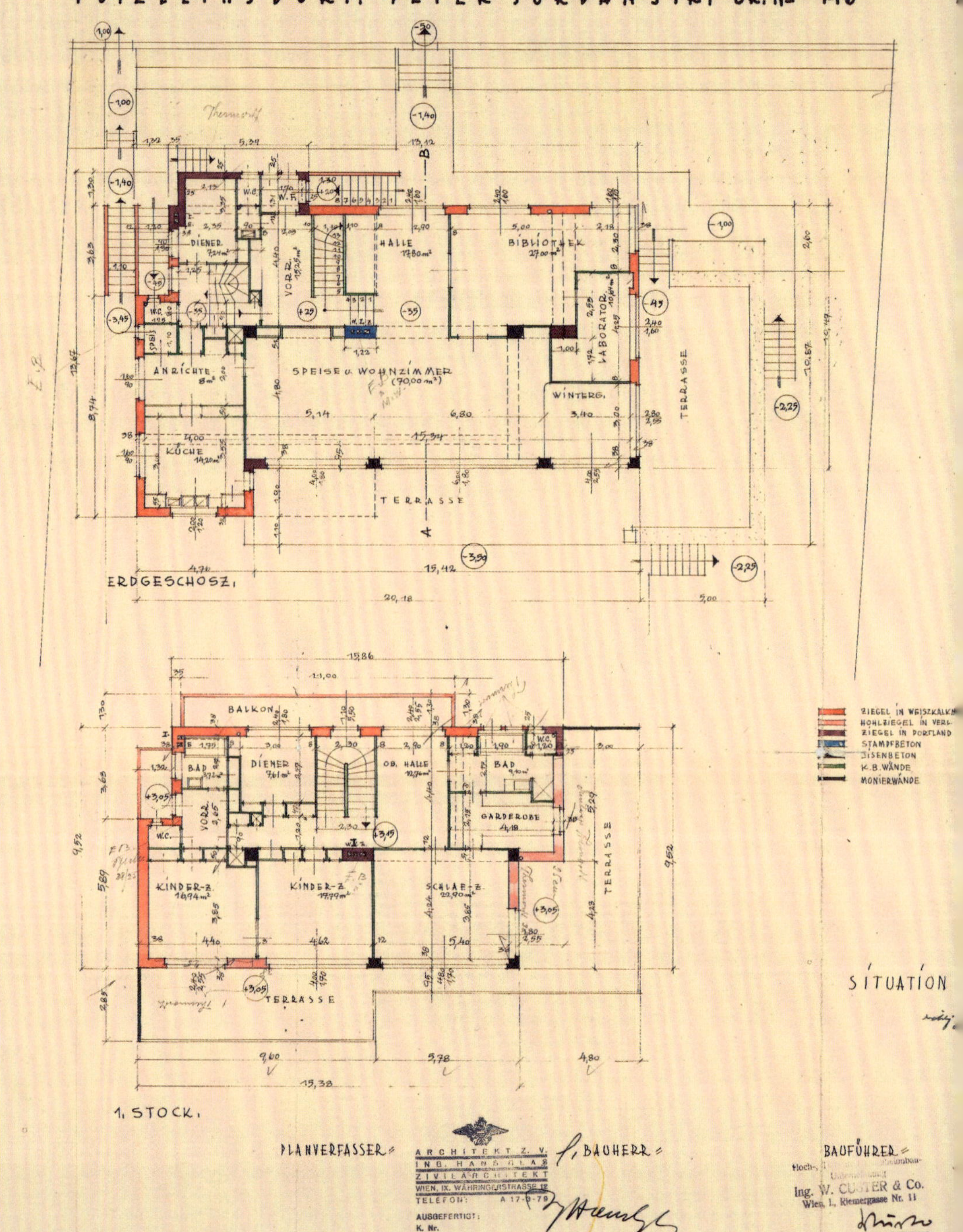

PLAN ZUR ERRICHTUNG EINES EINFAMILIENHAUS
PÖTZLEINSDORF. PETER JORDANSTR. OR.№ 146
DIENER
W.C.
VORZ.
HALLE
BIBLIOTHEK
LABORATOR.
ANRICHTE
SPEISE u. WOHNZIMMER (70,00 m²)
WINTERG.
KÜCHE
TERRASSE
ERDGESCHOSZ.
BALKON
BAD
DIENER
OB. HALLE
GARDEROBE
KINDER-Z.
KINDER-Z.
SCHLAF-Z.
TERRASSE
1. STOCK.
ZIEGEL IN WEISZKALK
HOHLZIEGEL IN VERL.
ZIEGEL IN PORTLAND
STAMPFBETON
EISENBETON
K.B. WÄNDE
MONIERWÄNDE
SITUATION
PLANVERFASSER:
ARCHITEKT Z. V.
ING. HANS GLAS
ZIVILARCHITEKT
WIEN, IX. WÄHRINGERSTRASSE
TELEFON: A 17-9-79
AUSGEFERTIGT:
K. Nr.
BAUHERR:
BAUFÜHRER:
Ing. W. CUSTER & Co.
Wien, I., Riemergasse Nr. 11

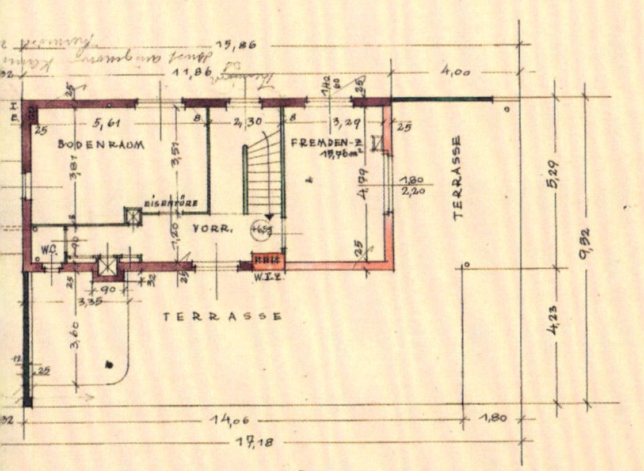

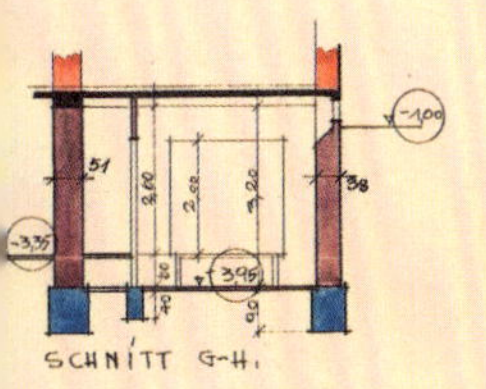

T–U
Plans for the Villa Rezek by Hans Glas, 1932–33.

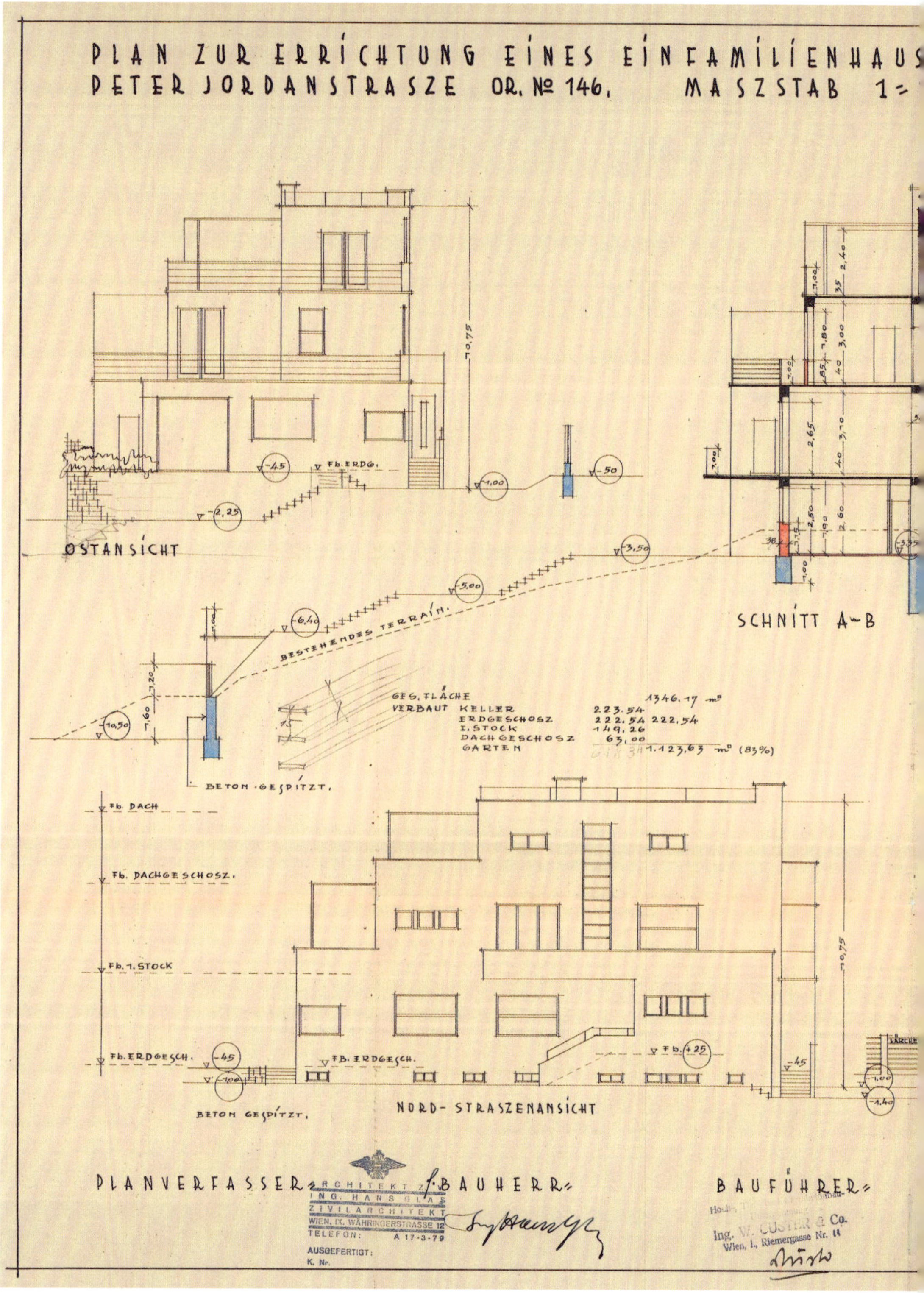

PLAN ZUR ERRICHTUNG EINES EINFAMILIENHAUS
PETER JORDANSTRASZE OR. № 146. MASZSTAB 1=

OSTANSICHT

SCHNITT A–B

BESTEHENDES TERRAIN

GES. FLÄCHE 1346.17 m²
VERBAUT KELLER 223.54
ERDGESCHOSZ 222.54 222.54
I. STOCK 149.26
DACHGESCHOSZ 63.00
GARTEN 1.123.63 m² (83%)

BETON GESPITZT.

Fb. DACH
Fb. DACHGESCHOSZ.
Fb. 1. STOCK
Fb. ERDGESCH.
FB. ERDGESCH.

BETON GESPITZT.

NORD-STRASZENANSICHT

PLANVERFASSER: ARCHITEKT Z. V. ING. HANS GLAS ZIVILARCHITEKT WIEN, IX. WÄHRINGERSTRASSE 12 TELEFON: A 17-3-79
AUSGEFERTIGT:
K. Nr.

f. BAUHERR:

BAUFÜHRER:

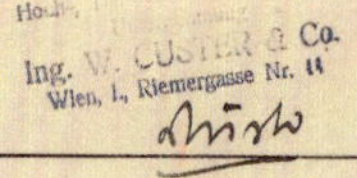

Z. № 1235 WIEN XVIII. KAT. GEM. PÖTZLEINSDORF.
PLAN № 2.

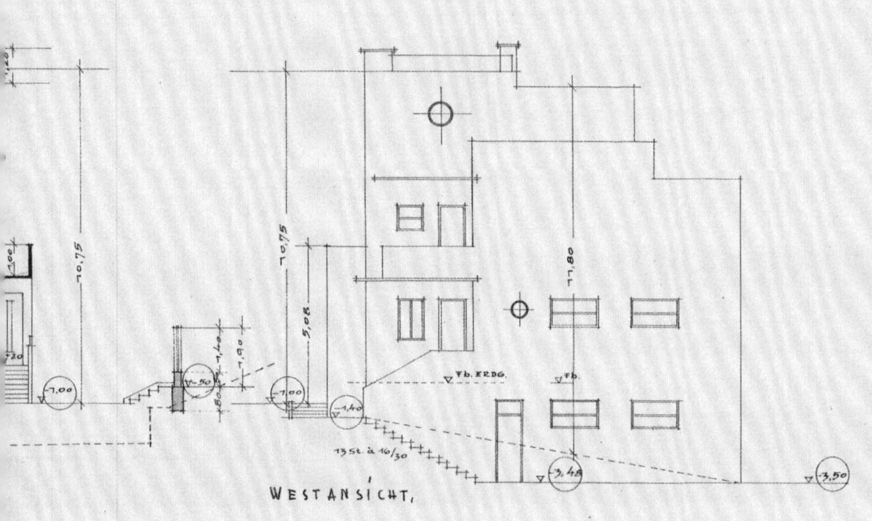

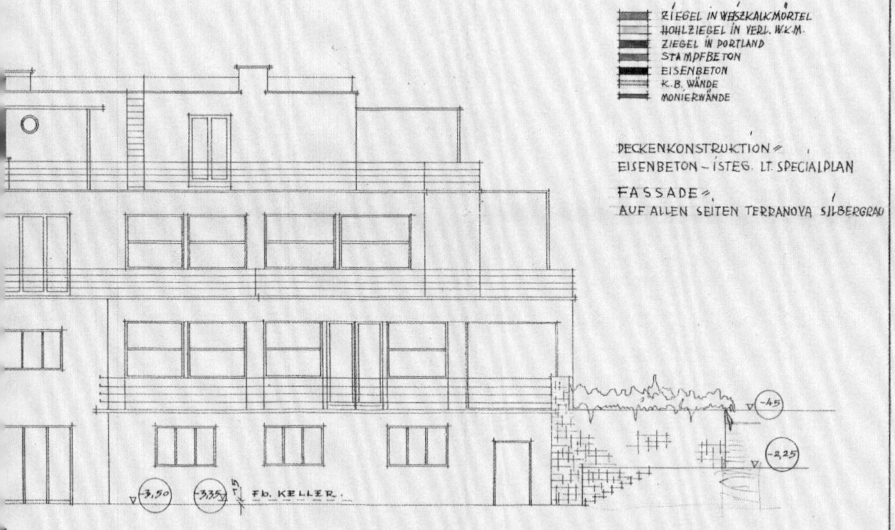

DANSICHT

PLANKOTE -50, IDENTISCH MIT PEGELKOTE 115,58.

Caroline Wohlgemuth

Albert Esch and the "Garten Dr. Rezek": The Melding of Architecture and Nature

House and garden as a harmonious entity

In 1933, Anna and Philipp Rezek commissioned one of Austria's best-known landscape architects of the time to plan the garden of their house, an approximately 1,500-square-meter expanse that sloped steeply from Wilbrandtgasse down to Peter-Jordan-Straße. Albert Esch (1883–1954), born in Eisgrub, Southern Moravia (today Lednice, Czech Republic), as the son of a director of court gardens for the Principality of Liechtenstein, studied in England, Belgium, and France before settling in Vienna and devoting himself to the planning of private gardens and parks.[1]

In the 1920s and 1930s, Esch designed gardens for houses planned by prominent Viennese architects like Josef Frank (1885–1967), Felix Augenfeld (1893–1984), and Karl Hofmann (1890–1962). In the Lower Austrian town of Ortmann, near Pernitz, Esch designed small gardens in 1920 for the houses in the workers' colony that Josef Frank had planned for the Bunzl & Biach company.[2] Bunzl & Biach was one of Austria's largest paper and felt producers; the client at the time was Hugo Bunzl (1883–1961), a first cousin of Anna Rezek.

Albert Esch also designed gardens in Belgrade, Brno, and Croatia. Moreover, in Vienna in the interwar period, he promoted qualified training for landscape architects. He taught at the horticulture school for girls, founded in 1912 by Yella Hertzka (1873–1948), at Kaasgraben 19 in Döbling. In addition to theoretical and practical training in gardening, fruit farming, and business economics, the students received a solid education in garden design that ranged from the planning of small private gardens to the design of parks, public squares, and gardens for children's homes and sanatoriums.[3]

In his 1931 book *Gärten von Albert Esch*, the Viennese author Karl Maria Grimme (1897–1983) wrote, "New attitudes toward life and new lifestyle habits have created the present-day house. It is obvious that they must influence the design of the garden as well."[4] In his book, Grimme poses the question of how the ideal modern garden should look, writing: "This is quite simple. One obtains the new garden by taking the considerations that are crucial for the construction of the new house and applying them to the design of the garden as well." Grimme continues: "The new garden thus evolves as the simplest and best

1 See Karl Maria Grimme, *Gärten von Albert Esch* (Michael Winkler, 1931), 7.

2 See Albert Esch and Albert Camillo Baumgartner, *Der Garten von heute. Sein Aufbau und seine Ausgestaltung* (Winkler-Verlag, 1933), 94. See also Caroline Wohlgemuth's essay "The Rezek Family: Expulsion and Flight from Vienna" in this volume.

3 See https://www.universaledition.com/News/Zum-75.-Todestag-von-Yella-Hertzka-Vielseitige-Netzwerkerin-Musikverlegerin-und-Kaempferin-fuer-Gleichberechtigung-Frieden-und-Freiheit/ (accessed Aug. 8, 2025).

4 Grimme, 1931, 3.

Gartenarchitekt
ALBERT ESCH

Ausgeführt in WIEN XII,
Längenfeldgasse Nr. 27

GÄRTEN
PARKS, SPORTANLAGEN
BERATUNG
ENTWURF
OBERLEITUNG
GARTENARCHITEKT
ALBERT ESCH
WIEN
XII, LÄNGENFELDG. 29
TELEPHON-NR. R-33-1-73

DRUCKSACHE

NEUE TELEPHON Nr.
R 35-2-49

A–B
Postcard depicting landscape architect Albert Esch, Vienna, ca. 1925.

satisfaction of those often-new requirements that we place on the garden, whereby the aesthetic demands placed on the result require the harmony of dimension ratios. . . . For it certainly makes no sense for the house to open itself not only to the entrance of light, air, and sun but also to the green area outside the house if this green area is merely a random result."[5] In his own book *Der Garten von heute. Sein Aufbau und seine Gestaltung,* Albert Esch also calls for a modern garden design: "Just as the 'house of today' and the modern apartment should open themselves completely to light, air, and sun, and just as the interior spaces are often colorfully and cozily furnished using the simplest means, the garden, based on the same concept, should also be designed in a colorful and sunny manner as an 'extended living space.'"[6]

Esch conceived the "Garten Dr. Rezek" as a direct continuation of the house, whose architecture was reflected in the garden design as well. On the property, which steeply sloped to the south, he laid out a garden over multiple levels. He planned the positions of trees, bushes, shrubs, and rose beds down

5 Ibid., 4.
6 Esch and Baumgartner, 1933, 4.

For the garden of the Villa Rezek, Albert Esch planned lush rose and shrub beds.

The garden of the Villa Rezek was laid out in terraces. Design: Albert Esch, 1933; photographed ca. 1935.

to the smallest detail, planting a total of 103 different trees, shrubs, and flower varieties in the garden.[7] For the balustrades between the terraces, Esch planted lush roses. He also planned a rose arch and a small pond.[8] In his writings about modern landscape architecture, Esch stressed that "A large part of life can take place in the out of doors, which is why the garden is treated like a living room in its planning as well. . . . The first precondition for the complete livability of the garden is its connection to the house, which is to be as close as possible. The entire plot of land is to be thought of as one whole living space, of which the house represents only one part. Large glass doors, which can be completely opened in summer, between the living room and terrace in front of the house create the ideal melding of both parts. . . . The house should open up from the living space directly to the garden."[9]

These thoughts were especially applicable to the garden that Esch designed for the Rezek family on Wilbrandtgasse: The villa and the surrounding garden represent a harmonious entity.

Johanna "Hanny" Strauß's Staudengärtnerei Windmühlhöhe

Very close to the Villa Rezek was the Staudengärtnerei Windmühlhöhe, a nursery run by Johanna "Hanny" Strauß (1890–1947), who lived with her family in the house at Wilbrandtgasse 11, planned by Josef Frank in 1913–14.[10] Hanny Strauß had founded the nursery in 1920 and operated it from her house and garden.

C
Albert Esch laid out a terraced garden for the Dos Santos House at Sternwartestraße 57 in Währing as well. Design: Karl Hofmann and Felix Augenfeld; landscape architecture: Albert Esch, 1929–30.

7 Albert Esch's original plans from 1933, titled "Garten Dr. Rezek, Wien 18," have been preserved in the Archive of Austrian Landscape Architecture at Vienna's BOKU University. Unfortunately, the legend to the detailed planting plan of the garden has not been preserved.

8 This pond was presumably never built.

9 Esch and Baumgartner, 1933, 10f.

10 Josef Frank worked at that time in a joint office with Oskar Strnad and Oskar Wlach. See the essay by Maria Welzig in this volume.

The self-taught horticulturalist had acquired her knowledge of shrub cultivation from many trips to shrub nurseries in the Netherlands and England.[11] She used her own garden for experimentation. Within only ten years, she enlarged the company grounds on Wilbrandtgasse from 500 to 15,000 square meters and increased her stock of plants from 2,000 to over 40,000, making hers one of the leading nurseries in Vienna.

The plants for the garden of the Krasny House on the Hohe Warte, designed by Josef Frank and Oskar Wlach, came from Strauß's shrub nursery. In 1932, she also supplied plants for the gardens of the houses planned by Oskar Strnad (1879–1935) and Josef Frank in the Werkbundsiedlung housing project in the thirteenth district. Moreover, Strauß was responsible for the garden design of the Austrian pavilion at the World Exhibition in Paris in 1937, for which she won numerous awards.[12]

In Vienna, Hanny Strauß was known for her colorful, unconventionally laid-out gardens with flowering shrub beds strongly reminiscent of English gardens.[13] The Rezek and Strauß families had a friendly relationship with each other, and it can thus be presumed that the plants in the garden of the Villa Rezek also came from the neighboring Staudengärtnerei Windmühlhöhe, but there is no confirmation of this.[14]

11 Ulrike Krippner, Sabine Plenk, and Valerie Ludescher, *Garten der Villa Beer. Anlagengeschichte und Empfehlungen für eine denkmalgerechte Sanierung* (BOKU University, Vienna, 2023), 17ff., https://boku.ac.at/fileadmin/data/H03000/H85000/H85200/TOPSTORY___Aktuelles/2025/Institutsprofil/Beer_Anlagengeschichte_BOKU_ILA_11-12-2023.pdf (accessed Aug. 8, 2025).

12 See *Österreichisches Biographisches Lexikon* (ÖBL), https://apis.acdh.oeaw.ac.at/person/30048 (accessed Aug. 8, 2025).

13 See Iris Meder (ed.), "Der Garten bestimmt den Innenraum," in Christoph Thun-Hohenstein, Hermann Czech, and Sebastian Hackenschmidt (eds.), *Josef Frank: Against Design*, exh. cat. (MAK Museum für angewandte Kunst Wien, 2015), 156–171.

14 The estate of the Rezek family contains a letter from Hanny Strauß to Philipp Rezek dated April 28, 1941. Both families lived in forced exile in the US. Philipp Rezek visited the Strauß family in New Jersey in 1941.

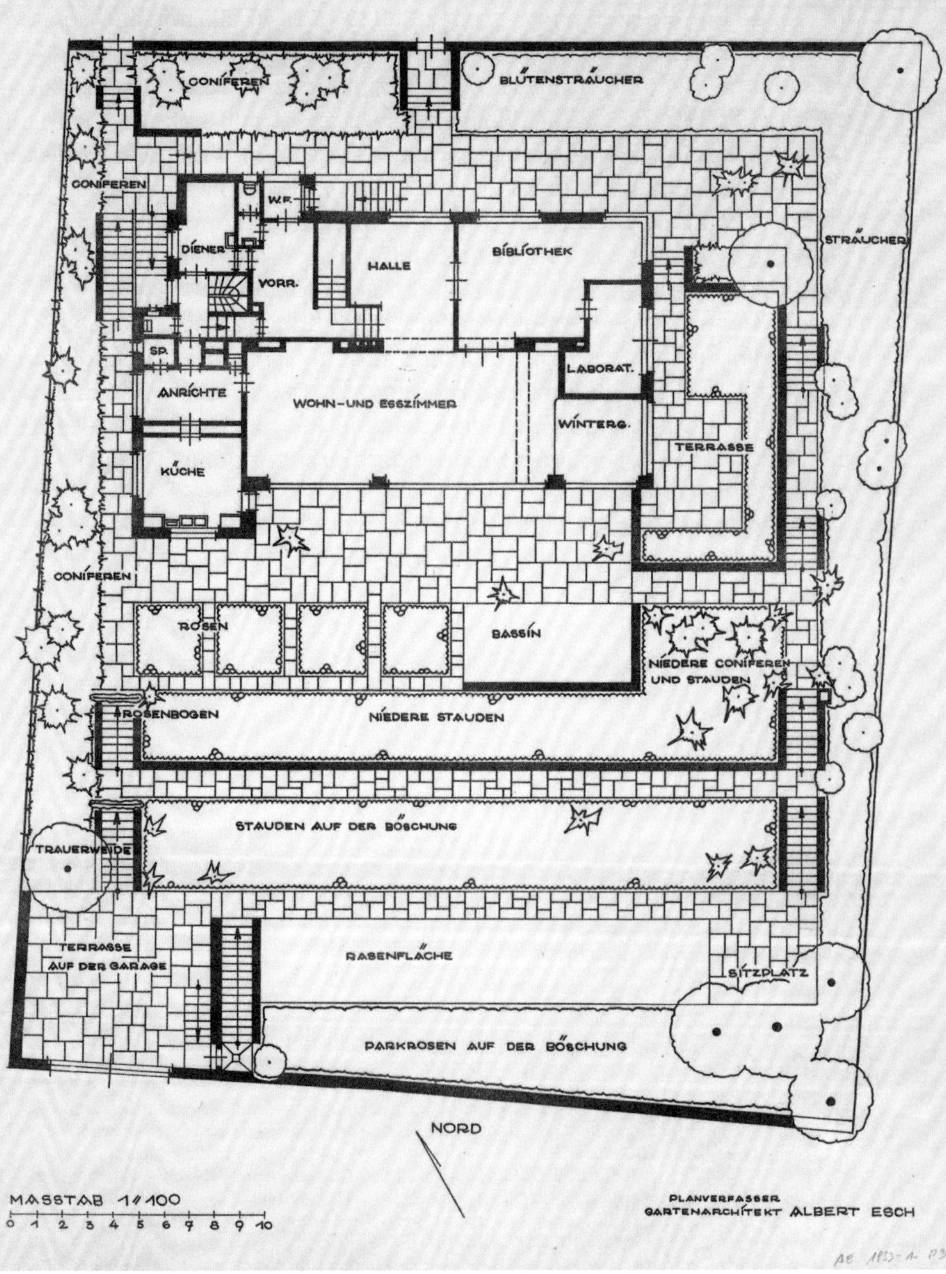

Master plan for the "Garten Dr. Rezek, Wien 18" by Albert Esch, 1933.

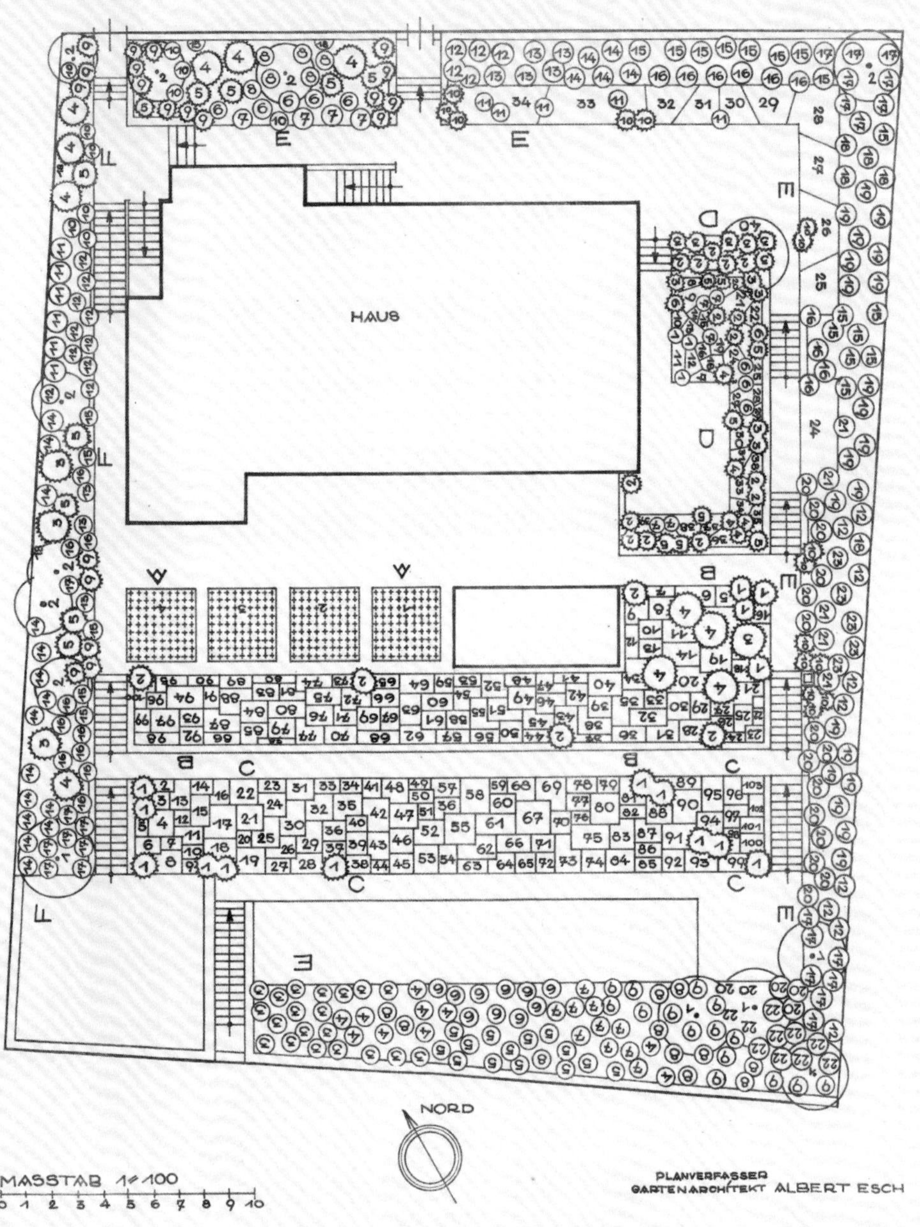

Detailed planting plan for the "Garten Dr. Rezek, Wien 18" by Albert Esch, 1933.

Caroline Wohlgemuth

A House from Tomorrow: Visionary Rooms, Interior Design, and Furniture

The collapse of the Habsburg Empire, the foundation of the Republic of Austria in 1918, and the widespread hardship suffered following World War I radically changed, among other things, the working conditions of architects and furniture designers in Vienna. Vienna became a large city in a small country with enormous artistic potential and academies for architecture and crafts that at the time were among the best and most modern in the world.[1]

While Josef Hoffmann (1870–1956) and Adolf Loos (1870–1933) designed luxe buildings, interiors, and furniture for Vienna's upper class before World War I, the architects of the interwar period were faced with completely new challenges. The housing situation in Vienna after 1918 was catastrophic. The primary concern at that time was to create affordable housing for the city's residents. In so-called Red Vienna, large-scale public housing programs were undertaken from 1919 to 1934. Following the slogan "light, air, and sun," a reform project began that was aimed at substantially improving people's living conditions. Hans Glas (1892–1969) was also involved in these City of Vienna housing projects.[2]

Architecture and furniture design

In the 1920s and 1930s, several generations of architects were active simultaneously. In addition to Josef Hoffmann and Loos, who both were forty-eight years old at the end of World War I, the younger generation became active as well, particularly Oskar Strnad (1879–1935), Josef Frank (1885–1967), Ernst Lichtblau (1883–1963), Walter Sobotka (1888–1972), Jacques Groag (1892–1962), Felix Augenfeld (1893–1984), and Otto Breuer (1897–1938). These men were joined by the country's first female architects, including Ella Briggs (1880–1977), Liane Zimbler (1892–1987), and Margarete Schütte-Lihotzky (1897–2000).

At that time, there was no specialized training yet for furniture design in Vienna; this was in most cases still the architects' domain. The Technische Hochschule,[3] the Arts and Crafts School,[4] and the Academy of Fine Arts (Akademie der bildenden Künste) trained furniture designers as well. Carl König (1841–1915) taught architecture for over four decades at the Technische Hochschule,

1 See Christian Witt-Dörring, *Wiener Innenraumgestaltung 1918–1938*, exh. cat. (Austrian Museum of Applied Arts, 1980), 27.

2 See Wolfgang Maderthaner: "Von der Zeit um 1860 bis zum Jahr 1945," in Peter Csendes and Ferdinand Opll (eds.), *Wien. Geschichte einer Stadt*, vol. 3: *Von 1790 bis zur Gegenwart* (Böhlau, 2006), 381f.

3 Founded in 1815 as the k. k. Polytechnisches Institut (Imperial and Royal Polytechnic Institute of Vienna), this institution became the Technische Hochschule in 1872. As of 1919, the school also officially admitted women as students. In 1975, it was renamed Technische Universität Wien, or simply TU Wien.

35 The Villa Rezek's 70-square-meter living space was used as a dining, living, and music room; design: Hans Glas, 1932–33; photographed ca. 1935.

leaving his mark on multiple generations of architects and furniture designers.[5] Otto Wagner (1841–1918) taught architecture at the Academy of Fine Arts until 1915. Josef Hoffmann held specialist architecture lectures at the Arts and Crafts School from 1898 to 1936 and also trained his students in interior design and furniture design. From 1909 onward, Oskar Strnad taught general theory of form at the Arts and Crafts School and as of 1914, alongside Josef Hoffmann, taught a specialized class for architecture. From 1919 to 1925, Josef Frank taught structural design at the Arts and Crafts School. Adolf Loos operated his own "Bauschule," a "building school," starting in 1912. Richard Neutra (1892–1970), Felix Augenfeld, Jacques Groag, Ernst Freud (1892–1970)—Sigmund Freud's son—Hans Glas, and Otto Breuer were among his first students.[6] They met at the Café Museum—whose interior Loos had designed—took strolls in Vienna and went on study trips together. Loos's school closed with the outbreak of World War I, but after the war, he resumed his teaching until moving to Paris in 1923.[7]

New furniture for a new age: the *Wiener Wohnkultur*

The students of Carl König, Josef Hoffmann, Oskar Strnad, Josef Frank, and Adolf Loos were deeply interested in furnishings and furniture design. Aside from their involvement in public housing projects, numerous architects were primarily active as furniture designers and interior designers, which led to a flourishing of interior furnishings and furniture design. The furnishings movement that developed in Vienna in the 1920s and 1930s became known as the *Wiener Wohnkultur* (Viennese domestic culture or dwelling culture) and *Neues Wiener Wohnen* (new Viennese living).[8] This new age demanded new furniture characterized by a diversity of forms and sophisticated details, by lightness and outstanding craftsmanship.[9]

4 Founded in 1867 as the k. k. Kunstgewerbeschule (Imperial and Royal Arts and Crafts School), this school was renamed the Hochschule für angewandte Kunst in 1945 and since 1999 bears the name Universität für angewandte Kunst—the University of Applied Arts Vienna. Women were allowed to study here as of 1868, but with restrictions and interruptions. Beginning in 1900, female students could enroll with no restrictions.

5 See Ursula Prokop, "Josef Frank und der kleine Kreis um Oskar Strnad und Viktor Lurje," in Christoph Thun-Hohenstein, Hermann Czech, and Sebastian Hackenschmidt (eds.), *Josef Frank: Against Design*, exh. cat. (MAK Museum für angewandte Kunst Wien, 2015), 48.

6 This according to the recollections of Gustav Schleicher, a former student of Adolf Loos. See Stefan Voglhofer, *Spurensuche Adolf Loos*, 2010, https://www.voglhofer.at/_rtf-voglhofer/CMS_fg4e735474df264_orig_1187.pdf (accessed May 1, 2024). See also Iris Meder, *Fragmente zu Leben und Werk des Architekten Otto Bauer: "Ihr Platz ist in der Welt,"* 2008, http://david.juden.at/2008/76/15_meder.htm (accessed May 1, 2024).

7 See Ruth Hanisch, "Die unsichtbare Raumkunst des Felix Augenfeld," in Matthias Boeckl (ed.), *Visionäre & Vertriebene. Österreichische Spuren in der modernen Architektur*, exh. cat. (Ernst & Sohn, 1995), 228, 327. See also Caroline Wohlgemuth's essay "Hans Glas – The (Un)forgotten Architect" in this volume.

8 See Erich Boltenstern, *Wiener Möbel in Lichtbildern und maßgeblichen Rissen* (Julius Hoffmann Verlag, 1935), VI; Marlene Ott-Wodni, *Josef Frank 1885–1967, Raumgestaltung und Möbeldesign* (Böhlau, 2015), 71.

9 See Ursula Prokop, *Zum jüdischen Erbe in der Wiener Architektur. Der Beitrag jüdischer ArchitektInnen am Wiener Baugeschehen 1868–1938* (Böhlau, 2016), 109; Eva B. Ottilinger (ed.), *Wohnen zwischen den Kriegen. Wiener Möbel 1914–1941* (Böhlau, 2009), 18.

A distinctive feature of the interior design and furniture that emerged in interwar Vienna is the interplay between old *and* new design ideas on the part of the architects—ideas that were made feasible on the one hand by highly specialized handicraft enterprises with decades of experience in furniture building, and on the other by a new lifestyle and a changed social order. In the area of interior and furniture design, the proponents of this new Viennese *Wohnkultur*—first and foremost Oskar Strnad, Josef Frank, Ernst Lichtblau, Felix Augenfeld, Karl Hofmann (1890–1962), Otto Breuer, and Liane Zimbler—followed similar principles: Furniture should fit the needs and preferences of the occupants, with old and new furniture combined in an unfussy manner. A piece of furniture should be comfortable, mobile, functional, light, and flexible. The interior design of that period displays a certain randomness and casualness in the positioning of furniture, something that Adolf Loos had long propagated.[10]

The Viennese art historian Max Eisler (1881–1937), the intellectual mentor of the *Wiener Wohnkultur*, referred to Oskar Strnad and Josef Frank as its pioneers. Strnad represented what for that time was an unconventional and modern approach to domestic culture. Spaces and furniture should be designed for people; they should come "from the soul" and "be harmonious in an inner, human sense."[11] "Strnad's furniture," wrote Eisler, "adheres to the original sense of the word [the German word for furniture is *Möbel*]: mobility. To remain moveable, it is made to be light: as thin as the structure permits and as small as its purposes allow. Not heavier, not thicker, and not larger than it needs to be to perform its assigned function. Proper proportions are retained: human proportions."[12] Josef Frank, as well, championed the use of graceful and mobile furniture, preferably made of wood, that could be placed freely and independently of each other in a room. His designs were characterized by lightness, transparency, and simple, organic forms.[13]

In 1925, following English models, Josef Frank and his former university classmate Oskar Wlach founded the firm Haus & Garten, which soon became the first name in furnishings and furniture design in Vienna. The first prominent commission for Haus & Garten was for the interior design, furnishings, garden landscaping, and the planning of a teahouse for the Krasny House on Fürfanggasse in the city's Döbling district, which had been built in 1927–28 for the industrialists Otto and Agathe Krasny by Arnold Karplus (1877–1943). This was quickly followed by another large-scale project: the planning of the Villa Beer in 1929–30 for the Viennese shoe-sole and rubber producer Julius Beer and his wife, Margarete, on Wenzgasse, in the Hietzing neighborhood.[14]

These two projects realized by Haus & Garten were portrayed in numerous architecture magazines; even Gio Ponti showed several rooms of the two villas in his architecture magazine *Domus*.[15] Clients came from far and near to patron-

10 See Witt-Dörring, 1980, 31.
11 Max Eisler, *Oskar Strnad* (Gerlach und Wiedling, 1936), 11f.
12 Ibid., 16f.
13 See Boeckl, 1995, 348; Ott-Wodni, 2015, 51–71.
14 See Ott-Wodni, 2015, 208.

A–B
A classic example of the *Wiener Wohnkultur*: the living space of the Krasr House on the Hohe War in Döbling; design: Arnold Karplus, 1927–28. The interior furnishings and furniture were designed by Josef Frank and Oskar Wlach for Ha & Garten; photographec ca. 1930.

C–D
The interior furnishings of the Villa Beer; design: Josef Frank and Oskar Wlach for Haus & Garten, Vienna, 1929–30.

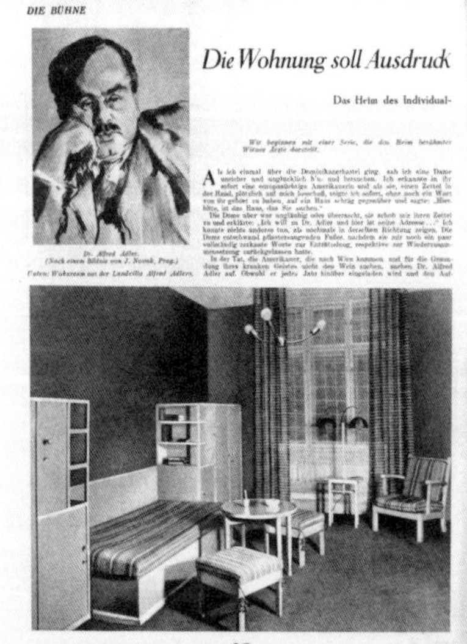

DIE BÜHNE

Die Wohnung soll Ausdruck

Das Heim des Individual-

30

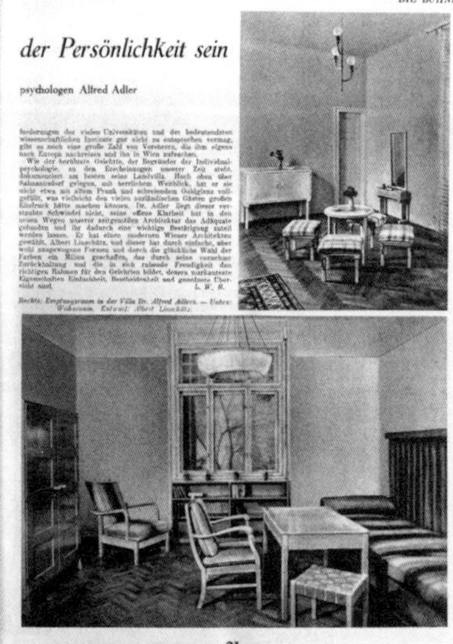

DIE BÜHNE

der Persönlichkeit sein

psychologen Alfred Adler

31

E
Albert Linschütz designe the interior furnishings and the furniture for the home of the renowned psychologist Dr. Alfred Adler; photographed for the magazine *Die Bühne*, 1929. The Villa Rezek wa furnished with similar furniture models created by Albert Linschütz.

ize Haus & Garten. According to the many enthusiastic voices, it was one of Europe's loveliest home-furnishing shops at the time.[16]

Just how decisive the influence of Josef Frank's interior-design philosophy was in interwar Vienna is demonstrated by the fact that numerous architects used not only their own designs for their projects but often furniture, lamps, and fabrics from Haus & Garten as well. The architectural team of Karl Hofmann and Felix Augenfeld, Fritz Groß (1895–1938), and Hans Glas were among those who made use of furnishings from this successful business to appoint the houses and apartments they planned. But it was not only the younger generation who frequently drew on the collections of Haus & Garten for their projects but also established architects like Oskar Strnad and Walter Sobotka.[17]

In the 1920s, Otto Breuer, a pupil of Adolf Loos who also attended the Bauhaus, and the architect Albert Linschütz (1900–1932), a graduate of Vienna's Technische Hochschule, operated a successful home-furnishings shop in Vienna as well.[18] Together, the two designed many interiors and light wooden furniture, with the emphasis on hygiene and comfort.[19] Near the end of the 1920s, Linschütz made a name for himself in Vienna as a bitter opponent of the construction of the city's first high-rise building, on Herrengasse, calling for protests against the planned structure. The young architect found a supporter in Josef Frank, who also had concerns with regard to the impact on the city's landscape.[20] Linschütz also designed the interior and furniture for the Salmannsdorf home of the renowned psychologist Alfred Adler, who lived there from 1929 onward, as well as for his country home.[21]

The new Viennese *Wohnkultur* was shaped by the close and creative collaboration between architects and highly specialized craftspeople and furniture manufacturers. In this regard, Vienna could look back on a long tradition of furniture-making. Gebrüder Thonet—founded in Vienna in 1849 by Michael Thonet, a pioneer of mass-produced furniture and modern furniture design—merged in 1923 with Mundus AG, a conglomeration of numerous small producers of bentwood furniture. The fusion proved successful. Under the direction of Leopold Pilzer, Thonet Mundus became the world's largest furniture manufacturer, with headquarters in Vienna, over twenty production plants, and more than 10,000 employees. In the following years, the company introduced several new models and was able to build on the past successes of Gebrüder Thonet.[22] In the interwar period, Viennese architects carried on their great fondness for bentwood furniture, often painted in vibrant colors. Josef Frank, a

15 See Claudia Cavallar and Sebastian Hackenschmidt, "Cover Versions," in Thun-Hohenstein, Czech, and Hackenschmidt, 2015, 231.
16 See Boeckl, 1995, 348; Ott-Wodni, 2015, 54.
17 See Ott-Wodni, 2015, 87.
18 See Witt-Dörring, 1980, 47–48.
19 See Otto Breuer, "Das redliche Bemühen," *Innendekoration*, 1927, 171.
20 See Isabel Termini and Peter Stuiber, "Wiens erstes Hochhaus, eine Stadterregung," http://www.hochhausherrengasse.at/wp-content/uploads/2016/12/Wien-Museum_Hochhaus-Herrengasse.pdf (accessed Apr. 20, 2024).
21 See https://magazin.wienmuseum.at/die-kakteenmode-der-zwischenkriegszeit (accessed Apr. 30, 2025).

vehement opponent of tubular steel furniture, also designed various bentwood models around 1930 for Thonet Mundus that were produced in series. He designed chairs and armchairs made from painted beech as well as stools and small tables.[23]

Bauhaus in the middle of Vienna

At the Bauhaus in the mid-1920s, a new material was discovered for the design and production of furniture: tubular steel. Thonet Mundus was one of the first furniture manufacturers in the world to respond to this new trend by launching production of tubular steel furniture. In the 1930s, with its execution of creative designs by Marcel Breuer, Le Corbusier, and Ludwig Mies van der Rohe, Thonet Mundus—in addition to its bentwood production—became the leading manufacturer of tubular steel furniture. Along with modern furniture designs using tubular steel, the form and silhouette of bentwood furniture changed as well.[24]

The influence of the Bauhaus was enormous: Many European architects who wanted to be seen as "modern" were now designing furniture made of tubular steel as well. In Vienna, too, there was a progressive group of young architects and designers at the time who experimented with tubular steel. Friedl Dicker (1898–1944) and Franz Singer (1896–1954), both of whom had studied at the Bauhaus, opened a joint studio in Vienna in 1926 that created not only innovative furnishings but also tubular steel furniture. As designers, they were both visionary: Together, they designed houses, apartments, shops, and a kindergarten, as well as a great deal of furniture, lamps, rugs, and fabrics. Bruno Pollak (1902–1975) worked for this studio as well and in 1927 designed a stacking tubular steel chair that was produced in small numbers by the Viennese iron-furniture company Josef & Leopold Quittner.[25] Bruno Pollak's chair was executed in nickel-plated tubular steel with a seat made either of woven cane, wooden slats, or fabric. A stacking chair with armrests, a stool, and a table designed by this successful furniture designer were also manufactured by Josef & Leopold Quittner.[26]

The zenith of the *Wiener Wohnkultur*

In 1932, under the direction of Josef Frank, the Werkbundsiedlung—a workers' association housing exhibition in Hietzing—was realized. The seventy completely

22 See Jiří Uhlír, "Thonet 1900–1938: Innovation und Krise," in Sebastian Hackenschmidt and Wolfgang Thillmann (eds.), *Bugholz, vielschichtig. Thonet und das moderne Möbeldesign* (Birkenhäuser, 2020), 48–63.
23 See Ott-Wodni, 2015, 106, 305–308.
24 See Ottilinger, 2009, 49.
25 See Katharina Hövelmann, *Bauhaus in Wien? Möbeldesign, Innenraumgestaltung und Architektur der Wiener Ateliergemeinschaft von Friedl Dicker und Franz Singer* (Brill, 2021) 195.
26 The tubular steel chair designed by Bruno Pollak in 1927 and originally made in Vienna was mass-produced in the 1930s under the name RP6 by the English furniture company Practical Equipment Ltd. (PEL) in cooperation with Accles & Pollock's Paddock Works in Oldbury and sold by the millions.

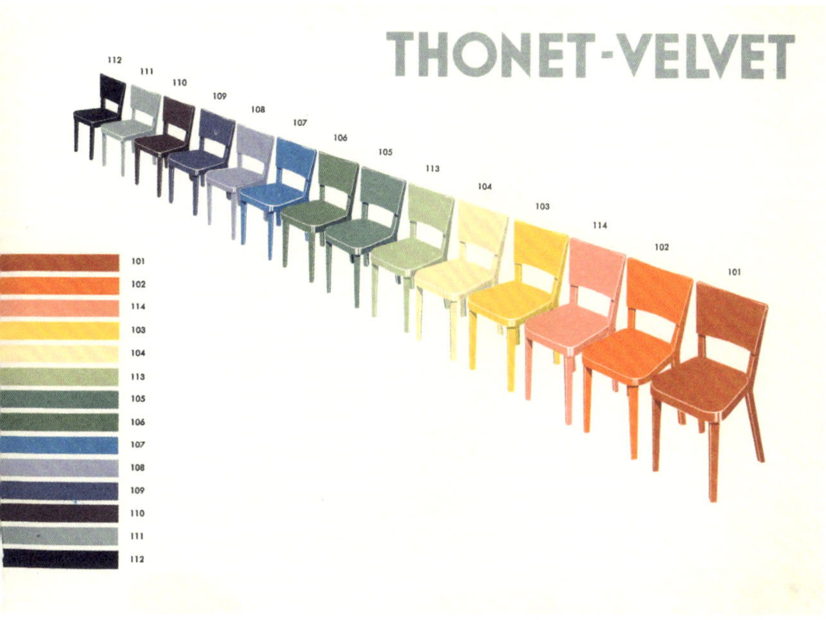

F
Design for a living room in a single-family home in Vienna; design: Albert Linschütz, 1928.

G
Thonet Mundus produced various colorfully painted bentwood models in the 1920s and 1930s; from a 1935 Thonet Mundus catalog.

furnished model homes—designed by architects such as Josef Hoffmann, Adolf Loos, Ernst Lichtblau, and Margarete Schütte-Lihotzky from Austria, André Lurçat from France, and Gerrit Rietveld from Holland—represented the zenith of Josef Frank's oeuvre as well as that of the *Wiener Wohnkultur*.[27] Unlike the Weißenhofsiedlung housing project in Stuttgart (1927), a number of the model homes in Hietzing were furnished in a homey and inviting manner very much in keeping with the philosophy of Josef Frank, with lightweight wooden furniture and colorfully upholstered furniture combined with cheerfully patterned draperies. By international standards, Frank was thus following a different path here, a personal, "typically Viennese" one.[28] Over 200 businesses were involved in Frank's project and provided their products for model furnishings—including modern household and kitchen appliances. Many of the houses featured furniture by Thonet Mundus and lamps by J. T. Kalmar; Haus & Garten alone completely furnished three model homes. It is notable that the leading figures of *Wiener Wohnkultur* were largely architects from Jewish families. To what extent the bond between the members of this group was the result of their training together at the Technische Hochschule, the Arts and Crafts School, or Adolf Loos's Bauschule, or of their common Jewish heritage is not clear. With their timeless, beautifully designed furniture and furnishings, the Jewish architects of this time created an identity of their own, in the middle of Vienna, in the form of

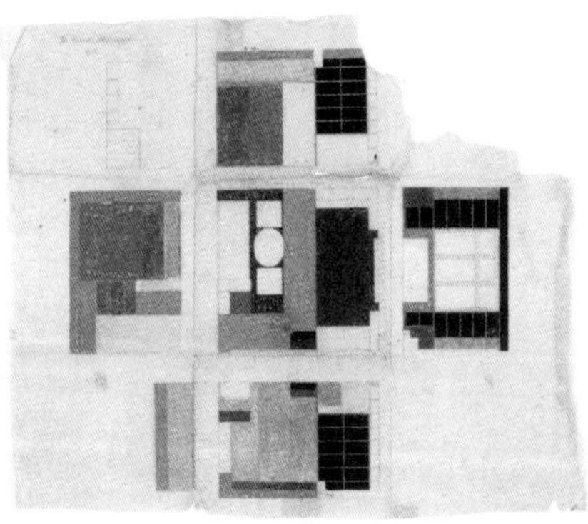

H
Sketch of the Reisner Apartment at Koschatgasse 110 in Währing, in the direct vicinity of Wilbrandtgasse; design: Friedl Dicker and Franz Singer, ca. 1930.

I
Multifunctional furniture in the Reisner Apartment; design: Friedl Dicker and Franz Singer, ca. 193

27 See Ott-Wodni, 2015, 104; Iris Meder (ed.), *Josef Frank. Eine Moderne der Unordnung* (Anton Prustet, 2008), 62.
28 Ott-Wodni, 2015, 107.

J
Interior furnishings of House No. 32 in the Werkbundsiedlung housing project in Hietzing; design: Oskar Wlach and Josef Frank for Haus & Garten, 1932.

K
Interior furnishings of House No. 12 in the Werkbundsiedlung in Hietzing; design: Josef Frank and Oskar Wlach for Haus & Garten, 1932.

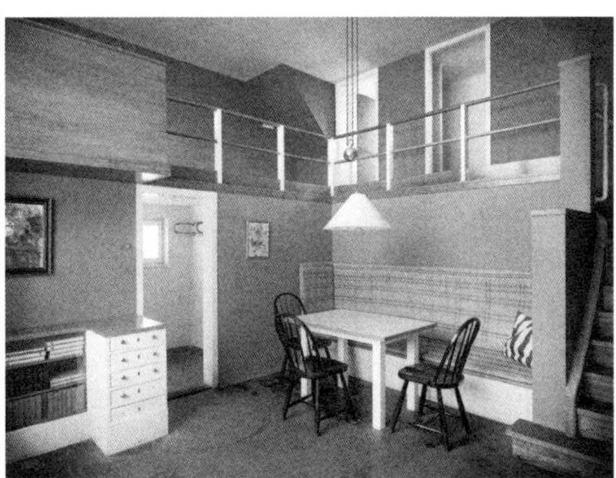

L
Interior furnishings of House No. 49 in the Werkbundsiedlung in Hietzing; design: Adolf Loos and Heinrich Kulka, 1932.

M
The children's room in House No. 46 in the Werkbundsiedlung in Hietzing, furnished with chairs by Thonet Mundus; design: Jacques Groag, 1932.

places of refuge and a feeling of hominess. Particularly in those politically unstable times, they were certainly concerned with creating spaces to which people could withdraw to find peace, serenity, and a bit of personal happiness.[29]

Hans Glas, Josef Frank, and the Tedesko, Bunzl, and Rezek families—a connection?

Hans Glas was born on September 11, 1892, into a Jewish family in Vienna. From 1911 to 1919, he studied at the Technische Hochschule[30] and at the same time attended Adolf Loos's private Bauschule.

When Anna and Philipp Rezek commissioned Hans Glas to plan their villa on Wilbrandtgasse, including the interior, the architect was forty years old. It is not entirely clear why these two wealthy physicians chose this little-known architect and not, for example, Josef Frank with his Haus & Garten. Frank, together with Oskar Strnad and Oskar Wlach, had in 1913 and 1914 already planned several houses on Wilbrandtgasse, including the Scholl House and the Strauß House.[31]

In addition to this spatial proximity, there were also family ties between Josef Frank and the Rezeks. Frank was not only close friends with the Bunzl and Tedesko families, and thus with the Rezeks as well; there were also family ties between them: In 1910, Josef Frank's younger sister Hedwig "Hexi" (1887–1966) had married Karl Tedesko (1874–1945), then the manager of Bunzl & Biach, one of the largest paper and felt companies in the Habsburg Empire, of which the Bunzl family was the owner. Karl Tedesko's parents were Salomon Tedesko (1845–1931) and Klara Tedesko (1854–1915), née Bunzl. Klara, Hedwig's mother-in-law, had five brothers, one of whom was Ludwig Lajos Bunzl, the father of Anna Rezek.[32]

The Tedeskos and Bunzls were among Josef Frank's first clients and later some of the most important customers of Haus & Garten. Even before the founding of the company, Frank had planned houses and apartments and designed furniture for both families. Planning the interior of Hedwig and Karl Tedesko's apartment on Untere Viaduktgasse in Vienna's third district in 1910 was Josef Frank's first commission in Vienna in the area of interior design and furniture design. In 1919, Hugo Bunzl (1883–1961), a first cousin of Anna Rezek and at the time the manager of the Bunzl & Biach company, commissioned Frank to build a country home for him in the Lower Austrian village of Ortmann, near Pernitz.

29 See Elana Shapira, "Sinn und Sinnlichkeit. Der Architekt Josef Frank und seine jüdische Klientel," in Thun-Hohenstein, Czech, and Hackenschmidt, 2015, 60–70.

30 Main catalog of fully enrolled students in 1911/12, entry 29 (Hans Glas), Archiv der Technischen Universität Wien (TUWA). Following an interruption due to the war, in 1918, Hans Glas again registered at the Technische Hochschule, now as an audit student.

31 See Josef Frank, "Das neuzeitliche Landhaus" (1919), reprinted in Johannes Spalt and Hermann Czech (eds.), *Josef Frank 1885–1967*, exh. cat. (Hochschule für angewandte Kunst in Wien, 1981), 15–17. Frank planned several houses on Wilbrandtgasse in 1913 and 1914, but not all were built. See also Maria Welzig's essay in this volume.

32 From the family archive and according to information provided by Prof. Peter Weinberger and his wife, Kitty Bunzl.

Frank designed not only the summer house there for Hugo and his wife, Olga Bunzl, but also a workers' housing estate and a day-care center for children.

At the end of 1933, Josef Frank and his wife emigrated to Stockholm. The previous year, he had overseen the planning of the Werkbundsiedlung—the culmination of his career. At the same time, Hans Glas was already working on the Villa Rezek. In 1935, Hugo Bunzl commissioned Haus & Garten to plan the Villa Bunzl, on Chimanistraße in Döbling.[33]

"Gaiety, cheery modernity, and affectionate room culture": the furnishings of the Villa Rezek

The design principles of Adolf Loos and Josef Frank as well as the ideas of the leading figures of the Viennese *Wohnkultur* are quite evident in the Villa Rezek. The house looks like the quintessence of modern architecture and the philosophy of domestic culture in 1930s Vienna.

In 1936, Max Eisler published an article in the English magazine *The Studio* about the modern villa, praising the furnishings of the visionary house as an

N–P
The Bunzl House at Chimanistraße 18 in Döbling; design: Josef Frank and Oskar Wlach for Haus & Garten, 1936.

33 See Ott-Wodni, 2015, 27–32, 181–182.

outstanding example of good taste in Vienna.[34] That same year, an article appeared in the journal *Österreichische Kunst* with the title "Eine neue Villa von Arch. Z.V.-Ing. Hans Glas," in which the "gaiety, cheery modernity, and affectionate room culture" of the house's interior was emphasized.[35]

Both articles showed photographs of the individual rooms and their furnishings, taken by the Viennese photographer Franz Gino Mayer (1891–1971) around 1935. Based on these some twenty pictures of the house's interior and exterior, and the accounts and private photographs supplied by Anna and Philipp Rezek's grandchildren, it is possible to reconstruct in detail the Villa Rezek's original interior design and furniture.[36]

How does the house's unadorned, modern façade fit with the "affectionate room culture" of its interior? The answer is perhaps given by Josef Frank himself: "The outward form of the houses we strive for today should again establish its uniformity in the simplest and most concise manner. A uniformity of this kind in the interior is not even desirable, and a conformity with the exterior makes it doubly senseless."[37] For the Villa Rezek, these words could scarcely be more fitting. "The conditions for the façade and for the interior are completely different and have nothing to do with each other," Frank continues. "The exterior and the interior as a unified whole is an idea that belongs to the past. . . . The most comfortable furnishings have always been the ones that the inhabitant has assembled himself over time and display no trace of deliberateness."[38]

Another design principle that Hans Glas took up in planning the Villa Rezek had already been applied by Josef Frank and Oskar Wlach in the Krasny House and the Villa Beer: the indivisible connection between inside and outside. The garden was to be perceived as an immediate, fluent continuation of the house.

"Modernism is that which gives us complete freedom" (Josef Frank)

Hans Glas designed the center of the house as an open, multifunctional living space characterized by spaciousness and abundance of light. Through the use of floor-length, woven draperies in natural tones, the various living areas—the open staircase, the vestibule, the library, and the large dining/living room—could be connected or completely separated from each other. Adolf Loos himself had already planned for his own apartment (1903) and for the Steiner House in Hietzing (1910) a large living space that could be divided into sitting, eating, and music areas through woven, room-length curtains. Oskar Strnad's Villa Wassermann in Döbling (1913–14) and Frank and Wlach's Krasny House (1927–

34 See Max Eisler, "A Viennese house in the district of cottage, architect Hans Glas," *The Studio*, 11, 1936, 45.
35 "Eine neue Villa von Arch. Z.-V.-Ing. Hans Glas," in *Österreichische Kunst*, 7, 1936, no. 2, 1936, 13.
36 The villa's original furnishings have not been preserved; in 2024–2025, they were reconstructed based on historic photographs.
37 Josef Frank, "Die Moderne Einrichtung des Wohnhauses" (1927), reprinted in Spalt and Czech, 84.
38 Josef Frank, "Fassade und Interieur" (1928), reprinted in ibid., 25–27.

28) also feature large, open living spaces that could be divided into smaller areas through the use of floor-length curtains of woven linen or wool. This way of dividing a space became one of the most popular interior design devices in interwar Vienna.[39]

The needs of the occupants were in any case the primary focus for Hans Glas in his design and furnishing of the villa's rooms. "In order to make the space as independent as possible, all of its walls and ceilings are white, as any color can then be used in such a room. The selection of the required objects in a room is not the business of the architect but that of the inhabitant, who in order to create a comfortable dwelling will use nothing he has no personal connection with," wrote Josef Frank in "Die Moderne Einrichtung des Wohnhauses,"[40] and Hans Glas applied this principle as well in planning the Villa Rezek. "The modern person, who is increasingly strained and exhausted by his occupation, needs a dwelling that is much more comfortable and cozier than in former times," wrote Frank. "Modernism is that which gives us complete freedom."[41]

Loosely following Josef Frank's unconventional principle "One can use everything that one can use,"[42] the furniture of the Villa Rezek came from a wide variety of sources. It almost seems that at that time, furnishing happened by chance. Anna and Philipp Rezek had married in 1921 in the Vienna synagogue and until they moved into the villa in 1934, they lived in the building belonging to Anna's parents, Ludwig and Julia Bunzl, at Grillparzerstraße 14 in Vienna's first district.

As photographs show, the young couple's apartment was decorated and furnished by Albert Linschütz, a graduate of the Technische Hochschule who was then just starting his career. Bearing the note "Wohnung Dr. Rezek," photographs of the interior furnishings and furniture appeared in 1929 in the German architecture magazine *Moderne Bauformen*.[43] The Rezek family apparently took numerous items with them when they moved into their modern villa, including several walnut armchairs and stools, a mahogany sideboard, wingback chairs, the parents' bed, a chaise longue, lamps, and the colorful, striped curtains of "English cretonne."

Entryway and open staircase

Hans Glas designed the house's foyer as a bright, colorful space with a cloakroom and two large mirrors that reflected the open staircase. The flooring was beige and brown linoleum with a rectangular pattern. In the cloakroom hung a

39 See Witt-Dörring, 1980, 32ff.
40 Josef Frank, "Die Moderne Einrichtung des Wohnhauses," reprinted in Spalt and Czech, 87.
41 Josef Frank, "Die Großstadtwohnung unserer Zeit" (1927), reprinted in Spalt and Czech, 33.
42 Josef Frank, "Der Gschnas fürs G'müt und der Gschnas als Problem" (1927), reprinted in Tano Bojankin, Christopher Long, and Iris Meder (eds.), *Josef Frank. Schriften*, vol. 1 (Löcker, 2012), 298.
43 *Moderne Bauformen*, 28, 1929, no. 10, 412–415.

curtain made of a robust cotton-linen blend with a striped pattern in bright red, yellow, and cream.[44] The oak stairs were covered with a red runner.

The open stairwell, which led both to the house's upper levels and to the afore-mentioned vestibule, also served as a waiting room for the patients of the husband-and-wife physicians. Next to the stairs, a bench seat, a display case, and a cherry bookcase were built into the wall. A wooden table, an armchair by Alfred Linschütz with a colorfully patterned linen cover, and a hand-woven rug gave this area a homey atmosphere. The vestibule led into the Rezeks' library and to the dining/living room, with its breathtaking view of the garden.

Open living space

The 70-square-meter living space was used as a dining, living, and music room and could be divided into smaller areas through the use of room-length curtains. The window curtains were made of delicate white cotton batiste, which let ample daylight into the room even when drawn. Beneath the windows of the room were distinctive curved radiator covers of macassar ebony, which could also be used as sideboards. On the left side of the room was an integrated, satin-covered settee with a glass-front cabinet and bar; in front of it stood a wingback chair from Haus & Garten, two round side tables from Thonet Mundus, and two walnut stools designed by Albert Linschütz, whose linen covers featured colorful plant and bird prints. In the middle of the room stood a baby grand piano from the C. Bechstein workshop, and next to it an extendable square wooden dinner table with several chairs from Thonet Mundus and a sideboard designed by Linschütz.

The living room, vestibule, and library were all uniformly furnished with a cube-patterned oak parquet floor covered with hand-woven rugs of various sizes.

Q
The apartment of Dr. Rezek at Grillparzerstraße 14 in the first district; interior design: Albert Linschütz; photographed for *Moderne Bauformen,* 1929. When they moved into the Villa Rezek in 1934, the Rezeks took furniture and fabrics with them from their city apartment.

44 This curtain was part of the furnishings of the Rezeks' city apartment; they apparently took it with them when they moved into the Villa Rezek.

Hans Glas designed the entryway of the Villa Rezek as a bright, colorful room with an open staircase; photographed ca. 1935.

The Villa Rezek's main hall served as a waiting room for patients of the physician couple.

51 View from the main hall into the Rezeks' library.

Library

Hans Glas had the elegant library paneled with Brazilian rosewood (Dalbergia nigra), and the illuminated bookshelves were outfitted with sliding glass doors. Very much in keeping with English models, this library space was furnished with armchairs by Albert Linschütz, two hand-woven rugs, and a round wooden table—featuring elephant-shaped legs—that the Rezeks had brought back with them from a trip to India. The library led into two separate rooms, connected by a small window—one that served Philipp and Anna Rezek as a laboratory the other as an examination room.

Conservatory

Glas also designed a conservatory for the villa's ground floor, with floor-to-ceiling doors and windows that could be completely opened or, if desired, fully retracted into the floor. This conservatory housed the family's many exotic plants and was the only interior space in the house furnished with modern tubular steel furniture: a cantilevered chair of tubular steel designed by Ludwig Mies van der Rohe (1886–1969), with an iron mesh lining, and a small étagère of tubular steel and wood, both made by Thonet Mundus. The southwest-facing conservatory picks up elements of the Villa Tugendhat, which Mies van der Rohe had built in Brno in 1929–30 for Fritz and Grete Tugendhat.

The furnishing of the rooms on the ground floor, with their various built-in seats and wall units of costly wood, the room-dividing curtains, the use—however sparing—of modern tubular steel furniture, and the colorful woven fabrics bring to mind the interiors of Ernst Lichtblau, Walter Loos, Jacques Groag, and Liane Zimbler, or those of the architectural team of Karl Hofmann and Felix Augenfeld, all of whom count among the progressive representatives of the *Wiener Wohnkultur.*

Kitchen and butler's pantry

The living room of the Villa Rezek led to the family of four's kitchen via a kind of butler's pantry used to plate the food. All of the kitchen furniture is made of wood, painted in a glossy white. With their modern and functional design, the kitchen cabinets are reminiscent of the Erdö kitchen cupboards that were popular in Vienna at the time and were also displayed in the 1932 Werkbundsiedlung exhibition.

The flooring was black and white rubber with a checkerboard pattern. The kitchen furnishings were highly functional and practical—obviously designed for a professional team that prepared and plated the food in the kitchen. The kitchen's state-of-the-art appliances were to be found in very few Viennese households at the time: an Elin[45] electric stove and the first built-in Elektrolux refrigerator (model no. L4) available back then.[46] According to the grandchildren, the modern Sunbeam Mixmaster mixer was a sensation not only for the Rezek chil-

The elegant library paneled with Brazilian rosewood on the Villa Rezek's ground floor.

The southwest-facing conservatory, with windows that could be fully retracted into the floor, black and white terrazzo floors, and a cantilevered chair of tubular steel designed by Ludwig Mies van der Rohe, picks up elements of the Villa Tugendhat, built in Brno in 1929–30 under the architectural direction of Mies.

dren but also for all the guests of the house. Thanks to an electric dumbwaiter, made by the Viennese company Ing. Stefan Sowitsch & Co., food could be easily served not only in the dining room but also in the upper levels of the house.[47]

The kitchen, the dining/living room, and the conservatory on the ground floor are all connected to the terrace by large doors. The expansive terraces were outfitted with wooden folding chairs and chaise longues with colorfully striped fabric coverings from Thonet Mundus. These were complemented by cantilevered chairs of white tubular steel and iron mesh lining—a design by Bruno Pollak, executed by Josef & Leopold Quittner—and colorful wooden sunshades with a red canopy.

The private rooms of the Rezek family

The open staircase leads to the first upper level of the house. For the Rezek family, Hans Glas planned a bedroom for the parents, two bedrooms for the children, a spacious cloakroom, two bathrooms, and a bedroom for the nanny, who lived in the house with the family. What today would be taken for granted was at that time rather rare in a floorplan design: the proximity of the two children's bedrooms to the parents' bedroom. In this case, too, Hans Glas seemed to consciously address the needs of the young family. The room arrangement reflects a close bond between the parents and their children and expresses the value placed on the two daughters within the family. In the furnishing of the two children's rooms, Glas paid great attention to affectionate details and a colorful design of the furniture: The wall units and shelves, the radiator covers, and the desk of Susanne, the younger daughter, were all made of wood and painted a light green. The architect complemented this with two bentwood chairs in red lacquer: model B 246 and model A 699, both from Thonet Mundus. Hans Glas also designed a multifunctional sofa bed especially for this room.

The two children's rooms were connected by a door with a frosted-glass window. The room of the elder daughter, Esther, was furnished with built-in wall units painted orange and cream; the desk chair, model A 283 from Thonet Mundus, was painted a light green. For hygienic reasons, the children's rooms had dark-green linoleum flooring. The brightly striped, translucent curtains picked up the cheery colors of the furniture.

According to accounts of the grandchildren of the family, during the planning phase, Hans Glas developed a close relationship not only with the parents but also with the children and tailored the furnishings of the individual rooms to

45 Elin stove, with oven and dish warmer, model no. 5545/33.

46 Elektrolux refrigerator, model no. L 3934. In 1937, only about 0.2 percent of all Austrian households had a refrigerator. See Ingeborg Micko, "Kühlschrank und Tiefkühltruhe," *Forum OÖ Geschichte. Virtuelles Museum Oberösterreich*, https://www.ooegeschichte.at/ausstellungen/das-bisschen-haushalt/kuehlschrank-tiefkuehltruhe (accessed May 1, 2024).

47 In 1914, the entrepreneur Stefan Sowitsch founded an elevator company in Vienna that cooperated with a Swiss firm after World War I. After World War II, it became the market leader in Austria. Among other things, the company built the express elevator for Vienna's Donauturm, completed in 1964, and for numerous public buildings

The "butler's pantry," an anteroom to the kitchen, was furnished in a functional, practical manner for serving the food.

Hans Glas designed kitchen furniture made of wood painted a glossy white. The flooring was black and white rubber with a checkerboard pattern.

For the bedroom of the elder daughter, Esther, Hans Glas designed a built-in wall unit and desk painted orange and cream. The desk chair, model A 283, manufactured by Thonet Mundus, was painted a light green.

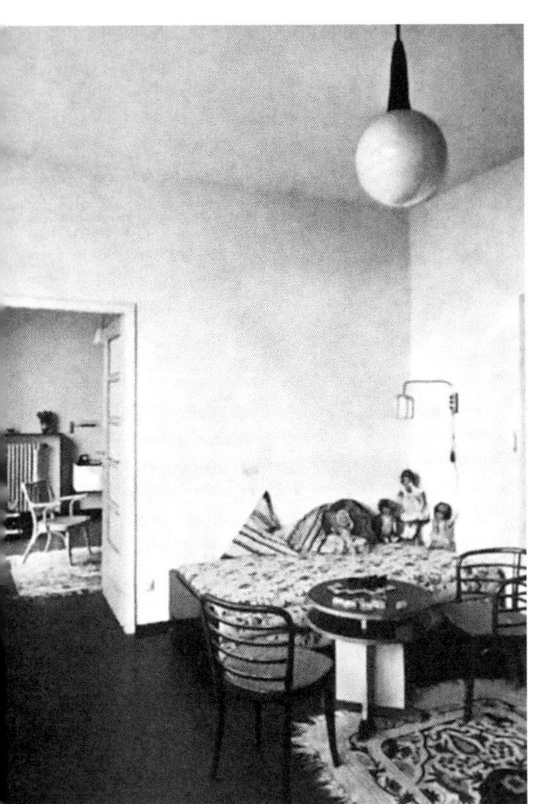

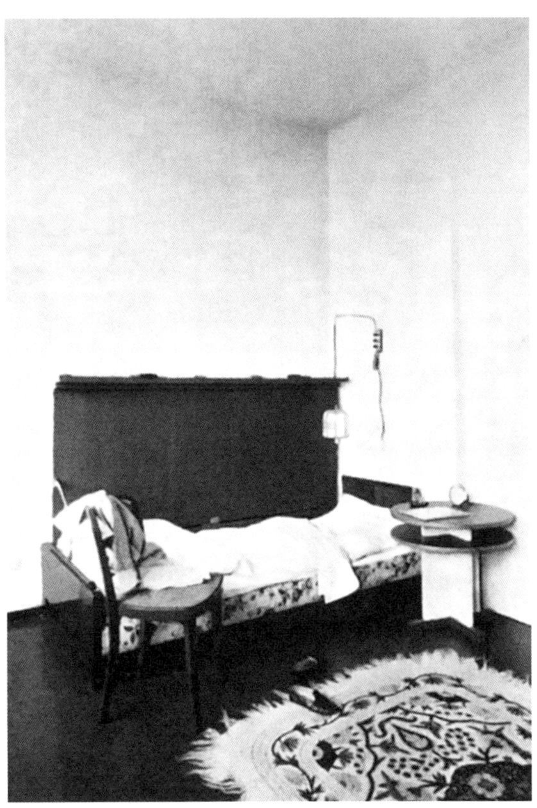

For hygienic reasons, the children's rooms had dark-green linoleum flooring.

For Susanne's room, Hans Glas designed a multifunctional sofa bed.

In furnishing the children's rooms, Glas paid great attention to affectionate details and a colorful design of the furniture.

For Anna Rezek, Hans Glas designed a dressing room of wood painted a lemon-yellow. The lamp was manufactured by J. T. Kalmar.

the wishes of the family. At the outset, the architect asked the family members about their preferences and also observed them over a lengthy period of time living in their former city apartment. He also watched how the domestic staff folded the laundry, for example, and only then planned the villa's laundry room and the changing room of the lady of the house on the first upper level. Hans Glas designed the latter room with a built-in dressing room painted a lemon-yellow and a vanity table with a white glass top and an outsized mirror. The delicate, adjustable pendant light with a spherical lampshade, brass ring, and passement was manufactured by the renowned Viennese lamp maker J.T. Kalmar. This company, founded in Vienna in 1881, worked closely with Haus & Garten and executed numerous designs, including those of Hans Glas.[48] Anna and Philipp Rezek's bedroom, directly next to the changing room, featured furniture by Albert Linschütz that came from their former city apartment.

The villa was remarkable for its state-of-the-art technical equipment and for its well-conceived, generous room layout of the main, auxiliary, and service rooms. The garden level housed a modern central-heating and ventilation system made by the J. L. Bacon Wien company, as well as a drying and ironing room, a laundry room with an electric washing machine and clothes wringer, a storage room, an additional kitchen, and an apartment for the caretaker. The architect also planned a special room for the careful storage of the Rezeks' furs, which at the time was customary in this kind of a grand house.

When the villa was finished in 1933 and the family moved in in spring 1934, the house was regarded as one of the most modern of its kind in the city. Not only guests of the family but also many passersby on Wilbrandtgasse marveled at the visionary design of the villa, its spaciousness, the distinctive windows, and the expansive terraces with their breathtaking view of Vienna. It was quite common, according to stories passed down to the grandchildren, for pedestrians to stop and gaze with amazement at the house.

The year 1938 and the end of *Wiener Wohnkultur*

Sadly, the Rezek family had only a few years to enjoy their modern villa. In 1934, when they moved in, Hitler had already taken power in Germany, and the political situation in Austria was coming to a dramatic head as well. The fabulous house on Wilbrandtgasse was certainly a reason the family remained in Vienna as long as it did. In spring 1938, only a few weeks after Austria's *Anschluss* with Nazi Germany, Philipp Rezek fled by way of France to the US. Anna Rezek escaped with their daughters, Susanne and Esther, via London to New York City, arriving there in November 1938. The Villa Rezek was Aryanized.[49] Nevertheless, the family was able to take a great deal of the villa's furnishings with them to

48 See the foreword in the 1938 J. T. Kalmar company catalog. The list of architects with whom the lamp manufacturer collaborated includes the name "Ing. Hans Glass" [*sic*].

49 See Caroline Wohlgemuth's essay "The Villa Rezek 1939–1953: Plunder and Restitution" in this volume.

their forced exile. According to the accounts of Anna and Philipp Rezek's grandchildren, most of the furniture, furnishings, and household goods from their grandparents' house made their way to the US and are still in the family's possession—from the table from India, the furniture designed by Albert Linschütz and Thonet Mundus, and dishes to books from the library in Vienna and the piano.

In 1938, Vienna lost some of its best and most creative minds within a very short time. It was a painful caesura, an irretrievable loss that was felt all across the arts and sciences and is still palpable today. In addition to all the human tragedies, 1938 also spelled an abrupt end to the golden age of Viennese furniture design. Many of the architects who at the beginning of the 1930s made Vienna into a modern and progressive city, and who were among the most important figures of the *Wiener Wohnkultur*, were Jews and had to flee Vienna after the *Anschluss*.[50]

Oskar Strnad died in Bad Aussee in 1935 and was thus spared the horrors perpetrated by the Nazis. Franz Singer and Bruno Pollak moved to London in 1934 and after 1938 never returned to Vienna. Jacques Groag and his wife, Jacqueline Groag, also fled to London, escaping in 1938 by way of Prague. After Josef Frank's emigration to Stockholm at the end of 1933, Oskar Wlach

R–T
An apartment in Vienna; design: Karl Hofmann and Felix Augenfeld, Vienna, ca. 1930.

50 See Oswald Oberhuber, Gabriele Koller, and Gloria Withalm, *Die Vertreibung des Geistigen aus Österreich. Zur Kulturpolitik des Nationalsozialismus*, ed. Zentralsparkasse und Kommerzialbank Wien and Hochschule für angewandte Kunst (Hochschule für angewandte Kunst, 1985), 197.

continued to run their joint business Haus & Garten in Vienna; in 1938, it was Aryanized by Julius Theodor Kalmar, the owner of J. T. Kalmar, who continued to operate it. The Frank and Wlach families survived the Holocaust in New York, the city to which Walter Sobotka, Felix Augenfeld, and Ernst Lichtblau had fled as well.

The country's first female architects, Ella Briggs and Liane Zimbler, were also forced to flee, Briggs emigrating to London in 1936 and Zimbler to Los Angeles in 1938. In 1938, Leopold Pilzer, the managing director of Thonet Mundus, fled to New York City. The art historian Max Eisler died in Vienna three months before the Nazis came to power in Austria; his son Martin—twenty-five years old at the time—fled with his family to Buenos Aires in 1938 and became one of the most sought-after furniture designers there. Arnold Karplus and his entire family emigrated to the US in 1938 and 1939. His son, Gerhard Karplus (1909–1995), also an architect, fled to New York City in 1938. Hans Glas fled to British India in 1938 and continued his career as an architect there. Albert Linschütz died before World War II in Vienna at the age of only thirty-two. Otto Breuer's entire possessions, including his furniture and interior design shop, were Aryanized shortly before the annexation of Austria. In the night of the November pogroms, on November 9, 1938, the architect—forty-one years old at the time—attempted suicide but failed. Only a few days later, he hanged himself at the Purkersdorf Sanatorium.[51] Friedl Dicker was murdered at the Auschwitz concentration camp on October 9, 1944.

The forced emigration deprived modern architecture not only of its creators but also of its clients and patrons. Jewish families such as the Krasnys, Beers, Tedeskos, and Bunzls, who made crucial contributions to the architecture of the interwar period, were forced to flee Vienna to escape the Nazis. Franz Gino Mayer also fled in 1938, settling in New York and continuing his career there as a sought-after photographer. After World War II, only very few of the displaced people returned to Vienna. The returnees were not made to feel welcome in Austria, and the City of Vienna did nothing to bring the displaced families back. The Rezek family and Hans Glas also did not move back to Vienna after World War II. Glas lived in Calcutta until his retirement, when he moved to Switzerland. The descendants of the Rezek family still live in the US.[52]

51 See Ott-Wodni, 2015, 359.
52 See Caroline Wohlgemuth's essay "The Rezek Family: Expulsion and Flight from Vienna" in this volume.

Maria Welzig

The Villa Rezek and the Viennese Modernism of the Interwar Period: Networks, Architectures, Memories

The basis: a "different" Viennese Modernism between 1900 and 1914

Hans Glas (1892–1969) is among the overlooked architects of Viennese Modernism, and there is also little known about the foundation he was able to build on: Aside from the familiar triumvirate of Otto Wagner, Josef Hoffmann, and Adolf Loos, a "different" Viennese Modernism existed between 1890 and 1914.[1] It was in those years that, for the first time in the city's history, Jewish architects emerged as influential figures.[2] They were largely the ones who, together with their building clients, artists, scientists, and entrepreneurs, succeeded in transforming Vienna into a cultural metropolis in this short period of time. Freed from formal traditions and artistic norms, architects such as Arthur Baron, Ernst Epstein, Leopold Fuchs, Emil Reitmann, and Ignaz Reiser made use of innovative technologies and materials to create completely new spatial possibilities and develop novel typologies. Hans Glas had close ties to one architect of this generation: Arnold Hatschek (1865–1931), a student of Carl König at Vienna's Technische Hochschule.[3] Glas also had his studio in a building designed in 1911–12 by Hatschek and his office partner, Karl Gärber.[4] The residential and office building at Währinger Straße 12 is a mixed-use, urban structure typical of that time that also housed cultural institutions such as Café Astoria and the Votivkino, the latter of which still exists today. From 1913, Hatschek & Gärber had their studio at this address as well. Glas spent his first internship years, from January 1921 to March 1923, with Hatschek. In 1924, as a freelance architect, he and Hatschek partnered to plan the villa at Cottagegasse 90–92 for Robert Wortmann, the director of the Nagel & Wortmann bank and vice president of the Vienna Stock Exchange.[5] What at first glance appears to be a nineteenth-century villa shows at second glance similarities with Josef Hoffmann's villas in

1 Otto Kapfinger initiated and with a team of researchers carried out the first reappraisal of this chapter of Viennese architectural history; Otto Kapfinger (ed.), *Anatomie einer Metropole. Bauen mit Eisenbeton in Wien, 1890–1914*, exh. cat. Wien Museum (Birkhäuser, 2025). The author of this essay was part of the research team.

2 On Jewish architects in Vienna, see the first and still most comprehensive exploration of this subject: Ursula Prokop, *Zum jüdischen Erbe in der Wiener Architektur. Der Beitrag jüdischer ArchitektInnen am Wiener Baugeschehen 1868–1938* (Böhlau, 2016).

3 In the previous generation, Carl König (1841–1915)—alongside Wilhelm Stiassny (1842–1910)—was, as an established architect of Jewish descent, still an exception.

4 Hans Glas was registered in *Adolph Lehmann's allgemeiner Wohnungs-Anzeiger: nebst Handels- u. Gewerbeadressbuch* with the studio address Währinger Straße 12 from 1928 until his emigration.

5 In 1909, Hatschek had planned a representative villa at Hohe Warte for Marie Auspitz, widow of the economist and banker Rudolf Auspitz.

the near vicinity—from the classicist formal language to the profiled wall design. It was presumably the prominent client himself who called for such a traditional, representative residence.

The Scholl and Strauß Houses on Wilbrandtgasse: Josef Frank and his circle

This period of new beginnings at the outset of the twentieth century also gave rise to the "Viennese School" that formed around the architect Josef Frank (1885–1967) in the 1920s and 1930s. Frank's first buildings, the Scholl and Strauß Houses (1913–14), are located on the same street as the Villa Rezek, at Wilbrandtgasse No. 3 and No. 11. The Windmühlhöhe, a knoll between the valleys of the Währinger Bach and the Krottenbach, was still undeveloped in the early twentieth century. With the Scholl and Strauß Houses, the first buildings in this neighborhood, Frank introduced a new type of town house to Vienna's suburbs.[6]

The Scholl House, built nearly twenty years before the Villa Rezek, anticipated key elements of the latter building: a cubic structural shell with a flat roof and on the street side a façade without conventional structuring elements.[7] As Hans Glas did with the Villa Rezek, Josef Frank responded to the view to the north, toward the Vienna Woods, with a large window opening and a balcony facing Wilbrandtgasse. On the south side, the Scholl House is largely terraced, with large window openings and a fluid connection to the garden. Both houses exhibit a prominent vertical window axis on the street-side façade that is intentionally unsymmetrical. Other common elements are the inconspicuous entry on the right side of the house and an open living/dining area. The Scholl and Strauß

A
The Scholl House at Wilbrandtgasse 3 in Währing; design: Josef Frank in collaboration with Oskar Strnad and Oskar Wlach, 1913–14.

6 Since 1919, the lane traversing this area has been called Wilbrandtgasse.
7 The permit plans show the façade completely without traditional structuring elements. Only in the execution—presumably stipulated by the building authority—were the delicate cornices, the applied corner pilasters, and the window surrounds added.

Houses both have a whitewashed, textured surface. The façade of the Villa Rezek, as well, is not smoothly plastered; rather, it had—and now again has—a scratchwork surface. What all three houses have in common are their light-colored façades.

Following a hiatus resulting from World War I, economic crises, and the political upheaval of the interwar period, the Villa Rezek was one of the first buildings constructed on Wilbrandtgasse after the Scholl and Strauß Houses. Both Hans Glas and his clients were certainly aware of the connection to these key buildings of early Viennese Modernism. The contemporary discussion of the Villa Rezek in the magazine *Österreichische Kunst* (1933) also referred to the pioneering structures of the Windmühlhöhe: The Villa Rezek, according to the article, "rises up next to the villas of Josef Frank and Oskar Strnad, which today have become nearly historic."[8]

There were close ties—also familial—between Josef Frank and the Bunzl family, from which Anna Rezek descended.[9]

With Frank's home furnishings company Haus & Garten, which he founded together with Oskar Wlach, he created a characteristically Viennese *Wohnkultur*, a distinctive style of living. One of the most remarkable examples of this Viennese Modernism in interior design, with its casual furnishings and the organic transition between house and garden, is the house built for Otto and Agathe Krasny on Fürfanggasse, in Vienna's nineteenth district (1927–28). Haus & Garten planned the furnishings and collaborated with Hanny Strauß (1890–1947), who commissioned the Strauß house, on the design of the garden. Arnold Karplus (1877–1943), who has unjustly fallen into oblivion today, designed the building very much in the spirit of modernism, with graduated transitions from the interior spaces via the terraces into the garden. This ensemble of house and garden is a significant precursor to the Villa Rezek.[10] Arnold Karplus was a member of the examination board at Glas's civil engineering exam.

In the context of the "Viennese School," with Josef Frank at its center, the Villa Rezek stands out for its pronounced modernity. New kinds of construction elements were consciously used here: floor-to-ceiling glass doors that can be completely retracted into the floor, ribbon windows, and horizontal sliding sash windows that glide into the wall and thus can be fully opened. In most of the residential buildings of the "Viennese School," the traditional window concept prevailed, and these kinds of innovative elements were rarely used. The corner window, like the one on the Villa Rezek's northeast corner, is a rarity in Viennese houses of this period, as is the tubular steel furniture used in outfitting the Villa Rezek, which was frowned upon by the "Viennese School" at the time.[11] Overall, however, the furnishings correspond to the principles of Viennese Modernism:

8 "Eine neue Villa von Arch. Z.-V.-Ing. Hans Glas," *Österreichische Kunst*, Feb. 7, 1936, no. 2, 12ff. This article bears no name, but it can be assumed that the explanatory text is by Dr. Else Hofmann, who was responsible for the architecture section of the magazine.

9 On these familial relationships, see Caroline Wohlgemuth's essay "A House from Tomorrow: Visionary Rooms, Interior Design, and Furniture" in this volume.

10 Ibid.

heterogeneous and adaptable, with comfortable armchairs and rugs, with textiles as room dividers and fitted cupboards integrated into the light-colored walls.

Wilbrandtgasse: the street of Viennese Modernism

In connection with the Scholl and Strauß Houses, Josef Frank also submitted a design proposal for the future development of Wilbrandtgasse.[12] Instead of single houses with an outward appearance that emphasized their individuality and a heterogeneous roof landscape, as had hitherto been the custom for villas in the Cottage quarter, he proposed a unified construction style with simple, cubic houses featuring flat roofs. The organizational concept of the structure was clear, with front gardens on the street side and uniform details such as fences.

The rediscovery of the Villa Rezek as well as three additional modern houses on Wilbrandtgasse shows that Frank's urban building proposal was implemented at least in part. After the early Scholl and Strauß Houses, it was nearly twenty years before further building was done on Wilbrandtgasse, but then three remarkable modernist houses were built within only a few years.

As early as January 1932, half a year before the Rezeks purchased their plot of land, plans were drawn up for a multifamily home at Wilbrandtgasse 43 (Peter-Jordan-Straße 152). The clients were Siegmund and Valentine Strum (1892–1960 and 1896–1980, respectively). Along with Samuel Strum and Rudolf Sogl, Siegmund Strum operated the Strum & Sogl building firm, which also planned the house.[13] The construction was done by the experienced reinforced-concrete company N. Rella & Neffe. All floors were constructed with reinforced concrete. In that same plan from 1932, Siegmund and Valentine Strum envisioned the construction of another multifamily residence, as semidetached houses, on the neighboring lot at Wilbrandtgasse 41 (Peter-Jordan-Straße 150), which was executed in 1936.

These houses consist of a semi-basement, two standard floors, each containing one apartment, and an additional third upper level recessed on all sides. These are cubic structures, with tar-and-gravel roofs, that are terraced down to the garden. They also feature terraces and balconies facing Wilbrandtgasse with views of the Vienna Woods. The windows are largely horizontal sliding sash windows. The result is an open street-side façade with broad balconies and expansive openings that was remarkable for that time. The sloped prop-

11 Josef Frank poked fun at Mies van der Rohe's famous cantilevered chair as a space-wasting tubular steel object; see Josef Frank, "Rum och Inredning," *Form* [Stockholm], 30, 1934, no. 19, 217ff.

12 The sketch for the further development of Wilbrandtgasse has been passed down in the form of a lecture slide, found in the Josef Frank Collection, ArkDes, the Swedish Centre for Architecture and Design. It is not known when the drawing was made.

13 Strum & Sogl, with offices at Mariahilfer Straße 76, also executed buildings of Viennese Modernism planned by Siegfried Drach, such as the duplex on Leopold-Steiner-Gasse, in the nineteenth district (1937), and the housing complex at Neulinggasse 52, in the third district (1935–38).

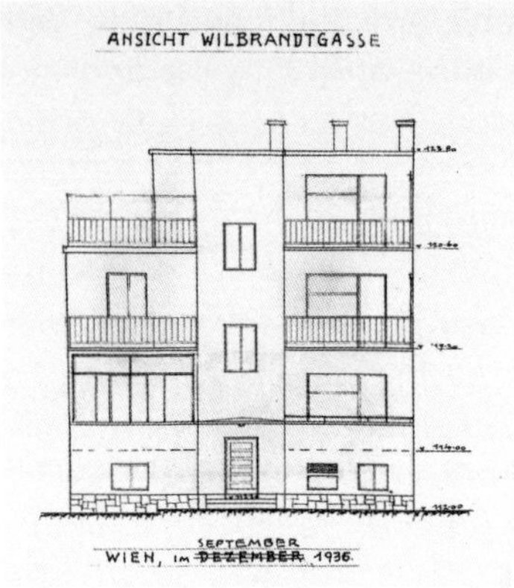

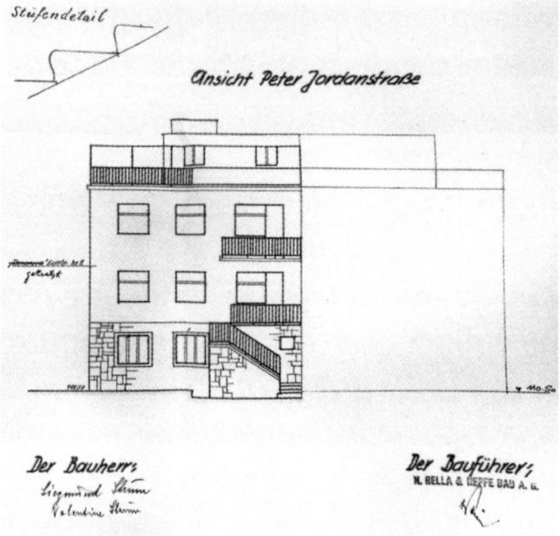

B–C
Plans for a multifamily house at Wilbrandtgass and 43 in Währing; desi Strum & Sogl, 1936.

erty is terraced and ends at Peter-Jordan-Straße with a front garden. As with the Villa Rezek, the garage is located on this street. The houses feature a "fine plaster with light-colored scratchwork" (originally, a "terranova fine plaster" was planned); on the planted west side, the house is clad with fiber-cement panels.

The semidetached multifamily houses by Strum & Sogl on Wilbrandtgasse represent a development of the urban building concept that Josef Frank had proposed for Wilbrandtgasse. They were some of the most typologically progressive private housing projects in Vienna at the time, rivaled only by the Am Modenapark residences, which were built somewhat later.[14] With their architectural conception and execution, they were among the most modern structures built in Vienna at that time. This is especially evident in the house at No. 41, from 1936, which, compared with No. 43, from 1932, conveys a modern impression—with more distinctive terracing and more transparency. It is reasonable to see this development as a response to the Villa Rezek, which had been built in the intervening time. Hans Glas, as well, explored this form of private residential building, which was more compatible with urban development at the periphery of the city: In 1929, for example, he planned a duplex, and in 1937 he built a multifamily home in Vienna.

Simultaneously with the Villa Rezek, a home for the young couple Ernst and Marianne Roubicek was built not far from the Scholl House. It was significantly smaller than the Rezeks' home but also of high quality. It was commissioned by Marianne Roubicek, née Tennenbaum (1908–1992), who at the time was only twenty-four years old.[15] The architect was Fritz Mellion (1900–1996). The building permit is dated October 1932. The house, built on a square ground-plan, is plain,

14 Strum & Sogl was, in fact, the construction manager of one of the residential buildings surrounding the Modenapark: Siegfried Drach's house at Neulinggasse 52.

15 George Roubicek, son of Ernst and Marianne Roubicek, born in 1935 in the house on Hermann-Pacher-Gasse, recalls the family's history in Vienna; see George Roubicek, in *Austria and us: 15 voices*, edited and published by the Federal Ministry for European and International Affairs and the Jewish Community of Vienna (Vienna, 2023), 106ff.

cubic, and terraced down to the garden over a quarter of the floor area. The closed, austere street frontage, with its centered, symmetrically arranged openings, calls to mind the Moller House and the buildings of Jacques Groag. The fence corresponds to those of the Moller and Rezek Houses. The window openings of various forms are reminiscent of Josef Frank's Villa Beer (1929–30), where the design of the windows just as consistently conforms to the demands of the interior space. With its ribbon corner window on the upper level—unusual in Viennese architecture—the retractable panorama window in the living room, and its advanced construction, the Roubicek House also displays distinct references to the Villa Rezek. The lavatory on the upper level is remarkable for its tower-like mounting on the flat roof with wired-glass skylight and louvered ventilator—a functional construction element that ensures lighting and ventilation and at the same time takes up the modernist principle of making functionality visible. Great emphasis was also placed on the landscaping of the garden, and the planning of a small pond was part of this. The garden extended the living area out into nature.

Despite its modest dimensions and the complete renunciation of outward representation, the Roubicek House is in its construction remarkably ambitious: All floors were constructed of reinforced concrete; as with the multifamily Strum House, the structural analysis was done by N. Rella & Neffe, a leading company in this field, which also completed formwork plans especially for this house.

The Roubicek House was discussed in the February 1935 edition of the Austrian fine-arts magazine *profil* and featured on the cover. A Siemens advertisement for a modern electric range used a drawing of the house. The art historian Iris Meder describes the house as "one of the most remarkable Viennese buildings of the 1930s" and as "among the outstanding structures of its time." Her assessment is based on the above-mentioned contemporary publication;

E
Haus Roubicek at Hermann-Pacher-Gasse 12 in Währing; design: Fritz Mellion, 1932.

she was not, however, able to determine the location of the house.[16] Because of its expropriation and the expulsion of both the clients and the architect, as well as the later transformation of the structure, the Roubicek House was largely lost to architectural history. All that is otherwise known about Fritz Mellion prior to his emigration to the US is his design for an electrically heated plant cabinet.[17]

The development of the property next to the Villa Rezek, at Wilbrandtgasse 35, took an interesting course. At the beginning of the 1950s, plans were drawn up for a single-family home in the midst of the houses on the Windmühlhöhe that had been expropriated from their former owners. This new house was completely consistent with the changed circumstances, with a steep, hipped gable roof, a traditional ground-plan solution, and equally traditional construction. The building permit for this house, which represents a stark contrast to the neighboring structures, had already been issued when the property changed owners. This time, once again, it was women who commissioned the building of the house, thus carrying on the tradition of female clients on Wilbrandtgasse. They realized a very different concept: a duplex clearly modeled after the Villa Rezek.

A new connection between house and nature

There was above all one key concern of modernism that the Villa Rezek modeled in an exemplary manner: the connection of the house with nature, the inside with the outside. Architectural modernism is often associated with technology and machines, but now the relationship to nature, the connection to the outside space, and human beings in their physicality became equally important. In the Villa Rezek, this is embodied in an exceptional manner.

To the south, alongside the slope, the building features five different terraces. The house is terraced on its east side as well, perpendicular to the slope and visible from the street. "Scarcely any other house in Vienna's Cottage quarter displays such complete utilization of all the possibilities of terracing as does this one, which offers five different gradations of light, space, and panoramas, from the sunny seating area in the front garden paved with flagstones up to an airy rooftop terrace with its splendid view of the hills of the Vienna Woods," wrote (presumably) Else Hofmann in 1936.[18]

The terracing of the house is carried over to the garden. The garage at the foot of the slope on Peter-Jordan-Straße is also included in this tiered principle:[19]

16 Iris Meder, *Offene Welten: Die Wiener Schule im Einfamilienhausbau*, PhD dissertation, University of Stuttgart, 2004, 279ff.; https://elib.uni-stuttgart.de/handle/11682/5256 (accessed Apr. 20, 2025).

17 Fritz Mellion was enrolled at the Technische Hochschule in Vienna in 1918/19. He worked as an architect and was a member of the ZF (Zentralvereinigung der Architekten Österreichs). He was married to Hildegard Altschul and lived in Grinzing. The exhibition *Contemporary American Industrial Design*, held at the Metropolitan Museum of Art in 1940, referred to him as an employee of the New York-based architect and designer Eugene Schoen, who studied, among other places, at Vienna's Academy of Fine Arts; see *Architectural Record*, vol. 87, June 1940, no. 6, 89.

18 "Eine neue Villa von Arch. Z.-V.-Ing. Hans Glas," 1936.

Its roof serves as a seating area and is flanked by a weeping willow. House and garden are closely interwoven. The house takes up the natural slopes of the terrain, and at the same time, the terraces provide the garden with an architectural structure through the use of concrete and natural-stone walls. The terraces are intended as actual outdoor living spaces, equipped with outdoor showers, and correspond to a new, free physical awareness. The conservatory acts as a transitional room between house and garden: Plants find their way into the house, and thanks to its fully retractable glass walls, the room can be completely transformed into an outdoor space. The great importance the garden had for the Rezeks is demonstrated not least by their commissioning of the renowned landscape architect Albert Esch.[20]

The strong connection between house, garden, and surrounding area did not go unnoticed in the contemporary reception. The art historian Max Eisler, for example, published an essay in 1933 with the title "Schutz der Landschaft vor der Architektur" (Protect the landscape from architecture), which dealt with the tension between landscape and city, a subject that he explored several times in previous writings. He apparently wrote the essay after a visit to the Villa Rezek: "Some time ago . . . I went out with a group of young people—students of art history and architecture—to look at a new house at the edge of the city. . . . The house we visited stands on a small knoll. To the north, one looks across a small valley with a lively mix of vineyards and small houses to the Kahlenberg; to the south, several terraces descend to a hillside lane lined with a row of recently constructed single-family homes and duplexes. . . . With their ponderous staidness that extends to their roofs, with the trite wantonness of their formal dalliances, with all their bourgeois unspiritualness, they are certainly among the most irksome structures to have appeared in the vicinity of Vienna in recent times. . . . Their coarse character is nowhere more out of place than in this area, which according to its nature would have called for a light, nimble, and garden-like formal design."[21]

The row of houses Eisler so harshly criticized was presumably the newly developed section of Peter-Jordan-Straße. This extension—like Wilbrandtgasse as well—was laid out only in the early 1930s. The development of the opposite side of Peter-Jordan-Straße occurred shortly before or at the same time as the construction of the Villa Rezek.[22] Eisler referred to them as buildings that "mar and even abuse" the landscape. On the other hand, he paid tribute to the Villa Rezek—which in contrast to this, he said, was composed in harmony with the

19 The garage of the Villa Rezek was accessed via Peter-Jordan-Straße, on the house's garden side.

20 See Caroline Wohlgemuth's essay "Albert Esch and the 'Garten Dr. Rezek': The Melding of Architecture and Nature" in this volume.

21 Max Eisler, "Schutz der Landschaft vor der Architektur," *profil, Österreichische Monatsschrift für bildende Kunst*, Zentralvereinigung der Architekten Österreichs (ed.), June 1, 1933, no. 6, III–V.

22 Peter-Jordan-Straße No. 193: 1932; No. 191: 1932; architect: P. Gutfreund; No. 189: 1932; architect: (F.?) Malecki; No. 187: 1931; architect: Alois Plessinger (student of Peter Behrens at Vienna's Academy of Fine Arts); see also Wien Kulturgut, https://www.wien.gv.at/kultur/kulturgut/architektur/gebaeudedaten.html (accessed May 19, 2025).

terrain and oriented toward the landscape—with an extensive essay in the renowned magazine *The Studio.*[23]

The connections to the Moller House (1927–28) and its designers: Loos, Groag, Dicker and Singer, Lang

If one follows the axis of Wilbrandtgasse farther toward the west, one comes to another house with a link to Hans Glas and the Villa Rezek: the Moller House at Starkfriedgasse 19 (1927–28). In 1927, Anny Moller-Wottitz (1900–1945) and her husband, Hans Moller (1896–1962), gave the task of creating a plan for a house to Adolf Loos—whose Bauschule (his private "building school") had counted Hans Glas among its first students.[24]

The triple terracing of the Villa Rezek on the street side can be read as a reference to Loos's groundbreaking Scheu House (1912–13), built twenty years before. However, the interconnecting of building and garden so characteristic of the Villa Rezek is not to be found there. Moreover, the Scheu House has no terraces on the garden side.

On the street side, the Moller House displays a largely cohesive, strictly symmetrical and expressive façade, with a centrally positioned, cuboid bay underscoring the cubic character. In contrast, the Villa Rezek—like Josef Frank's Scholl House—opens up to the street side with a balcony. The Villa Rezek exhibits a vertical ribbon window with symmetrical, flanking openings. Glas, however, integrated this axis into an overall free, asymmetrically structured house front. It is not a façade arranged according to formal principles, as with the Moller House, that is communicated outwardly, but rather the residents' desire for openness, transparency, and spaciousness. The broad, vertical ribbon of glass and the expansive windows of the Villa Rezek allow the light from the south to permeate from the garden all the way to the street. A detail: The fence of the Villa Rezek is identical to that of the Moller House. On the garden side, as well, the Moller house retains its cubic compactness despite its terraces and balcony, and as with all Loos buildings, there is a clear separation between architecture and nature.

Elements of the Villa Rezek that particularly bring Loos to mind are the staircase, with its multiple 90-degree twists, and the level differences in the area around the main hall. These have a surprising effect: One climbs several steps up to the entrance, but then from the first stair landing in the entrance hall, one

23 Max Eisler, "A Viennese house in the district of cottage, architect Hans Glas," *The Studio*, 11, 1936, 43–47. In September 1936, an article about the Villa Rezek, featuring numerous pictures, appeared in another international publication: *Het Landhuis. Het Tijdschrift voor het gezin.* The text is by F[riedrich] Mayreder (1905–1955), son of the architect Julius Mayreder.

24 The Loos student Gustav Schleicher recalled that an "architect Glass" was a student at Loos's private Bauschule in its first year of existence, 1912; see Burkhardt Rukschcio and Roland Schachel, *Adolf Loos. Leben und Werk*, 2nd ed. (Residenz Verlag, 1987), 171. In the literature, the years given for the periods when Hans Glas attended the Bauschule are 1912–1915 and 1919–1920; see Stefan Voglhofer, *Spurensuche Adolf Loos* (Schwertberg, 2010), 10.

F
The Moller House at Starkfriedgasse 19 in Währing; design: Adolf Loos; construction supervisor: Jacques Groag, 1927–28.

G
The garden side of the Moller House; design: Adolf Loos for Anny Moller-Wottitz and Hans Moller.

H
Left to right: Adolf Loos, Hans Moller, Anny Moller-Wottitz, and Heinrich Kulka on the terrace of the Moller House, 1928.

descends a few steps again to the main hall. On the other side of the entrance hall as well, steps lead down to the kitchen area.

The execution and part of the planning of the Moller House were done by Loos's associate Jacques Groag (1892–1962). Born the same year as Glas, he, like Glas, studied civil engineering at Vienna's Technische Hochschule prior to World War I. Moreover, before the war, both attended Adolf Loos's Bauschule and completed their studies after the war was over: Groag in 1919, Glas a year later. Max Eisler described Groag as "one of the best and most idiosyncratic talents of the "Viennese School."

Groag also oversaw the construction of two other milestones of Viennese Modernism: the Wittgenstein House (1926–1929), planned by Paul Engelmann and Ludwig Wittgenstein, and the Heller tennis clubhouse, designed by Friedl Dicker and Franz Singer (1928). Groag's urban residential buildings, such as those in Vienna's Werkbundsiedlung complex, demonstrate a greater, usually symmetrical, stringency than that of the Villa Rezek. In contrast, Groag's design for the Pollak weekend house (ca.1931), near the Moravian city of Olomouc, is remarkable for its lightness and openness. The single-level wooden house, built on stilts, with a wraparound veranda and an overhanging roof on slender supports, looks like a predecessor to Ernst Plischke's Gamerith House (1934).

Groag, who emigrated to London in 1938, was—like Glas—among the generation of architects and designers who were long forgotten in their native land. With a 2005 publication, the architectural historian Ursula Prokop revived the awareness of him and his wife, the designer Jacqueline Groag, and with her research corrected the one-sided image of Viennese architectural history. Just as Ernst Epstein's substantial contribution to the Goldman & Salatsch Building ("Looshaus") on Michaelerplatz (1910) has to this day scarcely been recognized, Groag's crucial involvement in the planning of the Moller House was also long unappreciated.[25]

I
Garden house for the Moller House; design: Friedl Dicker and Franz Singer, 1931.

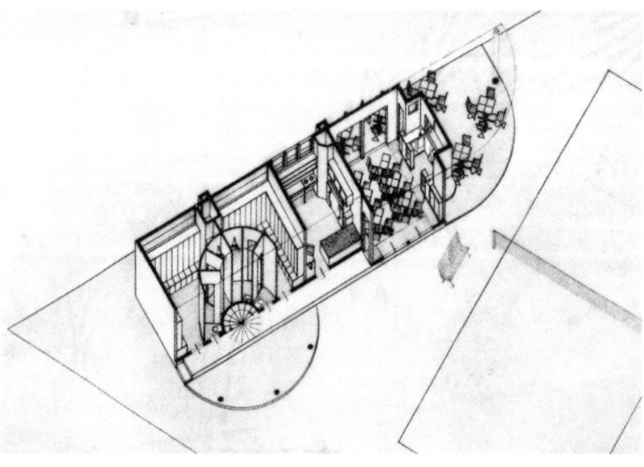

J
Sketch for a tennis clubhouse for Hans Heller in Hietzing; design: Friedl Dicker and Franz Singer, 1928.

25 Ursula Prokop conducted the first reappraisal of the design history of the Moller House on the basis of the correspondence between Groag and Loos, who was living in Paris at the time, thus shedding new light on Viennese Modernism; see Ursula Prokop, *Das Architekten- und Designerehepaar Jacques und Jacqueline Groag. Zwei vergessene Künstler der Wiener Moderne* (Böhlau, 2005).

The garden house of the Moller House (1931) and parts of the furnishings on the upper level were designed by Friedl Dicker and Franz Singer's studio. As early as 1928, with the Heller tennis clubhouse, Dicker and Singer realized a building that—through its lightness, transparency, and the dynamic formal language reminiscent of J. J. P. Oud—was unique in Vienna. Their studio was also known for its tubular steel furniture, which was used in the Villa Rezek as well.[26]

Like the Rezeks, Anny and Hans Moller enlisted a landscape architect for their house: Anna Lang, née Schwitzer (1895–1983). The design of the garden was not done until several years after the construction of the house, namely in 1932, the same time the Villa Rezek was built. Like Albert Esch, Anna Lang saw the garden as an organic and indivisible extension of the residence. At the time of the garden design for the Moller House, Anna Lang was already working with another architect of Hans Glas's generation: Ernst A. Plischke, whom she married in 1935.[27]

The Windmühlhöhe as a cultural and social biotope[28]

There were manifold connections among the residents of this axis of modernism from Wilbrandtgasse to the Moller House on Starkfriedgasse. This row of buildings was not only a street of the cultural avant-garde but also one of women's liberation: Many of the pioneering buildings of modernism were actually commissioned by women. In the case of the Scholl House, it was Agnes Scholl, née Eissler (1884–1944), who was the sole client and owner.[29] The same applies to the Roubicek House, where Marianne Roubicek was the official client.[30] In the case of the Villa Rezek, as well, it was Anna Rezek, née Bunzl, who facilitated the financing of the building project and was the de facto contact person with regard to the construction of the house. With the Moller House, Anny Moller-Wottitz was the decisive force in artistic matters. Moreover, two female designers were also involved in the project: Friedl Dicker and Anna Lang. The females of the modernist buildings on the Windmühlhöhe were all working women—which was highly unusual at that time. Anna Rezek and Marianne Roubicek were physicians, while Anny Moller-Wottitz was an artist. Hanny Strauß, née Jellinek,

26 See Caroline Wohlgemuth's essay "A House from Tomorrow: Visionary Rooms, Interior Design, and Furniture" in this volume.

27 On Anna Lang-Plischke, see Ulrike Krippner and Lilli Lička, "'A Garden for Pleasure'. Die Gartenarchitektin Anna Plischke (1895–1983) und ihre Werke in Wien und Wellington," in Hubertus Fischer and Joachim Wolschke-Bulmahn (eds.), *Gärten und Parks im Leben der jüdischen Bevölkerung nach 1933* (Martin Meidenbauer, 2008), 365–384; Ulrike Krippner and Iris Meder, "Anna Plischke and Helene Wolf: designing gardens in early twentieth-century Austria," in Sonja Dümpelmann and John Beardsley (eds.), *Women, Modernity, and Landscape Architecture* (Routledge, 2015), 81–102.

28 On the Windmühlhöhe, see the first reappraisal of the largely obliterated Pötzleinsdorf society of that time, conducted by Marie-Theres Arnbom, which uncovered extensive, hitherto unknown biographical material: Marie-Theres Arnbom, *Die Villen von Pötzleinsdorf. Wenn Häuser Geschichten erzählen* (Almathea, 2020).

29 *Neues Wiener Tagblatt (Tages-Ausgabe)*, Oct. 20, 1913. On the Scholl family history, see also Susanne Scholl, *Elsas Großväter* (Picus, 2003).

30 Marianne Roubicek's father, Ludwig Ernst Tennenbaum, was the head of a paper factory in the Lower Austrian town of Schlöglmühl.

the young woman who commissioned the Strauß House (1913–14), completed a degree in philosophy at the University of Vienna and in 1920 founded the Staudengärtnerei Windmühlhöhe, which she operated very successfully until 1938, making it one of Vienna's leading nurseries.[31]

In 1933, Hanny and Oskar Strauß acquired a piece of property in what was then the British Mandate of Palestine, as did Anna and Philipp Rezek that same year. In 1938, the couple, along with their son Walter, found a safe haven there. Even before 1938, Hans Moller, as well, had the wise foresight to move parts of his textile business to what would become Israel.[32]

Marianne Roubicek, née Tennenbaum, came from a family with close contact to many artists, including Arthur Schnitzler and Richard Tauber.[33] Agnes Scholl's husband, Emil Scholl (1875–1944), was a writer. Among the residents of the house at Wilbrandtgasse 43 was Erwin Stein (1885–1958), a composer, Arnold Schoenberg pupil,[34] music theorist, and member of the well-known Manz publishing family. The remarkable role these female clients and designers played on the Windmühlhöhe stands in disturbing contrast to the fate that many of them were to suffer yet in the 1930s. From 1938, all homeowners—and, with the exception of Loos and Esch, all architects and designers as well—and their families were dispossessed of their houses and expelled or deported and murdered.

Other connections to Viennese architects

In 1912, Adolf Loos's Bauschule was attended not only by Hans Glas and Jacques Groag but also by the architects Paul Engelmann (1891–1965), Helmut Wagner-Freynsheim (1889–1968), Richard Neutra (1892–1970), and Ernst Freud (1892–1970), the son of Sigmund Freud. Neutra and Freud, both born in Vienna in 1892, left the Austrian capital already at the beginning of the 1920s and, as Glas did with the Villa Rezek, set off on new architectural paths. From 1908 to 1912, Wagner-Freynsheim had studied at Vienna's Technische Hochschule, where he was classmates with Glas, before attending Adolf Loos's Bauschule. His pavilion for the Österreichisch-Alpine Montangesellschaft at the 1929 Vienna Fair, a steel-and-glass construction, was—along with Singer and Dicker's works and Ernst A. Plischke's public employment office—among the most modern Viennese buildings of that time.

The furnishings reveal a connection between Wagner-Freynsheim, Singer and Dicker, and Glas: In the 1929 pavilion, in keeping with the steel-and-glass

31 On Hanny Strauß, see Erika Karner, "Hanny Strauss und die Stauden – eine Liebesgeschichte," in *Historische Gärten*, 1/2011, no. 1, 4–8; Ulrike Krippner, Sabine Plenk, and Valerie Ludescher, *Garten der Villa Beer. Anlagengeschichte und Empfehlungen für eine denkmalgerechte Sanierung* (BOKU University, Vienna, 2023), 17–19, 22, 42, 48f., https://boku.ac.at/fileadmin/data/H03000/H85000/H85200/TOPSTORY___Aktuelles/2025/Institutsprofil/Beer_Anlagengeschichte_BOKU_ILA_11-12-2023.pdf (accessed July 28, 2025).

32 Arnbom, 2020, 174.

33 Roubicek, 2023.

34 Anny Wottitz and Friedl Dicker were also students of Schoenberg in 1918.

architecture, a "B[runo] P[ollak] steel seating furniture system by the Jos. and Leopold Quittner Company, Vienna XXI" was used.[35] Singer and Dicker often utilized tubular steel furniture, designed by Bruno Pollak and produced by the Quittner company—as Hans Glas did to furnish the Villa Rezek.

Wagner-Freynsheim also used this kind of furniture—not only for industrial structures like the fair pavilion but also for residences. On the terraces and in the garden of the house he built for Stefan Auspitz (1869–1945) in Vienna's Döbling district (1929), Bruno Pollak's tubular steel furniture could be found, with woven seats and backrests, including cantilevered chairs—identical to the ones at the Villa Rezek. The house for Auspitz, director of the Auspitz, Lieben & Co. bank and a prominent art collector, was among the most remarkable homes of the interwar period in Vienna.[36] Apart from the furniture, there are other evident parallels to the Rezek House: the structure's cubic shape with a flat roof, the horizontal sliding sash windows, and particularly the crucial role of the terraces in the living environment. At the Auspitz House, these are three expansive open spaces, with different orientations and intended for different functions: Next to the terrace facing the garden by the living/dining room there is a covered outdoor sleeping terrace on the first upper level and a rooftop terrace with a pool. This rounded, protruding, windowed component is a reference to an iconic element of modernist architecture that has been stylistically influential since J. J. P. Oud's Hoek van Holland rowhouse complex (1927).

A duplex planned that same year, 1929, by Hans Glas is also notable for a rounded, protruding, windowed component for the living room, whose roof serves as a rounded terrace for the upper level. The use of the flat roof as a rooftop terrace and the horizontal sliding sash windows represents further references to the Auspitz House. The railings, with their nautical flavor, that Glas uses in place of the tall parapets favored by Wagner-Freynsheim give both the planned duplex and the Villa Rezek additional lightness.

Like Hans Glas with the Villa Rezek, Wagner-Freynsheim distinguished himself in Viennese architecture circles during the interwar period with a markedly modern formal language.[37]

The Viennese architects who, like Glas with the Villa Rezek, were more aligned with international modernism, also included Ernst A. Plischke (1903–1992). Influenced by his work in the Frank & Wlach architecture firm (1927–28), Plischke, however, developed a more explicit architectural language, inspired by Le Corbusier, that set it apart from the "Viennese School."

Although about a decade older than Hans Glas, Siegfried Drach (1881–1943) also counts among the Viennese architects who stand out for their more explicit modernism. He was particularly interested in innovative, constructional

35 "Bilder von der XVIII. Wiener Internationalen Messe," *Das interessante Blatt*, no. 13, Mar. 27, 1930, 12.

36 In 1942, Stefan Auspitz von Artenegg was deported to the Theresienstadt concentration camp due to his Jewish heritage, and his possessions were confiscated by the National Socialists.

37 This is also quite evident in Wagner-Freynsheim's houses in Vienna's Werkbundsiedlung.

solutions. From 1912, he held senior positions in leading businesses active in reinforced concrete, such as N. Rella & Neffe. Only in the 1930s did he become active as an independent architect and building contractor; he possessed the necessary flexibility and skills to now realize outstanding modernist works in Vienna. The Malfatti housing development (1930–1932)[38] and the apartment blocks at Am Modenapark 10 (1931) and Neulinggasse 52 (1935–38),[39] with their spatial conception, formal language, and state-of-the-art furnishings, were among the most progressive buildings in Vienna at the time.

The art historian Max Eisler as a link in Glas's milieu

From the 1910s, the art historian and writer Max Eisler (1881–1937) was probably the most important and prolific architecture critic and theorist of Viennese Modernism.[40] He published the most extensive article about the Villa Rezek and at the same time acted as a common thread in Hans Glas's milieu. He wrote essays on most of the buildings referred to in this essay for purposes of comparison. Eisler had an impressively broad array of interests: He also published articles about painting and sculpture and edited standard works such as the *Historischer Atlas des Wiener Stadtbildes* (Historic atlas of Vienna's cityscape) (1919).

With close ties to Josef Frank and his circle, Eisler also coined the term "Wiener Schule" ("Viennese School")[41] and was the first to write about the Jewish contribution to Vienna's modernist architecture. As a recognized expert on Dutch architecture, he unquestionably had a significant influence on Viennese architects. In 1920, his book on Hendrik Petrus Berlage (1856–1934) was published, the first German-language biography of the Dutch architect.[42] Despite his great professional expertise, the art and architectural historian was never granted a professorship: His teacher Josef Strzygowski thwarted all appointments because of Eisler's Judaism.[43]

With the accession to power of the Nazis in Germany in 1933 and the enactment of the Nuremberg Race Laws in 1935, any hope Jews had for a peaceful life in Central Europe was destroyed. An impressive testimony to this lost hope was left behind by Max Eisler. During a stay in Tel Aviv in 1936, he wrote: "You do not yet recognize it, but your body feels it: Suddenly, after two thousand years, it again knows how it can move; it does not fear any malignant

38 Interestingly, Arnold Karplus's son Gerhard designed the furnishings for an apartment in the Malfatti housing development.

39 The firm Strum & Sogl oversaw the construction of the housing project; see the Strum Houses at Wilbrandtgasse 41 and 43.

40 Evelyn Adunka, *Max Eisler. Wiener Kunsthistoriker und Publizist zwischen orthodoxer Lebenspraxis, sozialem Engagement und wissenschaftlicher Exzellenz* (Hentrich & Hentrich, 2018).

41 Eisler, 1936.

42 Other publications by Eisler bear the titles *Die Geschichte eines holländischen Stadtbildes, Das holländische Interieur,* and *Alt-Delft.*

43 Iris Meder, "Josef Frank, Max Eisler and Austrian Architectural Criticism," in Christoph Thun-Hohenstein (ed.), *Josef Frank: Against Design. The Architect's Anti-Formalist Oeuvre* (Birkhäuser, 2021), 76.

glances, any offences. Its posture becomes upright, relaxed, and spirited. It enjoys the splendid happiness of freedom in its people's own infinite living space."[44]

One modernist building that is on a par with Mies van der Rohe's famous Villa Tugendhat, in the Czech city of Brno, in terms of architectural aspiration, technical refinement, and sumptuous furnishings is the country house in the Taunus that Peter Behrens (1868–1940) built between 1929 and 1931 for Clara Gans (1881–1959).[45] Max Eisler wrote a lavishly illustrated article about this house as well, published in *Moderne Bauformen* (1932).[46] His extensive essay on Frank and Wlach's Villa Beer had appeared two issues before.

In his article on the country estate for Clara Gans, Eisler particularly emphasized the house's integration into the landscape. The house, he wrote, had "due to its location alone grown together with the landscape in myriad ways."[47] The garden is divided into several terraces supported by drystone walls and represents an integral part of the architectural concept. This new connection with the landscape, a key characteristic of all the houses discussed here—including the Villa Rezek—manifests itself in the Villa Gans in the selection of material as well, such as regional Taunus slate and Naumburg marble.

The expansive cubic house opens to the garden via two spacious terraces facing east and west that are bordered by railings resembling those of a ship. In front of the dining room is a largely glassed-in conservatory whose windows can be electrically retracted into the floor. The living room, as well, opens into an almost completely glassed-in room extension, the so-called playroom. The casing of the radiator there is similar to that of the radiators in the Villa Rezek. The lighting in the living room comes indirectly from fixtures recessed into the ceiling.

Diversity of modern architecture in comparison: Holland, France, Vienna

International modernism in architecture was, despite its universal aspiration, multifarious. Later, the term "Bauhaus" erroneously became synonymous with the architecture of modernism as a whole. Beginning in the 1920s, representatives of modernism, especially in Austria and France, criticized the "German trend" for its dogmatism, labelling it dictatorial, monumental, overly dramatic, and lifeless.[48] A perceptive critic of the Bauhaus and the developments in Germany was Josef Frank.

44 Quoted in Adunka, 2018, 99.

45 I thank Elana Shapira for her information about the Villa Gans in connection with the Villa Rezek.

46 Max Eisler, "Peter Behrens: Landhaus einer Dame im Taunus," *Moderne Bauformen*, 36, 1932, 117–132; H. K. Zimmermann, "Ein Landsitz am Taunus, erbaut von Professor Peter Behrens, Berlin," *Deutsche Kunst und Dekoration*, 70, 1932, 32–39, both available digitally at digi.ub.uni-heidelberg.de.

47 Eisler, 1932, 117.

48 See Maria Welzig, *Josef Frank (1885–1967). Das architektonische Werk* (Böhlau,1998), 142ff.

The formative impetuses for the development of modern architecture came in the early 1920s, also primarily from Holland and France, and they were groundbreaking for the Viennese Modernism of the interwar period. The Low Countries, which remained neutral in World War I, were the site of pioneering work in public housing even during the war and then at the beginning of the 1920s. With architects such as Hendrik Petrus Berlage, Michel de Klerk, and J. J. P. Oud, the cities of Amsterdam, Rotterdam, and Den Haag set new standards in innovative social housing. Oud and the group *De Stijl*, founded in 1917, as well as Jan Duiker, were influential figures of modernist architecture.

Paris saw the erection of Henri Sauvage's stepped-terrace houses—even built as part of public housing projects in the French capital—which are regarded as architectural and constructional milestones. They remain today just as exemplary and inspiring for urban residential building as they were for Le Corbusier's "Immeuble-Villas" projects (beginning in 1922). In contrast, Loos's corresponding plans for stepped-terrace houses for public housing in Vienna (1923–24) were rejected.

Despite the international diversity in architecture, the later reception reduced the image of Central European modernist architecture to the Bauhaus. The Villa Rezek, however, is an especially good example of how broad the panorama actually was.

An instructive comparison is with the French architect Robert Mallet-Stevens (1886–1945), who had links both to early Viennese Modernism (Josef Hoffmann) and to the Dutch group *De Stijl*. With structures such as the Villa Paul Poiret (1921–1923), the Villa Noailles (1923), the buildings on Paris's Rue Mallet-Stevens, later named for him, (1926–27) and the Villa Cavrois (1929–1932), he was among the early and innovative influential figures of modernism. In addition to the cubic complex with terraces, ship railings, and the special role played by the garden, similarities to the Villa Rezek are also evident in details, such as the corner windows and the radiator covers of macassar ebony veneer in Art Deco style in the living room of the Villa Rezek.

Architectural relationships between Vienna, Brno, and Prague

Even after the political separation of Austria and the Czech Lands as a result of the collapse of the Habsburg Empire in 1918, the architectural networks remained in place across the new borders. Hans Glas, Walter Sobotka, Arnold Karplus, Jacques Groag, Heinrich Kulka, Adolf Loos, Friedl Dicker, and Franz Singer: all of them and many other architects as well were active in the newly founded nation of Czechoslovakia. Glas, for example, planned a villa for Ladislav and Věra Szathmáry in Prague at Pod Žvahovem 8.

Most of the Viennese architects of modernism originally came from the eastern countries of the Austro-Hungarian Empire and were German speakers or bilingual. Hans Glas, born in Vienna, was one of the few exceptions. Many of the German-speaking architects and clients who were still socialized in the Habsburg Empire continued to live in Prague and Brno until 1939. Most of them had received their training in Vienna and maintained close ties to the city. Max Eisler was a key link in this network. He published essays on Brno- and Prague-based architects such as Ernst Wiesner, Josef Kranz, Hugo Foltyn, and Karl and Otto Kohn.

The newly founded Czech state positioned itself as a center for modern art and architecture. With its functionalist new buildings, the city of Brno, located near the border to Austria, left the former capital of the Habsburg Empire far behind it in its progressiveness. The Villa Rezek displays striking parallels to Ernst Wiesner's (1890–1971) Münz (1924–1926) and Haas (1928–1930) Houses in Brno, which were built several years before the Rezek House: the terracing of the house, the transition to an equally terraced garden, railings similar to deck rails, and a glazed corner conservatory—in short: a striking example of spatial permeability. Ernst Wiesner studied from 1909 to 1911 at the Technische Hochschule in Vienna and from 1910 to 1913 at that city's Academy of Fine Arts with Friedrich Ohmann, whose studio he worked at in 1913–14. His villas in Brno from the 1920s clearly display the influence of Adolf Loos.

The commission to build the Haas House at Lipová 43, in Brno, came from Gustav Haas (1884–1965) and Gina (Race) Haas (1881–1961), who after World War I moved with their children from Vienna to Brno.[49] The expansive house, whose ground-level floor plan resembled that of the Villa Rezek, is stepped down a falling slope on the garden side with terraces. The terraced garden with natural-stone steps and shrub-covered slopes is organically carried over to the architecture of the house. As with the Villa Rezek, the terracing of the building is also displayed on the front of the house. The two houses also have in common their horizontally placed sliding sash windows, Mediterranean-looking exterior blinds, and the terrace railings with their nautical touch. Among the house's

K
The Haas House at Lipová 43 in Brno; design: Ernst Wiesner, 1928–1930.

49 John Selby, "Villa Haas, Brno, 1928. What Happened to the Family," *The Friends of Czech Heritage*, 26, Winter/Spring 2022, www.czechfriends.net/newsletter/from-previous-newsletters/people-places (accessed June 7, 2025). In 1939, the family was forced to emigrate to escape the Nazis, and the house was expropriated. Under the "anti-fascist" communist regimes that followed, there was no restitution to the Jewish owners. A younger relative of Gustav Haas was the later Austrian federal chancellor Bruno Kreisky.

furnishings are the iconic chairs of Oskar Strnad (1912), which today are regarded as virtually the quintessence of the modernist "Viennese School."

The house built for Grete and Fritz Tugendhat in Brno in 1929–30 to plans by Ludwig Mies van der Rohe became one of the iconic buildings of modernism. In the Villa Rezek's integration into the terrain, the horizontal structuring and the terracing down the slope, which extends beyond the actual structure into the garden, its transparency, modernity, and the use of new technologies, the Rezek house is closely related to Mies van der Rohe's building, which was completed two years before. Parallels are evident in the floorplan as well: The entrance of both houses lies on the right side of the building; from there, one turns left into the open living/dining area, which opens onto the garden. In both cases, a conservatory is situated in front of the living area at the southeast corner. A spectacular element that both houses share is the use of floor-to-ceiling plate-glass windows that can be completely retracted into the floor—at the Mies house electrically and at the Villa Rezek only through a mechanism requiring the effort of two people. As early as 1926, the architect Bohuslav Fuchs implemented this device for the first time at the Café Zeman in Brno. The Villa Rezek, with its haptic scratchwork façade, the delicate handrails reminiscent of a ship's railing—in contrast to Mies's massive balustrades—and the more direct dovetailing of house and garden, conveys an atmosphere that is at once warmer and more casual than that of the house in Brno. And yet, there is probably no building in Viennese Modernism that is so closely related to the Villa Tugendhat than the Villa Rezek. The Mies-designed tubular steel, cantilevered chairs in the Villa Rezek represent the conscious connection the clients and the architect had to the creative cosmos of Mies van der Rohe—in particular to the Villa Tugendhat.

Among the leading architects in Prague in the 1920s and 1930s were the brothers Karl and Otto Kohn,[50] who together operated an architecture office beginning in 1920. In 1931, Max Eisler published a book about the Kohn firm in which he emphasized the "stylistic neutrality of the two brothers, which allows them to choose a building design case-by-case, without losing the fundamental, consistent qualities of their work, their character, and their conception."[51] Such a stylistically unconstrained attitude can be observed with Hans Glas as well. The Kohns' Rindler summer house in the Czech village of Staré Splavy, built in 1927, speaks—in contrast to previous Kohn buildings—the language of modernism. With its rather blockish appearance, the rounded, protruding terrace, the base of natural stone, and the slender, high windows, with their Classical look, it is reminiscent of Glas's villa for Adolf Münch in Belgrade. The Villa Kohn in Prague's Smichov district (1936), built three years after the Villa Rezek, shares with the latter the modern formal language and the close connection between house and garden. Karl Kohn established modernist architecture in Quito,

51 Max Eisler, "Vorwort," in *Architekten Ing. Otto und Karl Kohn, Prag* (Waldes Verlag, 1931), quoted in Wikipedia, https://de.wikipedia.org/wiki/Karl_Kohn_(Architekt) (accessed May 19, 2025). On the occasion of the publication of that book, an exhibition of the architect's works was also held in his studio in the building housing the Adam apothecary (built 1911–1913) on Prague's Wenceslas Square.

Ecuador, the city to which he had emigrated, and to which he also imported the new reinforced concrete construction method.[52] Hans Glas achieved something comparable in Calcutta. What both architects possibly benefited from was their undogmatic approach to architecture, which was oriented toward the respective needs of their different clients.

Hans Glas—along with Jacques Groag, Friedl Singer and Franz Dicker, Ernst Plischke, Helmut Wagner-Freynsheim, Heinrich Kulka, Fritz Judtmann, Egon Riss, Anton Brenner, Paul Engelmann, Fritz Mellion, Richard Neutra, Ernst Freud, and others—was a member of the younger generation of Viennese architects after Josef Frank. When one surveys these architects, it becomes clear that in Vienna there were not merely exceptional individual figures who were consciously aligned with international modernism;[53] rather, this orientation can be observed with a host of Viennese architects of that generation.

However, in architecturally conservative Red Vienna—between 1923 and 1934, the city was by far the largest commissioner of building projects—there were only scant opportunities to put the new approaches of modernism into practice. Particularly because of the political development of the ensuing years, many architects of this generation were not able to realize their potential, and many of the few works they completed fell into oblivion. Therefore, the architectural history of Vienna that has been passed down is a fragmented one, making the examination of Hans Glas and his generation, which expands this view, all the more important. In this generation, a dense network of architectural relationships between Vienna, Brno, and Prague was also able to develop again.

Compared with the buildings of other Loos students—such as Groag, Kulka, Engelmann, and Wagner-Freynsheim—who carried on the cohesive, cubic formal language and severity of their teacher, the Villa Rezek is less Loosian. In its openness, the casual asymmetry, the organic connection between house and garden, and the heterogeneous, light furnishings, it is more closely aligned with Josef Frank. With the Villa Rezek, however, Hans Glas went beyond the "Viennese School": With its formal language, its technical ambitions, and the close link between architecture and landscape, it corresponded to the latest international trends of modernism. Scarcely any other single-family home in Vienna at that time reflected the avant-gardist developments of the interwar period so clearly. As the key architectural work of the "street of Viennese Modernism" on the Windmühlhöhe, the Villa Rezek marks a culmination of the brief phase in which Vienna was still part of an international architectural phase of new beginnings.

52 On the nearly forgotten architects Otto and Karl Kohn, see Zuzana Güllendi-Cimprichová, "Modernetransfer Tschechoslowakei – Ecuador. Zum Leben und Werk des deutschsprachigen jüdischen Architekten Karl Kohn (1894–1979)," *kunsttexte.de*, no. 1, 2014, https://edoc.hu-berlin.de/items/60e2245f-24a3-4f4a-be36-f9d2bc4d5bbc, (accessed June 7, 2025); Zdeněk Lukeš, "Otto a Karl Kohnovi – Praha, Paříž, Ekvádor," *Archinfo*, n.d., https://www.archinfo.sk/diskusia/blog/pamiatky-historia/otto-a-karl-kohnovi-praha-pariz-ekvador.html (accessed May 19, 2025).

53 This claim is usually made of Plischke and Singer and Dicker.

Caroline Wohlgemuth

Hans Glas – The (Un)forgotten Architect: Vienna 1892 – Lugano 1969

Hans Glas was born in Vienna on September 11, 1892, into a Jewish family. His father, Isidor Glas (1863–1937), worked as a master tailor for the former purveyor to the imperial and royal court E. Braun & Co, an elegant clothing and table-linen shop at Graben 8, in Vienna's first district. Isidor Glas was married to the Vienna-born Karoline (Caroline) Glas (1860–1941), née Schwarz.[1] The couple had four sons: Egon (1888–?), Richard (1890–1961), Hans, and Emil Glas (1894–1956). The family lived at Döblinger Hauptstraße 73, in the nineteenth district. After completing secondary school in the first district, Hans Glas began studying machine engineering at Vienna's Technische Hochschule in the 1911/12 academic year. After a year, he switched to the school of architecture at the same institution and studied there from 1912 to 1915 and again in 1918/19.[2]

From 1912 to 1915 and in 1919/20, Glas also attended Adolf Loos's (1870–1933) private Bauschule (architecture school) in Vienna, where his classmates included Richard Neutra (1892–1970), Rudolf Michael Schindler (1887–1953), Felix Augenfeld (1893–1984), and Ernst Freud (1892–1970), Sigmund Freud's youngest son.[3] In a letter from New York, dated October 1981, Felix Augenfeld, one of the first students to enroll at the Bauschule in 1912, recalled Adolf Loos's

A
Adolf Loos with his students on the roof of the Schwarzwaldschule in Vienna, ca. 1920. It is possible but not certain that Hans Glas is among the group in this photograph.

1 See Georg Gaugusch, *Wer einmal war – das jüdische Großbürgertum Wiens 1800–1938, S–T* (Amalthea Verlag, 2023), 3512.

2 After an interruption due to the war, Hans Glas again enrolled at the Technische Hochschule in 1918, now as an audit student. On the certificate of matriculation from the Technische Hochschule, dated October 4, 1911, Hans Glas listed as his place of residence Graben 8 in the first district as well as his parents' apartment at Döblinger Hauptstraße 73, in the nineteenth district. From the main catalog of fully enrolled students 1911/12, entry 29 (Hans Glas), Archiv der Technischen Universität Wien (TUWA).

3 According to the recollections of the German painter and architect Gustav Schleicher (1887–1973), "Hans Glass" [*sic*] was one of the first students at Loos's private Bauschule, attending the school from 1912 to 1915 and again in the 1919/20 academic year. See Stefan Voglhofer, *Spurensuche Adolf Loos* (2010), in https://www.voglhofer.at/_rtf-voglhofer/CMS_fg4e735474df264_orig_1187.pdf (accessed July 30, 2025).

The architect Hans Glas at the age of forty-one, photographed by "Antios," Vienna, 1933.

classes: "The word 'school' was scarcely applicable to this small work group. Nor was the word 'work.' It was a kind of seminar, a loose group of students, united by a common mindset, who met not in a lecture hall or studio but on improvised walks or around a table in the city, in the Kärntner Bar, which had been designed by Loos, in cabarets and nightclubs, at marble-storage sites, and in apartments renovated and furnished by Loos. At the time, he had a small circle of wealthy clients and was usually quite busy. . . . Our lives and our work would be nearly inconceivable without his influence."[4]

During World War I, Hans Glas had to interrupt his architecture studies due to his military service, resuming them in 1918. On October 29, 1920, Glas passed the second state examination for architecture at Vienna's Technische Hochschule. Already as a student, he began working for the Vienna construction company Anton Robert Fleischl. As of 1921, Hans Glas was employed by the Jewish architect Arnold Hatschek (1865–1931), who had made a name for himself with the renovation of the E. Braun & Co shop on the Graben and with the planning of numerous villas and residential and commercial buildings in Vienna. Arnold Hatschek had also studied architecture at the Technische Hochschule and as of 1901 worked in a joint office with the architect Karl Bernhard Gärber (1870–1926).[5] Hatschek & Gärber was initially located on Salvatorgasse, in the first district. In 1913, the firm moved to Währinger Straße 12/Türkenstraße 1, in the ninth district, setting up its office in a residential/commercial building that Hatschek & Gärber had built around 1910. It was at this address that Hans Glas maintained his architecture studio from the beginning of his career—later residing in the building as well—until 1938.[6] Arnold Hatschek also had his architecture office at this address until his death in 1931. In 1924, together with Hatschek, Glas built a villa for Robert (1869–1928) and Bertha (1877–1942) Wortmann at Cottagegasse 90–92 in Döbling. Robert Wortmann was at the time the owner of the Nagel & Wortmann bank.[7]

On March 23, 1922, Hans Glas married Olga Taussig (1896–1937) in the town of Plzeň (today in the Czech Republic). Olga Taussig, known as "Ola," was born in the Bohemian town of Louny, at that time still part of the Habsburg Empire, into a Jewish family. Her parents, Julius Taussig (1868–1932) and Olga Taussig, née Fanta (1873–1896), were from Bohemia.

One of Glas's first independent projects came around 1923: planning an additional level for a vintner house at Cobenzlgasse 16 in Grinzing, commis-

4 Felix Augenfeld, "Erinnerungen an Adolf Loos," letter from New York, dated October 1981, to the German architect and architecture historian Dietrich Worbs (1939–2022), Architecture Collection in the Archive of the Albertina, Vienna. Hans Glas is not mentioned by name in this letter. Felix Augenfeld fled from Vienna to New York City in 1938 to escape the Nazis, never returning to his native city.

5 See https://www.architektenlexikon.at/de/210.htm (accessed July 21, 2025).

6 Hans Glas signed all of his plans with "Architekt Ing. Hans Glas, Wien IX, Währingerstr. Nr. 12."

7 See examination certificate of the attainment of the certification as civil architect, Office of the Vienna Provincial Government, B.D., 5490/29, from Jan. 15, 1930. An examination request lists those projects that Hans Glas had carried out in 1923 as an independent architect.

B
Vienna municipal housing complex at Handelskai 210; design: Hans Glas, 1928–29.

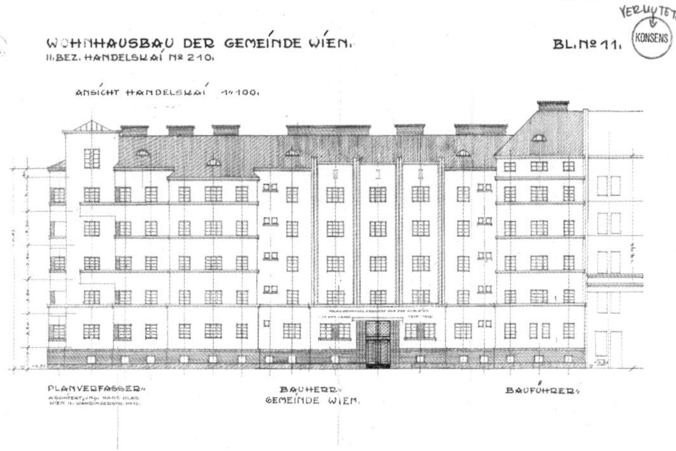

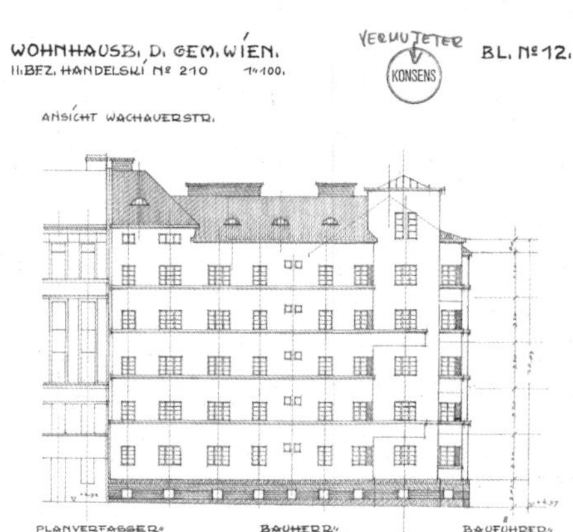

C–D
Plans for the Vienna municipal housing complex at Handelskai 210 by Hans Glas, 1928–29.

sioned by Otto Klein. In the 1928/29 academic year, Hans Glas again enrolled at the Technische Hochschule, this time as an audit student.[8]

In so-called Red Vienna, public housing projects were carried out on a large scale between 1919 and 1934 in order to improve the housing situation and the overall health conditions of the Viennese. By 1934, 382 *Gemeindebauten* (public housing complexes) with some 65,000 dwellings had been created.[9]

Hans Glas, as well, began working for the City of Vienna at the end of the 1920s. In 1928–1929, he designed a small residential complex with about fifty-four apartments at Handelskai 210, at the intersection with Wachaustraße, in the second district.[10] With its symmetrical, representational façade, balconies, brick accents, and cornices, Glas's *Gemeindebau*, which today is protected as a historic monument, conforms to the typical architectural image of Red Vienna.

Hans Glas addressed the idea of affordable housing not only in his architectural work but also in his writings. In 1929, he published an article with the title "Die Eigenwohnung im Zweifamilienhaus als Beispiel für die Anwendung des Wohnbauförderungsgesetzes" (The owner-occupied apartment in a duplex as an example of the application of the Housing Construction Subsidy Act) in the magazine *Zeitschrift des Österreichischen Ingenieur- und Architektenvereins*. Glas used the example of the planning of a duplex and a detailed sample calculation to explain the best possible utilization of the Housing Construction Subsidy Act and the savings compared with a single-family home. The architect also stressed the advantages of a flat "sunroof."[11]

On January 15, 1930, Hans Glas passed the civil engineering examination in Vienna. The Viennese architect Arnold Karplus (1877–1943)—who in 1927–1928 had designed the Villa Krasny on Fürfanggasse, on the Hohe Warte, in partnership with Josef Frank (1885–1967), Oskar Wlach (1881–1963), and Frank and Wlach's company Haus & Garten—was a member of the examination board.[12]

In the 1930s, Hans Glas worked not only in Vienna but also in Austria's neighboring countries. In Belgrade, Glas planned a villa in 1931–1932 for the Jewish industrialist Adolf Münch (1880–1941) and his wife Elizabeth Maria Treichel Münch (1879–?).[13] In 1933, the house was featured in the magazine *Architektur und Bautechnik* under the title "Einfamilienhaus Direktor M., Beograd."[14]

8 As his place of residence, Hans Glas gave the address Währinger Straße 12 in the ninth district.

9 See Wolfgang Maderthaner, "Von der Zeit um 1860 bis zum Jahr 1945," in Peter Csendes and Ferdinand Opll (eds.), *Wien. Geschichte einer Stadt*, vol. 3: *Von 1790 bis zur Gegenwart* (Böhlau, 2006), 381f.

10 On the Wiener Wohnen website, this public housing project is incorrectly attributed to the Viennese architect Hans Glaser; see www.wienerwohnen.at/hof/360/Handelskai-210.html (accessed July 22, 2025). The historic plans, however, were signed by Hans Glas.

11 Hans Glas, "Die Eigenwohnung im Zweifamilienhaus als Beispiel für die Anwendung des Wohnbauförderungsgesetzes," *Zeitschrift des Österreichischen Ingenieur- und Architektenvereins* [Vienna], 1929, nos. 45/46, 455, and 456. It is not known if this duplex was ever built.

12 See examination certificate, 1930.

13 This villa has not been preserved.

The article included a photograph of the villa, a model, a plan, and a detailed description of the architect's project. "Because the construction site was in Belgrade, only building materials from Belgrade and vicinity could be used.... The building lies on a hill sloping down from southeast to northwest with a splendid view of the confluence of the Danube and the Sava Rivers and of the city of Zemun," wrote Hans Glas enthusiastically in the article about his villa project.[15] For the living space of the house, which extended over more than 500 square meters and was built on a natural-stone base, the architect designed a rounded, protruding building element with narrow, upright, rectangular windows, a flat roof, and generously proportioned terraces. The client, Adolf Münch, was at the time president of the Trifailer Kohlenwerks-Aktiengesellschaft coal company.[16] Subsequently, Adolf Münch and his brother Julius Münch (1873–1932) commissioned Glas to build living quarters for the employees of the coal company in Boljevac, a small town in what is today the Zaječar District of Serbia.[17]

Shortly thereafter, in 1932, the physician couple Anna (1895–1974) and Philipp Rezek (1894–1963) commissioned Glas to plan the villa at Wilbrandtgasse 37 in Pötzleinsdorf. The architect was forty years old at the time, and the Villa Rezek is today regarded as the culmination of his oeuvre in Vienna. In 1936, the Austrian art historian Max Eisler (1881–1937) published an article in the English magazine *The Studio* about the house, praising the furnishings of the visionary house as an outstanding example of good taste in Vienna.[18]

That same year, an article appeared in the journal *Österreichische Kunst* with the title "Eine neue Villa von Arch. Z.V.-Ing. Hans Glas," in which the "gaiety, cheery modernity, and affectionate room culture" of the house's interior was emphasized.[19] Both articles showed photographs of the house taken by the Viennese photographer Franz Gino Mayer (1891–1971) around 1935. In 1936, the Dutch architecture magazine *Het Landhuis* reported on the Villa Rezek as well.[20]

In 1937, Glas realized a multifamily residence at Pfarrwiesengasse 22 in Döbling. The building contained twelve apartments. The building supervisor was Walter Custer (1882–1957), with whom Hans Glas had already worked on the construction of the Villa Rezek.[21] In 1937, the building was presented in the magazine *Österreichische Kunst* under the title "Ein neues Haus in Döbling von

14 Hans Glas, "Einfamilienhaus Direktor M., Beograd," *Architektur und Bautechnik* [Vienna], special issue "Dein Heim," vol. 20, nos. 5/6, March 12, 1933, 23ff.

15 Ibid., 24.

16 The Trifailer Kohlenwerks-Aktiengesellschaft, founded in 1872, was one of the most important coal companies in the Habsburg Empire.

17 See examination certificate, 1930. Hans Glas oversaw these projects. An examination request lists those projects that Hans Glas had carried out in 1923 as an independent architect. It is not known if these workers' quarters in Boljevac are still standing today.

18 See Max Eisler, "A Viennese house in the district of cottage, architect Hans Glas," *The Studio*, 11, 1936, 45.

19 "Eine neue Villa von Arch. Z.-V.-Ing. Hans Glas," *Österreichische Kunst*, 7, 1936, no. 2, 1936, 13.

20 "Woonhuis van een arts, Weenen – Pötzleinsdorf," *Huit Landhaus*, September 1936.

21 See Maximilian Eisenköck's essay "Walter Custer: Civil Engineer and Entrepreneur of Viennese Modernism" in this volume.

E
A villa for Elizabeth Maria Treichel Münch and Adolf Münch in Belgrade, Kingdom of Yugoslavia; design: Hans Glas, 1931.

F
A model of the Villa Rezek; design: Hans Glas, 1933.

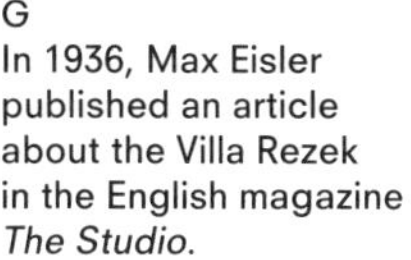

G
In 1936, Max Eisler published an article about the Villa Rezek in the English magazine *The Studio*.

ARCHITECT
HANS GLAS

A VIENNESE HOUSE
in the district of Cottage

Above is a view of the garden, from the south of the house designed by HANS GLAS. The terrace in the foreground forms the roof of the garage. At right is the front façade. Street level is one storey above garden level

BY DR. MAX EISLER

THE terrace house, designed for a married doctor with two children, is situated on a low hill on the outskirts of Vienna. From the flat roof there is a magnificent unimpeded view of the vine-clad and wooded hills in the vicinity. On account of this beautiful view there are several windows and a balcony in the street frontage, although it faces north. The terraces of the house are on the south side, facing on the garden, which is planted with shrubs and rose bushes and slopes gradually to the bottom of the hill. Consequently the rooms are sunny, airy and well lighted.

On the garden side the house consists of three storeys and a basement. The basement contains the apparatus for central heating, the storerooms and the spacious laundry, which is

43

H
A multifamily home at Pfarrwiesengasse 22 in Döbling; design: Hans Glas, 1937.

Arch. Hans Glas."[22] This, his final building project in Vienna, was praised in the article with the words: "The building that the architect Hans Glas planned on Pfarrwiesengasse in Döbling, with its delightfully calm modernism and clean execution inside and out, is among the city's most harmonious and pleasant. The apartments, as well, display all advantages of a new *Wohnkultur* in pleasing dimensions."[23]

In 1937, Rudolf Zeitschke and Berty Glass commissioned Glas to build a multifamily home in the town of Olomouc, today in the Czech Republic, at the corner of Štítného ulice 1 and Wolkerova. Around 1938, he was commissioned by Věra and Ladislav Szathmáry to design a villa for them in Prague, his last architectural work in Europe.[24]

For Hans Glas, the 1930s were marked by great misfortune. His father, Isidor Glas, took his own life on January 4, 1937. On September 28 of that same year, his wife, Olga, committed suicide as well. After the *Anschluss* in March 1938 and the Nazis' rise to power, life became unbearable for Austrian Jews. With the *Verordnung zur Neuordnung des österreichischen Berufsbeamtentums* (Decree on the Reorganization of the Austrian Civil Service) of June 1, 1938, Jewish civil servants, including architects and civil engineers in the public service, were barred from practicing their profession.[25] There were virtually no private commissions for Jewish architects, either. The provincial direction of the Reich Chamber of the Fine Arts, established in Vienna in 1938, henceforth regulated all areas of cultural life and everyone involved in the culture sector. Jewish artists and architects were barred from becoming members of the chamber.

In July 1938, Hans Glas—forty-six years old at the time—fled from Vienna to British India to escape the Nazis. On July 23, 1938, he boarded the *Conte Biancomano* in Genoa, sailing to Naples, through the Suez Canal, and on to Bombay (since 1995 Mumbai). From there, he traveled by train to Calcutta (since 2001 Kolkata), arriving on August 1, 1938. In his forced exile, Hans Glas was able to successfully continue his career as an architect. From the very beginning, he worked for Hindusthan Co-operative Insurance Society Ltd, a large insurance company. He planned the company's headquarters, the Hindusthan Building on Calcutta's Central Avenue, in 1943, as well as numerous villa projects. A 1943 issue of *Victory Magazine* praised the architectural work by one of Adolf Loos's outstanding pupils.[26]

22 See "Ein neues Haus in Döbling von Arch. Hans Glas," *Österreichische Kunst*, vol. 8, 1937, no. 11, 24.

23 Dr. Else Hofmann (1893–1960), at that time a renowned Jewish art historian, philosopher, and editor, was head of the Vienna office of the magazine *Österreichische Kunst* from 1931 to 1938. In 1938, she was forced to flee from the Nazis, first to Paris and then to New York City. The essay does not bear an author's name, but it can be assumed that it was written by Hofmann.

24 Both structures still exist today.

25 "Verordnung zur Neuordnung des österreichischen Berufsbeamtentums vom 1. Juni 1938," https://alex.onb.ac.at/cgi-content/alex?aid=dra&datum=1938&page=785&size=45 (accessed July 20, 2015).

26 See the essay by Margit Franz in this volume.

Immediately after his arrival in Calcutta, Hans Glas began efforts to help his siblings still in Vienna, as well as his lover, the well-known Viennese dancer and choreographer Hilde Holger (1905–2001), flee Austria. After a long odyssey, his youngest brother, the inventor and engineer Emil Glas, and his wife, Elsa Glas, reached Calcutta in March 1939. Holger was able to escape the Nazis in 1939 as well, fleeing to Bombay. Hans Glas's elder brother, the physician Richard Glas, and his family fled to Tel Aviv, while Egon Glas and his wife, Clara Glas, emigrated to New York City. The mother of the four siblings, Karoline (Caroline) Glas, was deported on Transport No. IX/509 to the Łódź ghetto in Poland on September 21, 1941, and murdered by the Nazis.

After retiring, Hans Glas returned to Europe in 1959, settling in Switzerland, at Via Massagno 14 in Lugano. He never returned to his native city of Vienna. On January 28, 1969, Hans Glas died in Lugano at the age of seventy-six.

I
Hilde Holger, Hans Glas's lover, photographed by "Antios," Vienna, 1933. In 1939, the well-known Viennese dancer fled Vienna to Bombay to escape the Nazis.

Margit Franz

Hans Glas in Calcutta (1938–1959): Exile and Architectural Work

"Too hot, too cold, too wet, too dry"—this is how an American soldier described the tropical climate of the huge port city of Calcutta (since 2001 Kolkata) in the early 1940s.[1] This metropolis situated on the Hugli River was enormously diverse in social and economic terms as well. As an "arrival city" for Chinese, Japanese, Armenian, and other refugees, Calcutta was until 1911 the capital of the crown colony of British India. In 1941, reaching a population of over 2.1 million, it became the "second city of the British Empire."[2] In the interwar period, this industrial and intellectual stronghold of British India also developed into a geographical center of India's struggle for independence and endeavored to redefine itself architecturally as well. This ranged from the British-influenced Indo-Saracenic style, Gothic Revival, and Baroque elements to modern forms of expression in steel, such as the Howrah Bridge, built in 1943, one of the world's largest steel-frame cantilever bridges.

The Viennese architect Hans Glas (1892–1969), who arrived in Calcutta at the beginning of August 1938 as an exile, was responsible for a number of the city's most important modern buildings. One of the architectural landmarks of Calcutta's new urbanity, Glas's Hindusthan Building,[3] completed in 1943, became a symbol of India's efforts—long before its political independence—to establish an autonomous version of architectural modernism. Highly qualified, technically inclined, mostly Jewish specialists from Central Europe who had fled from the Nazis did pioneering work for this Indian modernization project, which was launched during British colonial rule.

Arrival in Calcutta

Hans Glas's letters to his longtime Viennese girlfriend, the expressionist dancer Hilde Holger (1905–2001),[4] provide insights into the emotional world of a European refugee who had to leave behind family members threatened by the Nazi regime—including his sick mother and his brothers with their wives—as well as his friends and his lover for a completely unknown continent. And this was at a time when only recently his wife Olga ("Ola") Glas had committed suicide and

1 United States Army, A Pocket Guide to India, Washington, D.C., 1942, https://books.google.at/books?id=ONFOAQAAMAAJ&pg=PP1&source=gbs_selected_pages&cad=1#v=onepage&q&f=false, 6, (accessed Apr. 17, 2024).

2 On Calcutta's special significance within the British Empire, see Tristram Hunt, *Ten Cities that Made an Empire* (Allen Lane, 2014).

3 The spelling of this name varies between Hindustan and Hindusthan. As the sign on the building itself reads "Hindusthan," this spelling has been retained for the present article, except in quotations.

4 Hilde Holger was the stage name of Hans Glas's girlfriend. She was born Hilde Sofer, taking the name Boman-Behram when she married. See Wikipedia, "Hilde Holger," https://en.wikipedia.org/wiki/Hilde_Holger (accessed May 11, 2025).

A
Aerial photograph of Calcutta's city center with the Hindusthan Building in the background (above left), ca. 1945

his father had died as well. Apart from terse statements in administrative files, these letters are the only personal testimonies by the Vienna-born architect that have been passed down.[5] A few excerpts from them are intended to give Hans Glas himself a voice—this one from a letter he wrote to Holger on July 23, 1938, on board the ship *Conte Biancomano*:

"When I entered my cabin on the ship after having bid farewell to Hella[6] in Genoa, I was completely dazed by the events of the past days—and also a bit sad to be completely alone now. Then the door opens and the steward brings me your letter—yours and one from my brother Emil and a bouquet of red roses from him. Now I was no longer alone; I was bonded in thought with those I love by virtue of common blood and bonded with you through the force of the greatest mystery of life—bonded through the divine power of love. When I read your letter, my lover, I was again and again greatly uplifted by your emotions, but also deeply sad—I had to think of Ola[7] (please don't be angry, my child, or hurt if I write to you so sincerely), who loved me unwaveringly for half of her lifetime, and who left me—I don't know why."

The passage took him from Genoa to Naples and through the Suez Canal to the West Indian metropolis of Bombay (since 1995 Mumbai). Unlike other refugees, he received a warm welcome and was waved through customs by the British border officials at the port without any lengthy questioning. Hans Glas was, after all, entering India with a firm employment contract containing, in ad-

4 Hilde Holger was the stage name of Hans Glas's girlfriend. She was born Hilde Sofer, taking the name Boman-Behram when she married. See Wikipedia, "Hilde Holger," https://en.wikipedia.org/wiki/Hilde_Holger (accessed May 11, 2025).

5 Hans Glas's letters are kept in the Hilde Holger Archive, Primavera Boman-Behram, London. Heartfelt thanks to Primavera Boman-Behram, Hilde Holger's daughter and administrator of her estate, for the opportunity to visit on numerous occasions between 2003 and 2017 and to view various archival material and letters.

6 Dr. Helene Heller, the sister of Glas's late wife.

7 Olga Glas, Glas's late wife, who had committed suicide in December 1937.

dition to an affidavit, a lifelong guarantee in the case of illness, or social or political misconduct, as well as the assumption of all incurred costs in the host country. "I left Vienna for India after the invasion of Germany, having been deprived of the possibility to continue my profession under the then prevailing circumstances, and to escape the deportation into a concentration camp. I arrived in India on the 1st of August 1938 and have been living since this time in Calcutta. I am working here in my line as an Architect with Messrs. Hindustan Cooperative Insurance Society Ltd. to build up their Head-office building at Chittaranjan Avenue and others," he wrote in an official statement in December 1940.[8]

The Hindusthan Building: headquarters of a national insurance company

Hindusthan Co-operative Insurance Society Ltd was founded in 1907 "with highly patriotic motives."[9] The ceremony took place at Jorasanko Thakur Bari, the ancestral residence of the Tagore family. Rabindranath Tagore (1861–1941), the winner of the 1913 Nobel Prize in Literature and an eloquent spokesperson for the cause of Indian independence, descended from this distinguished family.[10] The British insurance companies on the Indian subcontinent initially excluded Indians completely as customers; they later accepted them but charged them high additional premiums. In 1870, the Bombay Mutual Life Assurance Society became the first Indian insurance company to offer insurance policies to Indians at standard rates, followed by the Bharat Insurance Company in 1896. The boycott of British goods declared in 1905 in Bengal by the Swadeshi movement (from the Sanskrit *swa desh*: "of one's own country") resulted in the establishment of additional national insurance companies. By 1938, India's insurance market had expanded to 176 businesses. Hindusthan Co-operative Insurance Society Ltd was one of the largest and most successful in the country. In 1956, all existing insurance companies were nationalized and merged to create the Life Insurance Company (LIC). The building designed by Hans Glas in Kolkata is still owned by this company, and several blue billboards with the LIC logo still hang on its façade.

In the fall of 1938, Hans Glas wrote to Hilde Holger: "I want to tell you now what I have experienced personally since landing in India and how I am living (I already wrote to you about the splendid sea voyage). In Bombay, I was given a touching welcome by Fred on the steamer. Everything was taken care of for me, and I was received at the Hindustan company with money. Spent the night with

8 Letter from Hans Glas to the Jewish Refugees' Relief Association, Calcutta, Dec. 31, 1940, in the National Archive of India (NAI), HOME_POLITICAL_E_1940_NA_F-72-3-34, Recommendation of the AAC Bengal Case No 34-Glass, Mr JH, 13.

9 "LIC (Life Insurance Corporation of India)," *Brief History Of Insurance*, https://licindia.in/history (accessed Apr. 18, 2024).

10 In honor of Rabindranath Tagore's 100th birthday, Rabindra Bharati University was established at Jorasanko Thakur Bari in 1961.

a friend (his name is Bund).[11] The next evening I took the sleeper to Calcutta. The journey took two nights and one day. . . . Arrival in Calcutta: Was welcomed on the platform by an engineer from the company with two servants. Accommodated at the finest of hotels. Settled accounts with the company and with my sponsor, Finance Minister Sarker: Should live well here—company pays for everything."[12]

Nalini Ranjan Sarkar as Hans Glas's sponsor

Nalini Ranjan Sarkar (1882–1953), whom Hans Glas refers to as his sponsor, was a Bengali industrialist, politician, and philanthropist who was greatly involved in Bengal's economic development.[13] The region was at the time a British-East Indian province in the area of the Ganges-Brahmaputra delta. With the founding of the Republic of India in 1947, it was divided into West and East Bengal, with the former claimed by India and the latter by Pakistan. This was the industrial and economic center of the British colonial empire in India and at the same time the most populous part of the occupied subcontinent.

Sarkar became involved early on in India's independence movement and supported Mahatma Gandhi's (1869–1948) nonviolent resistance to British colonial rule. He cultivated close contacts to the country's cultural elite—such as the writer and social reformer Rabindranath Tagore—and was also well connected to India's political circles. Nalini Sarkar became a member of the Indian National Congress (INC), the political party led intermittently by Gandhi that was primarily devoted to the Indian movement for independence from Great Britain. The young, politically motivated supporter of the non-cooperation movement vigorously pursued its goals of national self-rule and economic self-sufficiency (*swaraj*). Later, Sarkar was a member of several governmental bodies and from 1937 to 1939 was the finance minister of Bengal Province. In addition, he was actively involved in the municipal administration of Calcutta, becoming a city councilor in 1932 and mayor in 1934.[14] In 1941, Nalini Sarkar joined the Viceroy's Executive Council in New Delhi, the highest advisory body and cabinet in British India under the British viceroy, first in charge of education and health and later of commerce and industry. In 1943, to protest Gandhi's detention by the British, he resigned from all his functions and resumed his professional career.

11 Glas is referring here to the Austrian Lorenz Achilles Bund (b. 1886 in Lemberg/Lwiw), who settled in Bombay's Fort area with his wife and daughter as a "Manufacturer's Representative" and was granted British citizenship on Aug. 1, 1936. See NAI, Home Department, GoI 112/39 Public: List of persons of Austrian, German and Italian origin naturalised as British subjects since 1930.

12 In his letters to Hilde Holger, Hans Glas consistently used the spelling Sarker instead of Sarkar. Even in India, both spellings are common.

13 See "Sarkar, Nalini Ranjan," in *Banglapedia: National Encyclopedia of Bangladesh*, https://en.banglapedia.org/index.php/Sarkar,_Nalini_Ranjan (accessed Apr. 18, 2024); Wikipedia, "Nalini Ranjan Sarkar," https://en.wikipedia.org/wiki/Nalini_Ranjan_Sarkar (accessed Aug. 18, 2025).

14 Sarkar served as mayor in 1934 and 1935. At the beginning, mayors of Calcutta were elected only to a one-year term. See Wikipedia, "List of mayors of Kolkata," https://en.wikipedia.org/wiki/List_of_mayors_of_Kolkata (accessed Apr. 18, 2024).

B
A portrait of Nalini Ranjan Sarkar, Hans Glas's "sponsor," 1942.

In 1911, only four years after the founding of Hindusthan Co-operative Insurance Society Ltd, Sarkar had joined this insurance company as a low-level employee. He quickly moved up to become general manager and then company president, a position he held until his death in 1953. His vision of continuous growth in the prospering national insurance market, along with keen foresight with regard to business and a political commitment to the independence of India, made him a pioneer of the national insurance sector.[15] In addition, he sat on the advisory boards of several large firms and infrastructure projects in the area, including the port of Calcutta, and for years was director of the Bengal Chamber of Commerce and Industry. After India gained independence, he again became politically active, serving as finance minister of West Bengal beginning in 1948 and as chief minister of West Bengal for a few months in 1949.[16] He focused particular attention on higher education, devoting himself, for example, to crafting educational policy for India's first universities in Calcutta, Benares (today Varanasi), Delhi, and Dacca (today Dhaka).

Hans Glas and the establishment of technical universities in post-colonial India

Nalini Ranjan Sarkar also became an important part of the history of independent India for championing the establishment of the Indian Institutes of Technology (IITs).[17] From 1946 to 1952, he was head of the All India Council for Technical Education (AICTE), also known as the Sarkar Committee. This body recommended that the technical education system be modeled after the Massachusetts Institute of Technology (MIT) and established as a permanent institution.

15 *Hindustan Building LIC*, https://in.worldorgs.com/catalog/kolkata/insurance-agency/hindustan-building-lic (accessed May 23, 2025).
16 See Wikipedia, "Nalini Ranjan Sarkar."
17 See Salim Saquib, "Nalini Ranjan Sarkar: The Real Father of IIT," *Heritage Times*, Jan. 8, 2021, https://www.heritagetimes.in/nalini-ranjan-sarkar-the-real-father-of-iit/ (accessed Apr. 18, 2024).

There are presently twenty-three IITs in the country that are under the purview of the Ministry of Education, and today they represent the success story of the technical higher-education system in post-colonial India. They have developed into a training ground for highly qualified specialists who are in demand all over the world and not infrequently headhunted by tech companies from Silicon Valley and other global innovation centers.

Sarkar also played a crucial role in the foundation of the first IIT, in the West Bengal city of Kharagpur. This region, with its high density of industrial companies, was chosen to be the site of India's first technical university. In May 1950, the Eastern Higher Technical Institute was established, at that time still located in central Calcutta. Already by September of that same year, it was moved to Kharagpur, 120 kilometers to the south, and in August 1951, four years after the passing of the Indian Independence Act, the institute was officially recognized as the country's first IIT.[18]

It is also in this context of higher-education policy that the role of Hans Glas is to be seen, the role of an architect whose professional career in India was linked to the institutional reforms of those years and especially to the influence of Sarkar. From the day he arrived in his Indian exile, Glas could count on an extensive network that opened crucial doors for him in Calcutta as well as in Bengal. Through his employment with the financially strong Hindusthan Cooperative Insurance Society Ltd, and thanks to the regional and economic policymaker Nalini Ranjan Sarkar, he found himself in a privileged position during the entire period of his exile: After the friendly reception in the strange land, he was guaranteed a permanent position; his job as a well-paid architect provided him with a comfortable life and ultimately the opportunity to spend his retirement in Switzerland. As Glas bears the title of "Professor" in later documents, it is quite possible that, through Sarkar's considerable influence, he was given a position at IIT Kharagpur teaching architecture.[19]

In any case, Glas was undoubtedly well integrated into the elite and wealthy circles of Bengal. "I have received a *very* warm welcome everywhere. Sarker has seen to it that I have a fabulous reputation here. Difficult to live up to?! I am very much appreciated here—I'm constantly getting invitations—from Sarker as well," he wrote to his girlfriend in the autumn of 1938 in his second letter from Calcutta.

Refugee networks

"Hans Glas, an architect from Vienna, was among the refugees. Years previously he was offered a lucrative post by the Calcutta municipality but turned it down. Fate, however, played queer tricks. Bearing the offer in mind in the incep-

18 Nalini Ranjan Sarkar Avenue, on the campus of IIT Kharagpur, is named for the institute's founder.

19 Repeated attempts to contact the archive of IIT Kharagpur by email and phone were unfortunately unsuccessful.

tion of the Nazi brutality, he made his way to Calcutta where he became an architect of distinction."[20] According to Ezekiel Musleah, former rabbi of the Morgan David Synagogue in Calcutta, Hans Glas had received an invitation from the Calcutta municipality even before 1938. This came from Sarkar himself, who was the mayor of Calcutta from July 1934 until the end of April 1935. "I had met the former Mayor of Calcutta, Mr. N.L. Sircar [*sic*], when he was studying municipal questions in Vienna: he wrote to say that he will give me employment, a[nd] I got this job in the Hindusthan Insurance Co[mpany] of which Sircar is the managing director. I now get Rs. 1,000 a month as architect of its head office now being built,"[21] Hans Glas wrote to the British colonial administration in India around 1940.

In April 1934, the *Kleine Volks-Zeitung* announced the visit of the mayor of Calcutta to Vienna with the headline "Calcutta learns from Vienna."[22] Red Vienna, with its social and educational policies as well as its municipal housing programs, attracted great interest internationally, and local politicians from the Indian subcontinent followed the activities in Vienna closely. The article refers to a fellow party member and Sarkar's predecessor as Calcutta's mayor, Subhas Chandra Bose (1897–1945), who held the office from August 1930 to April 1931.[23] From 1933, Bose visited Austria on several occasions, the first time to recover from a bout with tuberculosis, which he had contracted in British prisons in India. During this stay, he wrote his book *The Indian Struggle*, which covered the years 1920–1934 and was published in London in 1935. In 1937, he married a Viennese woman, Emilie Schenkl (1910–1996), in Bad Gastein, with the result that his name appeared several times in the Austrian press in this period.

Simultaneously, Austria was showing a growing interest in India. In 1934, this led to the founding of a society that was to promote economic and cultural exchange between the two: the Vienna-based Indian Central-European Society, of which Subhas Chandra Bose was a founding member.[24] With its world-renowned medical institutions, the Austrian capital attracted not only many Indian patients but also medical students from India who—because of the lack of study opportunities at home—completed their studies at Vienna's university clinics. The Indian students and scientists[25] in Vienna formed the Hindustan Academical Association.[26]

20 Ezekiel N. Musleah, *On the Banks of the Ganga: The Sojourn of Jews in Calcutta* (Christopher Publishing House, 1975), 396.

21 Note by Hans Glas, in NAI, HOME_POLITICAL_E_1940_NA_F-72-3-34, Recommendation of the AAC Bengal Case No 34-Glass, Mr JH, 9.

22 "Kalkutta lernt von Wien. Bürgermeister Subhas Chandra Bose kommt zu Besuch," *Kleine Volks-Zeitung*, Apr. 18, 1934, 7. Available digitally at *ANNO. Historische österreichische Zeitungen und Zeitschriften*, https://anno.onb.ac.at/cgi-content/anno?aid=kvz&datum=19340418 (accessed Aug. 18, 2025).

23 Subhas Chandra Bose later led the armed resistance against the British colonial government in India. Unlike his allies and fellow party members Mahatma Gandhi and Jawaharlal Nehru, he employed more and more military means to attain independence for India, which ultimately resulted in an alliance with authoritarian Japan (1943–1945).

24 See Otto Faltis, "India and Austria," *The Modern Review*, 59, Feb. 1936, 205–207, https://archive.org/details/in.ernet.dli.2015.277486/page/n235/mode/1up (accessed Apr. 18, 2024).

25 According to recent research, these were exclusively male students and scientists.

These manifold relationships were strengthened through reciprocal visits: For example, Anna and Philipp Rezek, a physician couple from Vienna, traveled to India in the early 1930s to conduct research into liver diseases.[27] Following Austria's annexation by the German Reich in March 1938, which resulted in many people being forced to flee due to their ethnic background, religion, or political affiliation, these connections proved helpful for the swift establishment of efficient networks. From 1938 to 1939, for instance, the Austro-Indian Association, with its economic institute in Vienna, together with the Indian Institute of Science and Commerce, tried to provide refugees with visas for India as well as employment opportunities in that country. However, as is not uncommon with refugee aid, there were cases of abuse in the middle of this life-threatening situation.[28] In any case, a letter dated October 16, 1938, from Hans Glas to his girlfriend, Hilde Holger, who was stranded in Vienna, reveals that a Viennese representative of the Austro-Indian Association demanded a sizable sum of money from him and his brother Richard Glas (1890–1961) without providing any service in return. At that time, Holger was desperately seeking a visa for herself and her sister Hedi, who was later murdered along with their parents by the Nazis in a concentration camp.

To date, it has not been possible to precisely reconstruct the details of Hans Glas's flight to India. There are no archival documents regarding his visa for India. It is also not known with absolute certainty who signed the affidavit—the declaration of personal guarantee for all immigrants—for him. Beginning in mid-March 1938, all refugees from annexed Austria to British India needed a guarantee of financial security. As of the beginning of 1939, thanks to the lobbying of British-Jewish organizations, the Jewish Refugees' Relief Association in India was able to provide this guarantee as well. In the previously mentioned letter, Hans Glas referred to Nalini Ranjan Sarkar as his "sponsor." Most likely, it was Sarkar himself or a representative of the Hindusthan Co-operative Insurance Society Ltd who signed the life-saving affidavit for the ambitious Viennese architect on the run.

Arrival City: Calcutta

Several hundred people persecuted by the Nazis in Germany and Austria found refuge in and around Calcutta. The city's financially strong Jewish community established relief networks for threatened Jewish refugees. Sir David Elias Ezra (1871–1947)—a successful businessman, director of the Reserve Bank of India,

26 See Swami Agehananda Bharati (born as Leopold Fischer), *The Ochre Robe* (George Allen & Unwin, 1961), 35f.

27 See "Rezek, Philipp Raphael," in Herbert A. Strauss and Werner Röder (eds.), *International Biographical Dictionary of Central European Emigrés 1933–1945*, vol. II, part 2: *L–Z, The Arts, Sciences, and Literature* (Research Foundation for Jewish Immigration, Inc., 1983), 964f.

28 See Ernst Ritter, *So habe ich es erlebt*, 1958, 9 (manuscript, Leo Baeck Institute: ME 1264. MM III 2), https://digipres.cjh.org/delivery/DeliveryManagerServlet?dps_pid=IE8917300 (accessed May 10, 2024).

and president of the Jewish Refugees' Relief Association—and major Jewish companies such as B. N. Elias & Co. employed Central European Jewish refugees, among them Emil Glas (1894–1956), one of the architect's three brothers.[29] The Jewish Refugees' Relief Association supported Jews fleeing Germany and Austria by helping them find accommodations, jobs, and schools and kindergartens for their children. A remarkably large number of Austrian and German physicians found a safe haven in Calcutta between 1933 and 1938. Many technical specialists were provided with well-paid positions in the many factories and in the region's wood and steel industry. Western art, particularly classical music, was broadcast daily by the Western Music Department of All India Radio, including concerts given by musicians who had escaped from Austria and Germany.[30] According to the current state of research, however, there was only one other architect who fled to Calcutta: Victor Lurje (1883–1944), an inlay artist and a member of the Wiener Werkstätte. But unlike Glas, he came to Calcutta by way of Shanghai and Singapore with no confirmed employment. Because he lacked a job and contacts, Lurje and his wife, Leopoldine, were interned outside Calcutta during the early war years by the British as "enemy aliens." Only in 1944 did he receive short-term employment as a "consulting architect" to the Maharaja of Jodhpur, some 2,000 kilometers west of Calcutta. He did not survive the long, strenuous return journey, however: he died of a heart attack at the train station in Jaipur.[31]

Forms of refugee solidarity

From Calcutta, Hans Glas tried to obtain a visa for British India for his girlfriend, the expressionist dancer Hilde Holger, as well. In his first letter, from July 23, 1938, he wrote, still euphoric: "I will make every effort to find something for you in Calcutta—a job that corresponds to your artistic individuality. . . . I will speak with your and my new friends, and it should work!" In his second letter, dated October 16, 1938—only three months after his arrival in Calcutta—he already sounds more disillusioned: "I've asked around here about prospects for you, my darling—for the time being haven't met the right people—but it will work out." He sounds disappointed, even helpless: "I am so very sorry, dear Hilde, that I can't help you—you of all people, for whom it would be so important to me. For you to simply come without any kind of employment and then look for something here is endlessly difficult. . . . I wouldn't dare to even have one of my brothers come over."

29 See NAI Home_Political_EW_1940_NA_F-72-3-33: Recommendation of the ACC Bengal Case No-33 Glass MrE Mrs, 15.

30 On the situation regarding the admission of refugees into the Indian labor market, see Margit Franz, *Gateway India. Deutschsprachiges Exil in Indien zwischen britischer Kolonialherrschaft Maharadschas und Gandhi* (CLIO, 2015), 133ff.

31 See Leopoldine Lurje's letter to the Allied Control Commission Austria, Sept. 21, 1946, in the British Library (BL) IOR/L/PJ/32, 167, quoted in Franz, 2015, 284.

C
Calcutta, the "second city of the British Empire," ca. 1945

But Hans Glas did eventually accomplish this!

On December 21, 1938, Hans Glas wrote, "It looks as if Egon has been rescued—he is getting an affidavit for America. Richard and Emil and their wives have only me to support them. After months of work, I think that Emil and his wife can now get out—both will live with me—and now I will concentrate my efforts on Richard. I will manage this as well, and then there will be five of us here—you know how devoted I am to my brothers, we still won't have an easy time of it—but we'll make it."

With regard to his girlfriend, there was a mixture of bitterness about his fruitless efforts and disappointment on her part about her insufficient qualifications to make it in a local, male-dominated, oversaturated labor market. In Hans Glas's words: "This hinterland is today completely inundated with locals who, even if they have only primitive abilities, work for such ridiculously low wages that a European cannot compete. These are the prospects, my darling!"[32]

The chance of being granted refuge in British India was significantly better for technically or medically qualified people, or for those with legal rights through marriage into affluent Indian families.

Emil Carol Glas—engineer, inventor, and brother of Hans Glas—and his wife, the secretary Elsa Glas (née Dubsky, 1895–?), reached India in March 1939. After a short internment immediately after the beginning of World War II, in September 1939, and another internment in summer 1940, Emil was quickly released due to his technical inventions, which were seen as a possible contribution to the war effort. He collaborated with the British military authorities in India throughout the entire war. Officially, Emil was initially employed by a tobacco producer and as an assistant to his brother in his architectural office. In 1946 and 1947, he is listed as a "consulting engineer" with the Hindustan Development Cooperation,[33] his brother's employer.[34]

32 Letter from Hans Glas, Calcutta, to Hilde Holger, Oct. 16, 1938, Hilde Holger Archive.
33 In 1946, the company wrote its name as "Hindustan Development Cooperation."
34 See NAI Home_Political_EW_1940_NA_F-72-3-33: Recommendation of the ACC Bengal Case No-33 Glass MrE Mrs.

The cohesion of the Glas family is evident in the fact that the three family members lived together in the Temple Chambers building for the entire duration of their stay in Calcutta. Even later, Hans Glas lived with his sister-in-law under one roof in Ticino, Switzerland. With regard to exile in Canada—and applicable to other countries of exile, particularly British India—Patrick Farges observes: "Life stories by exiles show that they were considering less a refuge *country* and more a refuge *address*."[35] In exile, refugees activated various forms of solidarity, depending on their "family social capital."[36] In the case of the Glas family, it was "family solidarities," rooted in deep, mutual affection and a sense of responsibility. Hans Glas failed, however, in his efforts to bring his second brother to Calcutta as well. Dr. Richard Glas, urologist and assistant to Julius Tandler, was able to emigrate to Palestine with his wife, Elisabeth, née Hirschenhauser.[37] Egon Glas fled to the US with his wife, Clara.

The daily work and architectural activities of Hans Glas

Above the rooftops of Calcutta, in the most exclusive part of town between the Town Hall and the Calcutta High Court, Hans Glas had his office in one of the most prestigious commercial and residential buildings of the time, Temple Chambers on the Old Post Office Street, a structure in simple classicist style.

"I have my own apartment with a separate studio space, very lovely area, centrally located but still a bit open—view of palm and olive trees, high above the rooftops of Calcutta. It's hot as well. I have company when I like, but I am *very often* alone and brood too much. I have sufficient work—a large office and commercial building, plans for government buildings for civil servants, plans for complete build-outs, a subdivision plan for a large villa colony where I then want to build a few villas—I can't complain. The pay is enough for a nice life—but not more."[38]

The completed villa colony Glas mentioned is a housing complex in New Alipore, an upscale residential neighborhood in what is now South Kolkata. Hindusthan Co-operative Insurance Society Ltd invested considerable financial resources in the acquisition of large parcels of land in the southwestern part of the city in order to build a modern satellite settlement for more upmarket residences.[39]

In December 1938, he wrote to his girlfriend in Vienna: "I'm still doing well—working on a parcel of land with 700 building sites where I will then build a number of houses."[40] In his studio in Temple Chambers, Glas planned modern office buildings for Calcutta. In 1943, the city's most modern and impressive

35 Patrick Farges, "Exil in Kanada – ein Exil der 'kleinen Leute'?," in Daniel Azuelos (ed.), *Alltag im Exil* (Königshausen & Neumann, 2011), 22.
36 See ibid, 28.
37 See Österreichische Nationalbibliothek (ed.), *Handbuch österreichischer Autorinnen und Autoren jüdischer Herkunft*, vol. 1 (De Gruyter, 2002), 420.
38 Letter from Hans Glas, Calcutta, to Hilde Holger, Oct. 16, 1938, Hilde Holger Archive.
39 See Wikipedia, "Nalini Ranjan Sarkar."
40 Letter from Hans Glas, Calcutta, to Hilde Holger, Dec. 22, 1938, Hilde Holger Archive.

D
The Temple Chambers building, where Hans Glas lived and worked, was located only 300 meters from the mighty Hugli River.

E
Hindusthan Building; design: Hans Glas, 1943.

structure was about to be completed: the Hindusthan Building, a monumental, unadorned, modernist administrative and office building on a triangular plot of land directly on Central Avenue. The façade design is limited to simple structural elements that by means of uniform balcony units achieve a clearly defined, three-dimensional effect. The sides of the office complex are interrupted by plain, tower-like elements, each of which serves as a modernist entrance portal. Architecturally, they draw attention to themselves, thus fulfilling their social function as reception halls. The corner solution is formally reminiscent of the distinct architectural design of Viennese public housing; in Calcutta, however, this is adapted to the tropical climate, equipped with balconies and modeled after the façade design of the side walls. The flat roof contains another level: a recessed floor whose façade structure is a deliberate contrast to that of the lower floors.

As it happened, the building was occupied by the US Army immediately after its completion and served as the central military administrative and services building. The photographer Clyde Waddell, who was stationed as a US soldier in Calcutta during World War II, described its use this way: "Hindusthan building, one of the most modern in Calcutta, was built for an Insurance company but occupied upon its completion by the U.S. Army. Located in the heart of the city, it is the nerve center of all military business, containing post office, finance office, Base Section offices, air, rail booking offices, a radio station, giant post exchange, Officers mess and living quarters, signal offices and others."[41]

Victory Magazine, a US military periodical, also paid tribute to Hans Glas's work: "The famous Labor Quarters of Vienna were the work of one of Adolf Loos' outstanding pupils who is the architect responsible for the New Hindustan Insurance Co-operative Society building on Central Avenue, the biggest office premises to be constructed in Calcutta. He also made the plans for a new hospital to be erected in the city in the near future," referring to today's Chittaranjan Cancer Hospital.[42]

In India, Hans Glas frequently collaborated in the area of interior design with avant-garde artists, including the Bengali sculptor Prodosh Das Gupta (or Dasgupta, 1912–1991), co-founder of the *Calcutta Group*, which searched for a global aesthetic between East and West while drawing on ancient Indian traditions. Das Gupta created a bust of Hans Glas in 1952, later recalling, "Temperamentally an artist, he is an architect of renown and is responsible for designing many important buildings in India. I came in touch with him in connection with some works I did for a building he designed and was charmed with his informal manners and the broken, 'continental' English he spoke with gusto."[43]

As a member of the Rotary Club and the Freemasons, Glas also supported the Jewish Refugees' Relief Association[44] and provided employment for refugees in his architectural office, including for the Austrian engineer Egon Kars, who as a result of this was released from internment.[45] As early as December 1938, Glas

F
Bust of Hans Glas by Prodosh Das Gupta, 1952.

41 Clyde Waddell, photo no. 4 in *Clyde Waddell photograph album of Calcutta*, 1945, University of Pennsylvania, Rare Book & Manuscript Library: Ms. Coll. 802, https://openn.library.upenn.edu/Data/0002/html/mscoll802.html (accessed May 11, 2025).

42 Dora Newfield, "Mr. Strauss Comes to Town," *Victory Magazine* V (February 1943), n. p.; courtesy of Ken Robbins.

43 Prodosh Das Gupta, *My Sculpture* (Oxford Book & Stationery Co., 1955), 25.

44 Musleah, 1975, 396.

45 WBSA/HO/Political Branch/W1036/41: "List of released detainees and those provided with guarantees by the Jewish Refugees' Relief Association (JRRA), Calcutta," quoted in Kaustav Chakrabarti, *European Jewish Immigrants in India Between the Two World Wars* (Priyashilpa Prakashan, 2008), 63.

presented his ideas to the Rotary Club, writing the following day, "Yesterday, I gave a lecture on modern architecture at the local Rotary Club—with slides—which was quite a success."[46]

Calcutta's turbulent 1940s

Hans Glas's letters to Hilde Holger end in December 1938. In summer 1939, with the help of the journalist Karl Petrasch (later Charles Petras),[47] Holger was able to flee to India as well, but to the city of Bombay, some 2,000 west of Calcutta.[48] In Calcutta, Hans Glas experienced World War II, India's independence in 1947, and the turbulent developmental years of the young nation up to 1959. It cannot be precisely reconstructed how he perceived this historic period, as no letters or personal documents have survived from this phase of his life.

No decade changed Calcutta so profoundly in such a short time—politically, economically, architecturally, socially, culturally, but also militarily—as did the 1940s. The outbreak of World War II in Europe in September 1939 ushered in a new decade of bellicose actions; three years later, the war had become a reality in Calcutta as well. It fundamentally altered the everyday life of the country's people—through rationing, flows of refugees from Malaya (today part of Peninsular Malaysia), the massive presence of British and American troops, Japanese air strikes, the construction of plane runways in the middle of the city, and a great deal of new infrastructure facilities. The Hindusthan Building, for example, was first used as the command center of the US military in Calcutta before it was able to serve its intended purpose as an insurance and administrative building after the war.

The immense strain placed on the city by the war also resulted in an intensification of colonial suppression and caused deep conflicts of loyalty among many Indians. Moreover, the 1940s were also a decade when India's struggle for independence heated up. In 1942, the Indian National Congress founded the nonviolent Quit India Movement, while the former mayor of Calcutta, Subhas Chandra Bose, fled the city to establish the armed Indian National Army (INA), with the support of Imperial Japan. Meanwhile, the economic pressure applied by the British colonial power, combined with political neglect, led to severe civil catastrophes, including the famine in Bengal resulting from the war, ethni-

46 Letter from Hans Glas, Calcutta, to Hilde Holger, Dec. 22, 1938, Hilde Holger Archive.

47 On Petras, see Margit Franz, "Charles Petras," in *METROMOD Archive*, 2021, https://archive.metromod.net/viewer.p/69/2951/object/5138-11945051, last changed on Sept. 14, 2021 (accessed May 11, 2025); Franz, 2015, 248–266.

48 On Hilde Holger in Bombay, see Rachel Lee, "Hilde Holger," in *METROMOD Archive*, 2021, https://archive.metromod.net/viewer.p/69/2951/object/5138-11945051, last changed on Sept. 7, 2021 (accessed May 11, 2025); Rachel Lee, "Hilde Holger: Vienna > Bombay > London. An expressionist dancer's route through exile," in *METROMOD*, https://metromod.net/2019/04/04/hilde-holger/ (accessed May 11, 2025); Margit Franz, "Exile meets Avantgarde: ExilantInnen-Kunstnetzwerke in Bombay," in Margit Franz and Heimo Halbrainer (eds.), *Going East – Going South. Österreichisches Exil in Asien und Afrika* (CLIO, 2014), 403–431, esp. 408–413; Denny Hirschbach and Rick Takvorian (eds.), *Die Kraft des Tanzes. Hilde Holger. Wien–Bombay–London. Über das Leben und Werk der Tänzerin, Choreographin und Tanzpädagogin* (Zeichen und Spuren, 1990).

G
American soldiers were part of Calcutta's cityscape in the 1940s. Photo by Clyde Waddell, 1945.

cally motivated massacres in Calcutta in the course of the Partition of Bengal, the refugee crisis, and the abusive treatment of some INA combatants. These events left behind deep scars in the social landscape of the city of arts and industry. After India's independence, British residents as well as many Muslim Bengalis, Anglo-Indians, and other formerly influential groups left Calcutta, which had a sustained effect on the city's political and economic structure in the post-liberation period. The arrival of refugees from East Bengal brought new resources but also many problems and great turbulence for the city. Calcutta underwent fundamental changes. By 1911, the political power center had already shifted to Delhi, and while Bombay rose to become the economic capital of independent India, Calcutta was struggling with economic decline, social tensions, and the loss of its former status. The city found itself in an inexorable transformation.[49]

In the transitional period around the country's year of independence, 1947, the young democracy and the fragile state of India were faced with immense political, administrative, and infrastructure-related challenges, in addition to millions of refugees from East and West Pakistan and a war over Kashmir, which began in the year of the country's foundation. In the midst of all this upheaval, Hans Glas planned and built office and residential buildings as well as settlements that are not individually documented. The history of Calcutta's modern architecture has not yet been written; the hot, humid climate of the metropolis is not conducive to long-term archiving of records and plans, and the archive of Hindusthan Co-operative Insurance Society Ltd is inaccessible. One can only hope for a surprising find in an Indian or British governmental archive, although investigations to date have proven fruitless.

According to recent research, Hans Glas left behind no records from these turbulent years—neither personal nor professional. Nevertheless, he lived and

49 See "Dramatic Events," in *1940s Calcutta of a Changing City*, http://www.calcutta1940s.org/Frames.html (accessed May 10, 2024).

worked in Calcutta during this transformative period and exerted a lasting influence on this city both architecturally and with regard to higher-education policy.

In the first year of his stay in Calcutta, 1938, he wrote to Hilde Holger, who was able to emigrate to India in 1939: "I'm convinced, dear Hilde, that you will feel at home here—when the Indians are nice, they are delightful—I have had the best of experiences with them."[50] These positive experiences appear to have been confirmed for him in the years of profound transformation in Calcutta as well. It was not until 1959, after twenty-one years in the country—nearly half of his professional life—that Hans Glas left the old Bengali city and the young nation of India. At the age of 67, he was financially so secure that he was able to spend the final ten years of his life living with his sister-in-law in retirement in Central Europe—not in Austria but in the Mediterranean city of Lugano, in the south of Switzerland.

50 Letter from Hans Glas, Calcutta, to Hilde Holger, Dec. 21, 1938, Hilde Holger Archive.

"I have my own apartment with a separate studio space, very lovely area, centrally located but still a bit open—view of palm and olive trees, high above the rooftops of Calcutta. It's hot as well. I have company when I like, but I am very often alone and brood too much."

Hans Glas, October 1938

Hans Glas's last extant letter from Calcutta to Hilde Holger in Vienna, dated December 21, 1938.

Meine liebe Hilde! Aus deinem letzten Brief sehe ich, daß Du mich aber „missverstanden" hast. Du hast recht Hilde, man soll von Menschen, die man noch nicht erprobt hat, keine zu gute Meinung haben – die Enttäuschung ist zu schmerzlich. Wenn Du aber wüsstest Liebe, welche Verantwortung meiner Familie gegenüber auf meinen Schultern lastet, würdest Du mich verstehen können. Der Egon scheint gerettet zu sein – er bekommt ein Affidavit nach Amerika. Richard und Emil samt Frauen haben nur mich als einzige Stütze. Nach monatelangen Bemühungen glaube ich, daß der Emil und Frau nun herauskommen können – beide werden bei mir wohnen – nun bemühe ich mich bezgl. des Richard. Auch das wird gelingen, dann sind wir fünf hier – Du weißt mit welcher Liebe ich an meinen Brüdern hänge, aber immerhin werden wir's nicht leicht haben – aber es wird gehen. Soll ich mich nochmals entschuldigen bei Dir, Hilde – was soll ich tun. Für den jüdischen Arzt in Bamberg wird es wohl leichter sein – trotzdem ist deine Menschlichkeit auf das Höchste einzuschätzen. Ich bin überzeugt, daß er Dir auch bald Arbeit verschaffen wird – er hat doch seine Beziehungen und scheint nach seinem Schreiben entsprechend nett zu sein. Ich bin überzeugt, l. Hilde, daß Du Dich wohlfühlen wirst – wenn die Leute nett sind, sind sie entsprechend – ich habe da schon die beste Erfahrung gemacht. Hat der Arzt schon Schritte wegen Visum unternommen?

Caroline Wohlgemuth

The Rezek Family: Expulsion and Flight from Vienna

A modern physician couple: Anna and Philipp Rezek

Anna Rezek was born as Anna Bunzl on July 28, 1895, into a Jewish family in Vienna. Her father, Ludwig Lajos Bunzl (1857–1928), came from Pressburg (Bratislava), while her mother, Julia "Dolly" Bunzl (1867–1932), née Porges, was born in London. The couple had three daughters: Minnie (1893–1962), Anna, and Cornelia "Lily" (1898–1986) Bunzl. The family lived at Grillparzerstraße 14, in Vienna's first district.

Ludwig Lajos Bunzl, Anna's father, was at that time director of Bunzl & Biach, one of the largest paper and felt factories in Austria. The business had grown out of the company Emanuel Biach's Eidam, which had been founded in Pressburg in 1854 by Moritz Bunzl (1820–1875), Ludwig Lajos Bunzl's father. In addition to the business's headquarters in Vienna, it also owned numerous plants and subsidiaries in what at the time were the countries of the Habsburg Empire. Of great importance for the company was the location in Ortmann, near the Lower Austrian town of Pernitz: Hugo Bunzl (1883–1961), a first cousin of Anna Rezek, commissioned the architect Josef Frank (1885–1967) to build worker housing, a day-care center for children, and a summer house in this village.[1] Frank was not only close friends with the Bunzl family; there were also family ties between them: In 1910, Frank's younger sister Hedwig, known as "Hexi" (1887–1966), had married Karl Tedesko (1874–1945), then the manager of the Bunzl & Biach paper factory. Karl Tedesko's parents were Salomon Tedesko (1845–1931) and Klara Tedesko (1854–1915), née Bunzl. Klara Tedesko, Hexi's mother-in-law, had five brothers, one of whom was Ludwig Lajos Bunzl, Anna Rezek's father. The Tedesko and Bunzl families were among Josef Frank's first clients and later some of the most important customers of his home-furnishing business Haus & Garten.[2]

Philipp Rezek was born in Vienna on August 23, 1894—also into a Jewish family. His father, Adolf Rezek (1857–1928), came from Prague and was a butcher; his mother Gisella Rezek (1867–1948), née Goldstein, was a native Viennese. Philipp Rezek had two brothers—Heinrich Rezek (1896–1972) and Paul Rezek (1898–1953)—and a sister, Stefanie Rezek, who died only a few weeks after her birth in Vienna in 1904. During World War I, Philipp Rezek served in the Austrian army, first as a soldier on the front and later in a hospital for epidemic diseases in Albania.[3]

1 See Maria Welzig's essay in this volume.

2 From the family archive and according to information provided by Prof. Peter Weinberger and his wife, Kitty Bunzl. See also Caroline Wohlgemuth's essay "A House from Tomorrow: Visionary Rooms, Interior Design, and Furniture" in this volume.

3 See Memorial Book for the Victims of National Socialism at the University of Vienna 1938, Philipp Rezek, https://gedenkbuch.univie.ac.at/person/philipp-rezek (accessed July 30, 2025).

Anna Bunzl and Philipp Rezek both studied medicine from 1917 to 1921 at the University of Vienna Medical School and were both awarded the title "Dr. med." on the same day: July 26, 1921. Shortly thereafter, on August 15, 1921, they married in the Vienna synagogue, on Seitenstettengasse, in the city's first district. The young couple initially lived in a building belonging to Anna's parents, Ludwig and Julia Bunzl, at Grillparzerstraße 14, in the first district. Their first daughter, Esther, was born on June 28, 1923, followed three years later, on July 2, 1926, by their second daughter, Susanne.[4] After his graduation, Philipp Rezek worked as an assistant at the First Medical University Clinic and taught neuropathology at the University of Vienna Medical School.[5] The young physician opened a private practice for internal medicine in the building belonging to his parents-in-law on Grillparzerstraße.

In 1928, Anna Rezek's father, Ludwig Lajos Bunzl, died, and her mother, Dolly Bunzl, four years later. Anna Rezek inherited a considerable fortune from her parents at that time. On September 9, 1932, the Rezeks purchased a plot of land at Wilbrandtgasse 37, at the corner of Peter-Jordan-Straße 146.[6] That same year, Anna and Philipp Rezek commissioned Hans Glas to design a modern house for the family on this site. In 1932–1933, during the construction of the villa, the young couple and their two daughters took research trips to British India (since 1948 India), Ceylon (since 1948 Sri Lanka), and Palestine (since 1948 Israel). Anna and Philipp Rezek were interested in the Zionist movement and in the early 1930s acquired 5,000 hectares of land in former Palestine that was planted with citrus trees.[7] Philipp Rezek, who was very enthusiastic about the new medium of film, preserved impressions of these journeys in the form of documentary films, which he then showed at his lectures at the university and at schools in Vienna.[8]

In spring 1934, according to the accounts of Anna and Philipp Rezek's grandchildren, the family of four moved into their new villa in Pötzleinsdorf, at the time one of the city's most modern houses. Anna and Philipp Rezek installed a small examination room and a research lab there. Not only guests and friends of the family but also patients of the couple and passersby on Wilbrandtgasse marveled at the visionary design of the terraced house, with its breathtaking views across Vienna. Music played a special role in the Rezek family. Philipp Rezek was an avid amateur pianist. In the living room stood a grand piano made by the German firm C. Bechstein, and the Rezek family organized house concerts there for friends and relatives.

4 According to information and documents from the archive of the Jewish Community of Vienna; email from Sabine Loitfellner, Nov. 9, 2023.

5 See Memorial Book for the Victims of National Socialism at the University of Vienna 1938, Philipp Rezek, https://gedenkbuch.univie.ac.at/person/philipp-rezek (accessed July 30, 2025).

6 Historic land register, register number 1235, cadastral district Pötzleinsdorf, house at Peter-Jordan-Straße 146 / Wilbrandtgasse 37.

7 Austrian State Archives, ÖStA/AdR/VVST/VA. Zl.4755, "Verzeichnis über das Vermögen von Juden" from April 24, 1938. According to these documents, the property was located in Israel near "Naane by Gan Hadar, South District, Palestine."

8 See Marie-Theres Arnbom, *Die Villen von Pötzleinsdorf. Wenn Häuser Geschichten erzählen* (Almathea, 2020), 159–168.

A
Dr. Anna and Dr. Philipp Rezek, Vienna, 1936.

B
The two Rezek daughters: Esther (left) and Susanne, Vienna, ca. 1935.

C
Anna Rezek shortly before fleeing Vienna to escape the Nazis, Vienna, 1938.

D
Anna and Philipp Rezek,
Miami, 1957.

E
Philipp Rezek, Miami, 1957

F
Anna Rezek, Miami, 1970

Jewish life and the year 1938 in Währing

In Währing, which back then counted among Vienna's most upscale residential areas, there was a Jewish community prior to World War II. According to statistics from 1934, 5,061 Jews lived in Währing that year, which amounted to about 16 percent of the district's population.[9] In 1888–89, a synagogue, designed by the Jewish architect Jakob Modern (1838–1912) was built for the "Israelitische Cultusgemeinde Währing" at Schopenhauerstraße 39. As early as 1873, the Rothschild Hospital opened at Währinger Gürtel 95–97, which enjoyed a top-notch medical reputation and drew patients from far beyond the district borders of Währing. Until the *Anschluss* with Nazi Germany, in March 1938, 114 physicians lived in the district, 67 of whom also had their practices there.[10] The Währing Cemetery was Vienna's second Jewish cemetery.[11] Arthur Schnitzler (1862–1932) lived at Sternwartestraße 71, Theodor Herzl's (1880–1904) last address was Haizingergasse 29, and Sigmund Freud (1856–1939) often spent his summer holidays in Pötzleinsdorf. In the summers of 1931 and 1932, Freud lived in the direct vicinity of Wilbrandtgasse in the Villa Mautner, at Khevenhüllerstraße 6.

The expulsion and flight of the Rezek family from Vienna

In 1938, the Rezek family was forced to flee Vienna to escape the Nazis. International colleagues and physician friends helped Philipp Rezek organize a lecture tour through the US. In spring 1938, Philipp Rezek fled from Vienna to Paris. On May 27 of that year, he then set sail on the *SS Britannic* from Le Havre to New York City, where he arrived on June 5. On July 14, he continued on by plane to Miami, where he took up residence. On October 13, 1938, Anna Rezek, along with the couple's two daughters, Esther and Susanne—at the time fifteen and twelve years old, respectively—and her mother-in-law, Gisella Rezek, fled from Vienna to London, where she had relatives.[12] On November 23, 1938, they arrived in New York City on the *SS Vendam* and then continued on to Miami, where Philipp Rezek had taken a position as a pathologist at Jackson Memorial Hospital in July of that year. He was forty-four years old at that time; his wife, forty-three.[13] On her immigration forms, Anna Rezek listed her occupation as "housewife."[14]

9 See *Topographie der Shoah in Währing – Orte, Häuser, Schicksale*, in https://www.oeaw.ac.at/ikw/shoah-in-waehring (accessed July 30, 2025). By comparison, in 1934, nearly ten times as many Jews lived in the district of Leopoldstadt: 50,922.

10 See *Jüdische Ärzte in Währing*, in https://www.oeaw.ac.at/ikw/shoah-in-waehring/ausschluesse/juedische-aerzte-und-aerztinnen-in-waehring (accessed Aug. 10, 2025).

11 See ibid.

12 Gisella Rezek's last address in Vienna was Rembrandtstraße 17, 1020 Vienna.

13 Document No. 3929, United States of America, Declaration of Intention, Philipp Rezek, dated Aug. 9,1938, from the archive of the Jewish Community of Vienna; email from Sabine Loitfellner, Nov. 11, 2023.

14 Document No. 6837, United States of America, Petition of Naturalization, Anna Rezek, dated April 12, 1939, from the archive of the Jewish Community of Vienna; email from Sabine Loitfellner, Nov. 11, 2023.

In 1941, proceedings were initiated against Anna and Philipp Rezek to rescind their citizenship; subsequently, all four family members were deprived of their Austrian citizenship.[15] On July 14, 1942, Anna and Philipp Rezek were also both stripped of the medical degrees bestowed upon them by the University of Vienna, because, in Anna's case, "As a Jewess, she is unworthy of an academic degree from a German university." It was not until thirteen years later that their title "Dr. med." was restored.[16] With Austria's *Anschluss* with Nazi Germany in 1938, some 70 percent of the professors and students of Vienna's medical school were barred from university because they were Jewish.[17]

Life in forced exile in Miami

In 1943 and 1944, all of the Rezeks were granted American citizenship. Until his death in 1963, Philipp Rezek worked as a pathologist at Miami's Jackson Memorial Hospital, where he was head of the hospital's laboratories until 1953 and then head of the department of pathological anatomy. He conducted teaching and training programs for pathology and clinical pathology and in 1947 established a training program for medical technicians. In 1954, he was named director of the newly founded department of pathological anatomy and held a professorship for pathology at the University of Miami Medical School. At the same time, he worked as a pathologist at Kendall Hospital, in South Miami, and at Miami's Victoria Hospital. Moreover, he was a medical advisor to the Lago Oil and Transportation Company in Aruba (until 1986 part of the Netherlands Antilles) and served as a guest lecturer for pathology at the Hebrew University in Jerusalem, Israel.[18]

Philipp and Anna Rezek never returned to Vienna after the Holocaust. Philipp Rezek died in Miami on June 23, 1963, at the age of sixty-nine; Anna Rezek in 1974. Susanne Rezek, the younger of the two daughters, died in 2016; her elder sister, Esther Rezek, who worked in the US as an art historian, in 2019. Anna and Philipp Rezek's grandchildren still live in the US with their families.

15 See Memorial Book for the Victims of National Socialism at the University of Vienna 1938, Philipp Rezek, in https://gedenkbuch.univie.ac.at/person/philipp-rezek (accessed Aug. 10, 2025).

16 Memorial Book for the Victims of National Socialism at the University of Vienna 1938, Anna Rezek (Bunzl), in https://gedenkbuch.univie.ac.at/person/anna-rezek-bunzl; Philipp Rezek in https://gedenkbuch.univie.ac.at/person/philipp-rezek (accessed July 30, 2025).

17 See Michael Hubenstorf, "Österreichische Ärzte-Emigration," in Friedrich Stadler (ed.), *Vertriebene Vernunft II. Emigration und Exil österreichischer Wissenschaft 1930–1940* (LIT Verlag, 2004), 359.

18 Memorial Book, Philipp Rezek.

U.S. DEPARTMENT OF LABOR

List 13

LIST OR MANIFEST OF ALIEN PASSENGERS FOR THE UNITED

ALL ALIENS arriving at a port of continental United States from a foreign port or a port of the insular possessions of the United States, and all aliens arriving at a port of said insular possessions from a foreign port, a port of continental United
This (yellow) sheet is for the listing of

CABIN CLASS PASSENGERS. S. S. "VEENDAM" Passengers sailing from SOUTHAMPTON, 12TH NOVEMBER, 1938.

1	2	3		4		5	6	7	8			9	10	11		12	13		14	15	
No. on List	HEAD-TAX STATUS (This column for use of Government officials only)	NAME IN FULL		Age		Sex	Married or single	Calling or occupation	Able to—			Nationality. (Country of which citizen or subject)	†Race or people	Place of birth		Immigration Visa, Passport Visa, or Reentry Permit number	Issued		Data concerning verifications of landings, etc. (This column for use of Government officials only)	*Last permanent residence	
		Family name	Given name	Yrs.	Mos.				Read	Read what language	Write			Country	City or town, State, Province or District		Place	Date		Country	City or town, State, Province or District
1		REZEK	ANNA	43		F	M	HOUSEWIFE	YES	GERMAN ENGLISH FRENCH	YES	Germany	Hebrew	Germany	Vienna	QIV.19741	Vienna	11-10-38		Germany	Vienna
2	No Head UNDER 16	REZEK	ESTHER	15		F	S	STUDENT	YES	GERMAN ENGLISH	YES	Germany	Hebrew	Germany	Vienna	QIV.19742	Vienna	11-10-38		Germany	Vienna
3	No Head UNDER 16	REZEK	SUSANNE	12		F	S	STUDENT	YES	GERMAN ENGLISH	YES	Germany	Hebrew	Germany	Vienna	QIV.19743	Vienna	11-10-38		Germany	Vienna
4																					
5																					
6																					
7																					
8																					
9																					
10																					
11																					
12																					
13																					
14																					
15																					
16																					
17																					
18																					
19																					
20																					
21																					
22																					
23																					
24																					
25																					
26																					
27																					
28																					
29																					
30																					

NOV 21 1938

13

Total passengers . . . . .
U.S. citizens . . . . .
Aliens . . . . .

* Permanent residence within the meaning of this manifest shall be actual or intended residence of one year or more.
† List of races will be found on the back of this sheet.

Anna, Esther, and Susanne Rezek arrive in the US on board the *SS Veendam* on November 12, 1938, as "Alien Passengers."

U. S. DEPARTMENT OF LABOR

IMMIGRATION AND NATURALIZATION SERVICE

No. 10 9948

CERTIFICATE OF ARRIVAL

I HEREBY CERTIFY that the immigration records show that the alien named below arrived at the port, on the date, and in the manner shown, and was lawfully admitted to the United States of America for permanent residence.

Name: Philipp Rezek
Port of entry: Miami, Florida
Date: July 14, 1938
Manner of arrival: Plane N.C. 80-V

I FURTHER CERTIFY that this certificate of arrival is issued under authority of, and in conformity with, the provisions of the Act of June 29, 1906, as amended, solely for the use of the alien herein named and only for naturalization purposes.

IN WITNESS WHEREOF, this certificate of arrival is issued AUG 1 1938

RECEIV... AUG 6 - 1938 Immigration and Naturalization Service JACKSONVILLE, FLA

mc

James L. Houghteling

IMMIGRANT IDENTIFICATION CARD ISSUED

Form 161 U. S. GOVERNMENT PRINTING OFFICE 14—2601

JAMES L. HOUGHTELING
Commissioner.

Arrival certificate for
Philipp Rezek, July 14, 1938,
Miami, Florida.

„March 13, 1938, was undoubtedly the most tragic day in the history of that little nation in Central Europe formerly known as Austria. … There was no doubt about it, the end had come. It just seemed a matter of time then. Our whole house seemed to be changed.“

Esther Rezek, end of November 1941

Postcard from a friend of Anna Rezek in Vienna, sent to Miami on January 18, 1940.

Esther Rezek

"What Really Happened on March 13, 1938": Memories of a Fifteen-Year-Old

March 13, 1938, in the Villa Rezek

March 13, 1938, was undoubtedly the most tragic day in the history of that little nation in Central Europe formerly known as Austria. Being a native of Vienna, I was on the scene where the drama of that eventful day unfolded.

While eating my breakfast, I, as usual, listened to the early news broadcast. Great was my surprise when I heard the announcer say that Chancellor Schuschnigg had ordered a plebiscite to be held in Austria. The purpose of it was to end those days of doubt which had prevailed during the last two weeks and to find out if the people of that nation wanted to unite with the German Reich. On my way to school I noticed that huge signs had already been posted in order to influence the population in its vote. To my dismay I saw little swastikas mingled with leaflets on the ground. There had been a strong opposition to the government in the past few days; Schuschnigg was even forced to take Seys-Inquart, a Nazi, into his cabinet as Minister of the Interior. Yet everybody was confident as to the positive outcome of the plebiscite.

After school, I had to go downtown in order to do some shopping. The atmosphere seemed very tense. People went around with worried faces. A silence prevailed which was only broken by the horns of cars. All of a sudden, I found myself in the middle of a big tumult. University students made a pro-Nazi demonstration. They wore the emblem of the National Socialist party and took [word illegible] in yelling "Heil Hitler" and "Down with the Jews." Right beside them the police were standing, making no attempts whatsoever to establish order. I finally managed to get away from the crowd and hurried home. There, I found my family very much disturbed. They had been listening to German as well as Austrian broadcasts all day long. The Germans had made propaganda programmes, telling of the "terrible mistreatments and abuses" which their brothers in Vienna had to go through. There was no doubt about it, the end had come. It just seemed a matter of time then.

Our whole house seemed to be changed. Everybody had just one desire: to get away from it all. To make matters worse, the radio, which we didn't dare to turn off, for fear we might miss some news broadcasts, kept proceeding all day. At about 8:30 p.m. the music, then on the air, suddenly stopped, and Chancellor Schuschnigg was introduced. He talked about the terrible pressure put on him by the German Government for the last few days, and finally about the ultimatum given him, either to give [in] peacefully, or to be prepared for shooting. He continued saying how he had appealed to every one of the democracies, only to find closed doors and deaf ears. He therefore, in order to avoid any bloodshed, had given the government into the hand of Dr. Seys-Inquart. Tears choked his voice when he concluded with the words, "God protect Austria."

Then we heard him say to somebody, "I am at your disposal," the sound of handcuffs, and after that for the last time the Austrian National Anthem. Soon Dr. Seys-Inquart was announced. He yelled that the change of government was a blessing for the Austrian people, and that independently from its German neighbors it would flourish as a National Socialist nation. His speech was followed by the song "Deutschland, Deutschland über alles" and the "Horst Wessel Lied." Dumbfounded, we sat around the radio. Our future lay before us in ruins. Being Jewish we would be persecuted and treated like dogs. Not many words were spoken, but many a silent tear was shed. At dawn we went to bed, only to fall into a restless slumber. Next morning we were awakened by the noise of airplanes. On looking out of the window, we saw about fifty German bombers. They dropped leaflets saying, "The National Socialistic Germany greets and welcomes its National Socialistic sister Austria." In the paper we saw the border between Austria and Germany had fallen at midnight.

The end had come. Germany gained glory—Austria lost its freedom. Civilization had given way to barbarism.[1]

Three years

1

Three years ago today I came to this country. I shall never forget November 23, 1938. Our boat was scheduled to arrive in Hoboken at seven o'clock in the morning. Nervous and excited with anticipation, I got up at four. Tears came to my eyes when I saw the first lights of New York through the early dawn. This was my new home, heaven opening its doors. I was determined to like everything I saw and everything I met.

This afternoon my friends here, celebrating the occasion, gave a little party for me. And now I sit at my desk and review the past three years in my mind. They were wonderful years. Their pleasantness was only interrupted by the worries about our friends and relatives abroad.

I did like everything I experienced, not because I was determined to do so, but because I could not help it. The healthy and democratic outlook of life I found here was and still is fascinating to me. After the pessimism that surrounded me in Europe, the optimistic views in this country were like balsam on a fresh wound.

My father was successful in his work and made a name for himself in Miami. My grandmother joined us and once again we were united. We lived the normal life of the average American family and made many valuable friendships.
Then I went off to college. It was not easy for my parents to send me, and [I] shall always appreciate their sacrifices in order to make their and my dream

1 For more information on the Rezek family, see Marie-Theres Arnbom, *Die Villen von Pötzleinsdorf. Wenn Häuser Geschichten erzählen* (Almathea, 2020), 159–168. The archives of Vanderbilt University contain numerous personal letters and records from the Rezek family as well as from relatives and friends of the family from the years 1939–1941, including the essays Esther Rezek wrote in exile: https://collections.library.vanderbilt.edu/repositories/2/archival_objects/92678 (accessed July 30, 2025).

come true. I realized that very few young refugees are fortunate enough to have such an opportunity and was determined to do my best in everything.

School was a completely new experience for me. I was surrounded by young people and formed lasting friendships with some of them. That and the education I got are things I shall never cease being thankful for.

During all these three years I never had the feeling of being a "foreigner." Maybe it was because people immediately counted me as one of their own, maybe because I never regarded myself as one. I never drew any comparisons with conditions in Europe. I never wanted to. Not once was there a desire to go back or a craving for Vienna. From the very first minute this was my home, this was what I always liked and loved.

Thanksgiving has a special significance for me. Not only because then I am thankful for the privilege of living in this country (I give thanks for that deeply), but because it always marks another year spent in the United States. Two years from today I shall be able to take out my citizenship papers. This will be one of the happiest days of my life. My most ardent wish will have come true.[2]

2 Ibid.; this text has been lightly edited for clarity.

Caroline Wohlgemuth

The Villa Rezek 1939–1953: Plunder and Restitution

The Aryanization of the Villa Rezek, 1939

With the "Verordnung über die Anmeldung des Vermögens von Juden" (Regulation on the Registration of the Assets of Jews) of April 26, 1938, the Nazis began their systematic plundering of property belonging to Jews in Germany and Austria. With this law, the policy of Aryanization—the expropriation and theft of all assets of the Jewish population—was declared legal.[1] According to this regulation, "Every Jew, in accordance with the First Regulation to the Reich Citizenship Law of November 14, 1935 ... is obliged to register and appraise all domestic and foreign assets as of the day this regulation takes effect. Jews with foreign citizenships must only register and appraise their domestic assets. This compulsory registration and appraisal also applies to the non-Jewish spouse of a Jew."[2] Assets did not include "movable property solely intended for the personal use of those affected by the compulsory registration, provided they are not luxury items."[3] Violation of this regulation was punishable by large fines, prison sentences, and "hard labor of up to ten years." By June 30, 1938, all Jews in Germany and Austria were compelled to declare their entire assets in writing.[4]

Henceforth, attorneys, expert witnesses, appraisers, judges, notaries public, moving companies, auction houses, and government authorities all participated in the expropriations and legalized plundering.[5] Anna and Philipp Rezek were also impacted by this regulation. In July 1938, their entire assets were appraised. The Austrian State Archives still hold detailed assessments of the value of the family's assets, including meticulously compiled lists with appraisals of carpets, silver, vases, plates, and other objects of value found in the villa at that time. The files also contain an "Itemization of the medical inventory of Dr. Philipp Rezek" in his practice at Grillparzerstraße 14, in Vienna's first district.[6]

With a ruling from April 29, 1939, issued by the "Finanzamt Innere Stadt-Ost Reichsfluchtsteuerstelle für das Land Österreich," Anna and Philipp Rezek were charged with a "Reich Flight Tax" amounting to 335,921 Reichsmark (RM). According to the historic currency converter of the Austrian National Bank, this

1 The term "Aryanization" is a Nazi neologism that refers to the forced expropriation and theft of the assets of Jews under the Nazi regime.

2 "Verordnung über die Anmeldung des Vermögens von Juden" (Regulation on the Registration of the Assets of Jews) from April 26, 1938, RGBl I 1938, 414, in ALEX, Historische Rechts- und Gesetzestexte Online, https://alex.onb.ac.at/cgicontent/alex?apm=0&aid=dra&datum=19380004&seite=00000414&zoom=2, (accessed July 20, 2025).

3 Ibid.

4 Ibid., http://ns-quellen.at/gesetz_anzeigen_detail.php?gesetz_id=29310&action=B_Read (accessed July 20, 2025).

5 See Gerhard Melinz and Gerald Hödl, "'Jüdisches' Liegenschaftseigentum in Wien zwischen Arisierungsstrategien und Rückstellungsverfahren," *Veröffentlichungen der Österreichischen Historikerkommission. Vermögensentzug während der NS-Zeit sowie Rückstellungen und Entschädigungen seit 1945 in Österreich*, vol. 13 (Böhlau, 2004), 20ff.

6 Austrian State Archives, ÖStA/AdR/VVST/VA. Zl.4755.

would be some 2,455,000 euros today.[7] The ruling stated that this sum was due retroactively on October 15, 1938.[8] The entire possessions of the Rezek family were confiscated. In July 1939, their house was Aryanized and their property thus effectively plundered. At this point, Anna and Philipp Rezek and their two daughters, Esther and Susanne, were already living in forced exile in the US.

Their property was appraised by the Viennese architect Gustav Gröger (1875–1958)[9] at 80,000 RM (today equal to about 585,000 euros). Gröber assessed the value of the house at 77,333 RM and the interior furnishings and household goods to be worth 2,667 RM. According to the files on the "Registration of Revoked Assets," the "modern, single-family villa, built in 1933, with a garden, partially built-in furniture, central heating, ground level and first upper level, partially finished attic, garage," had a significantly higher value at the time, namely 312,104,44 schillings (today about 2,266,000 euros).[10]

As a private "Aryanizer," Oswald Hermsen acquired the house on July 26, 1939, for 80,000 RM (today about 585,000 euros), a significantly lower value. In 1939, Hermsen was chairman of the Hanf-, Jute-, und Textilindustrie AG Wien (HITIAG) textile producer, a subsidiary of the Vienna Creditanstalt Bankverein with headquarters at Börsegasse 18, in the first district.[11] Already on July 7, 1936, nearly two years before the *Anschluss*, Oswald Hermsen, as an illegal Nazi, had become a member of the local St. Pölten (Lower Austria) chapter of the National Socialist German Workers' Party (NSDAP), with the ID card no. 3053714/3839.[12] On May 1, 1938, he then became an official member of the NSDAP with the membership number 6383318.[13] He initially lived with his wife, Alexandra Hermsen, also a member of the NSDAP, in the Lower Austrian town of Pöchlarn and later at Hockegasse 95, in Vienna's thirteenth district. The couple had two children, Hugo and Hildegard Hermsen.

Under Nazi rule, Aryanizations by private persons like this one always maintained a semblance of legality: The Villa Rezek was offered for sale publicly through a newspaper advertisement, and Oswald Hermsen acquired the house with a purchase contract dated July 26, 1939.[14] He paid the purchase amount into a frozen account. The attorney Dr. Stephan Lehner[15] handled the forced

7 Historic currency converter of the Austrian National Bank, https://finanzbildung.oenb.at/docroot/waehrungsrechner/# (accessed July 20, 2025).

8 Austrian State Archives, ÖStA/AdR/VVST/VA. Zl.4755, "Reichsfluchtsteuerbescheid" (Reich Flight Tax Notification) of April 29, 1939.

9 Architect Gustav Gröger (1875–1958), Weihburggasse 10–12, 1010 Vienna.

10 Municipal and Provincial Archives of Vienna, M.Abt.119, A41-VEAV-Vermögensentziehungs-Anmeldungsverordung: 18th District Zl.284 (Rezek, Philipp Dr.), Registration of Revoked Assets from July 2, 1939; Claimant: Ing. Oswald Hermsen.

11 Adolf Gustav Oswald Hermsen was born on August 5, 1895, in Schiffbeck, near Hamburg, Germany. His father, Louis Friedrich Hermsen, was Swedish; the son consequently had Swedish citizenship as well. In 1929, Adolf Gustav Oswald Hermsen was granted German citizenship.

12 Staff questionnaire 5858 of the NSDAP, no.: 6383318; The Federal Archives, Berlin. File of the NSDAP, Oswald Hermsen; information from Sabine Gresens per email, July 23, 2025.

13 See ibid., NSDAP Central File.

14 On Feb. 26, 1940, the registration of the sale was entered in the land register.

15 Attorney Dr. Stephan Lehner, Meistersingerstraße 1, 1010 Vienna.

transaction for Hermsen. The Rezek family, who at this time was already living in forced exile in Miami, was represented by the attorney Dr. Josef Führer.[16] In winter 1939, the Hermsen family of four moved into the Villa Rezek.[17] In this period, the Rezeks' former domestic worker and cook, "Hedi," continued to live in the house. She maintained an affectionate relationship with the Rezek family and in those years wrote several letters to Anna Rezek in the US, in which she reported on the situation in Vienna and in the house.[18] During the war, additional residents moved into the villa, with the Reuter family taking up quarters with the Hermsens as so-called bombing victims. The two families divided the two levels of the house.

In July 1945, Oswald Hermsen was arrested in Vienna by the American occupying forces. Through a decree from August 20, 1945, the Villa Rezek was confiscated by the Military Government–Austria and henceforth served as quarters for American generals. The house was now under the administration of the American Property Control, with headquarters in Vienna. After serving a prison sentence in Vienna, Oswald Hermsen was interned first in the camp in Glasenbach (Camp Marcus W. Orr), near Salzburg, and later in the camp in Ludwigsburg, Germany. After his release from internment, he returned to Austria in 1946. In 1948, Oswald Hermsen and his two children, Hugo and Hildegard Hermsen, were granted Austrian citizenship.

The restitution: 1952–53

Between 1946 and 1949, seven Restitution Acts were passed in Austria that were to regulate the restitution of property stolen or expropriated from Jews. For private claims pursuant to the Third Restitution Act, the Federal Law of February 6, 1947, on the Nullification of Property Seizures,[19] such as the restitution of houses Aryanized by private persons, the responsible authority was the Restitution Commission at the Vienna Higher Civil Court Landesgericht für Zivilrechtssachen, established in 1947. The act regulated the recourse claims for expropriated assets that were currently in private ownership. It was on this legal basis that the majority of restitution proceedings in Austria were conducted.[20]

At the order of the Restitution Commission from March 10, 1949, restitution proceedings were initiated concerning the Villa Rezek, which dragged on over four years. Anna and Philipp Rezek, as claimants, were represented by their at-

16 Attorney Dr. Josef Führer, Freyung 6, Schottenhof, 1010 Vienna.

17 See "Arisierungen in Währing," https://www.oeaw.ac.at/ikw/shoah-inwaehring/arisierungen-in-waehring (accessed July 20, 2025) and https://hiko.univie.ac.at/PDF/13.pdf (accessed July 20, 2025).

18 The archives of Vanderbilt University contain numerous personal letters and records from the Rezek family as well as from relatives and friends of the family from the years 1939–1941, including the letters from "Hedi," https://collections.library.vanderbilt.edu/repositories/2/archival_objects/92678 (accessed July 30, 2025).

19 (BGBl 54/1947), http://nsquellen.at/gesetz_anzeigen_detail.php?gesetzid=10014910&action=B_Read (accessed July 30, 2025).

20 See Restitution, https://www.archiv-ikg-wien.at/archives/restitution/ (accessed July 30, 2025).

torney, Dr. Josef Führer. The defendant, Oswald Hermsen, was represented by his attorney, Dr. Karl Schachner.[21] On the basis of a legally binding partial decision by the Restitution Commission from January 31, 1952, the ownership of the villa was returned to Anna and Philipp Rezek, with each receiving half of the ownership. In further oral negotiations before the Restitution Commission on October 14, 1953, the two parties arrived at a settlement: The Rezeks agreed to make a "compensation payment" to Oswald Hermsen of 81,000 schillings within six weeks.[22]

In a letter dated May 18, 1946, which Dr. Josef Führer, the Rezek family's attorney, wrote as part of the restitution proceedings, he stated that only a small part of the house's furnishings of the house had been sold to Oswald Hermsen in July 1939 along with the villa. The Rezek family was able to take nearly all of the villa's furnishings with them to their exile. A large part of the furniture and the extensive library, as well as scientific equipment, rugs, and silver goods, were shipped to the US. However, the transport containers were apparently broken open by the Nazis in Hamburg and the most important and valuable objects confiscated.[23]

According to the accounts of the grandchildren, most of the furniture, furnishings, and household goods from their grandparents' house in Vienna nonetheless made their way to the US and are still in the family's possession today.

On June 2, 1954, Anna and Philipp Rezek sold the villa to Corrado and Amalie Bardi.

21 Attorney Dr. Karl Schachner, Mommsengasse 30, 1040 Vienna.

22 See Municipal and Provincial Archives of Vienna (WStLA), M.Abt.119, A41-VEAV-Vermögensentziehungs-Anmeldungsverordnung: 18th District Zl.284 (Rezek, Philipp Dr.); Vergleichsausfertigung der Rückstellungskommission.

23 According to information and documents from the archive of the Jewish Community of Vienna; email from Sabine Loitfellner from Nov. 9, 2023.

Wien, 12. April 1940

Liebe Frau Doktor!
Heute habe ich mit unendlicher Freude Ihren Brief vom 7. Februar erhalten, aber eine Karte mit dem Haus nicht, was mir sehr leid tut. Habe bei dieser unruhigen Zeit die Hoffnung auf ein Schreiben schon fast aufgegeben. Im Maerz habe ich einen Brief an Frau (Name) nach Triest geschickt und sie gebeten ihn von dort wegzuschicken, den muessten Sie wohl auch schon haben. Gottlob, dass die Grossmutter wohlbehalten gelandet ist. Der liebe Gott hat Ihnen Liebe Frau Doktor Ihre Guete belohnt. Wenn man von andern Leuten hoert haelt man Vieles nicht fuer moeglich. Wenn Sie im kochen so viel Erfolg haben, werden Sie die schwere Arbeit nicht so spueren. Das Geschirrwaschen ist verflucht graesslich, wenn man aber die Koechin ist so ist das halb so schlimm, denn nach dem grauslichen ist man dann bis zur naechsten Mahlzeit Freifrau, zur Jause hat man in der Glanzzeit ein Stubenkaetzchen gehabt, aber ueber Glanz Schwamm darueber. In meinem Beruf gibt es jetzt in Wien nichts zu tun, wirklich nichts zu tun; man zerbricht sich taeglich das Hirn was und woher! Die meiste Zeit ist man mit <u>nekram</u> auf der Jagd nach <u>lettimsnebel</u> und sie schreiben seelenruhig von Huelle und Fuelle. Wissen Sie was das heisst lange Zaehne und Wasser im Mund zusammenlaufen? und Sie schreiben einen guten Saft machen, Kunststueck, Fleisch, Braten, Gefluegel, oh Schmerz, lass bei mir nach, Grossmutter hat einmal in der Villa gesagt: gibt man gut hinein kann man gut herausnehmen, aber wir in Wien koennen jetzt nicht gut hineingeben.
Sonstige Neuigkeiten gibt es nicht zu berichten, sonst geht der Brief unter. Vergessen hab und werde ich nichts und spaeter einmal schreibe ich Ihnen so dick wie ein Buch. Es ist jetzt fast acht Monate, dass ich von Ihnen kein Schreiben hatte und da war ich oft so schwermuetig. In mir ist immer noch ein Gefuehl, aber das haette jetzt gerade am 9. & 10. April nicht sein sollen. Da wo die (Name)kinder sind, diese zwei armen ungluecklichen Geschoepfe. So geht es jetzt vielen. Frau (Name) sagt auch sie wuerde die Welt zu Fuss durchwandern wenn sie Mann und Kinder finden koennte, und wieviele sterben an der Krankheit wie Hans (Name), Friede und Brot sonst soll man sich nichts wuenschen.

Liebe Frau Doktor bleiben Sie gesund und gluecklich und schreiben Sie recht bald wieder. Recht herzliche Gruesse an alle und ich verbleibe in alter Liebe und Anhaenglichkeit

Ihre Alte.

Note: Underscored words are to be read from right to left. This is done in order to avoid German Censorship.

"Hedi," the Rezek family's former domestic worker and cook, continued to live in the Villa Rezek after its Aryanization and in those years wrote several letters to Anna Rezek in the US.

May 13, 1941

Wien,13.,V,1941

Liebe Frau Doktor!

(Name) war bei mir und hat gefragt was mit mir ist ,es geht mir ganz gut. Habe seit August 1940 keine Nachricht mehr von Ihnen.(Name)'s Schreiben war das letzte.Dass Onkel (Name) in Wien war hat mich ganz entsetzt,hab ihn auch im ersten Moment nicht erkannt.Haette gern mit ihm allein gesprochen.Vielleicht hat er die Spannung gemerkt die bei uns war.Oft habe ich Tage wo ich aus der Haut fahren koennte.Ich bin schon ganz truebsinnig,so plan und ziellos dahinleben ist eine Hoellenqual.Ihnen liebe Frau Doktor geht es sehr gut.Wie geht es (Name)?Was macht die Kleine?Wie lang ist sie schon?Mein Gott wo sind die Zeiten?Bitte koennt ich nicht einmal einige kleine Photos haben ,die Kinder werden sicher etwas haben.

Wir in Wien haben es noch ruhig.Hoffentlich werden sich die Voelker der Erde bald einigen,dass wir wieder Frieden und Ruhe haben,und Brot auch. Sie in Miami werden vom Krieg nichts spueren;ich fahre oft nach Theras zur Schwester,aber wenn ich jetzt in den schweren Zeiten noch meine Mutter haette!

Vom Besitzer der Villa hoert man nur Schandtaten-wir Frau Doktor koennen uns fest auf due Brust klopfen-Sie als Herrin und ich als Koechin-Sie verstehen mich schon.Frau Doktor Sie stehen im vollen Glanz in Glanzing. Wenn ich ab und zu einmal nach Poetz.komme und es begegnet mir jemand <u>alter Bekannter</u> so bleibt den meisten der Atem stehen:"Ja die Hedi!Ja wo sind denn Ihre Herrschaften?Na das sind Leut die jetzt drauf sind"frueher hat mich jeder angeschnauzt:"Na wo sind denn Ihre J. hin?"Selbst Frau Ebner spricht heute schon anders--aber uns ist damit nicht mehr geholfen-Vorbei------Bei uns ist es noch immer kalt und das Wetter ist schlecht.Bei Ihnen wird Hochsommer sein oder noch mehr.Jetzt muss ich einmal warten wie alles ausgeht,dann werde ich mir diese herrliche Gegend einmal anschauen.Ich hinterlasse niemand,da muss es doch ganz einfach gehen.Meine Schwester hoert auch schon 15 Monate nichts von ihren Verwandten aus Chicago.Liebe Frau Doktor,versuchen Sie es auch wieder einmal zu schreiben.Ich habe Ihnen das letzte Mal im Dezember 1940 geschrieben.Dann habe ich es aufgegeben.

Recht herzliche Gruesse an Herrn Doktor,Grossmutter und die Kinder. Bitte Frau doktor schreiben Sie mir bitte recht bald ob Sie diesen Brief bekommen haben,er geht einen seltsamen Weg--

Es gruesst Sie innigst Ihre <u>Alte</u>

****

Note:No signature.

Maximilian Eisenköck

Walter Custer: Civil Engineer and Entrepreneur of Viennese Modernism

The Swiss-born civil engineer Walter Custer (1882–1957) is among the figures in the building sector in interwar Vienna who have received little recognition until now. As a specialist for reinforced concrete, owner of an independent construction company, Freemason, Custer was part of the liberal, technically progressive movement that greatly influenced the architectural modernism of Vienna in the 1930s.

Walter Custer was born on February 15, 1882, in Rheineck, in the canton of St. Gallen, and between 1900 and 1905 completed a civil engineering degree at the ETH Zurich, where he was a student of the concrete pioneer Robert Mörsch.[1] Before World War I, he gained practical experience at large construction sites in the Alsatian town of Mülhausen/Mulhouse, Naples, Mannheim-Waldhof, and Trieste.[2]

In 1920, Custer began working in Vienna, where he founded Ing. W. Custer & Co., a company specializing in construction and civil engineering and especially in building with reinforced concrete. The company was located at Riemergasse 11, in the first district, and in its advertisements offered the turnkey construction of industrial plants, residential buildings, and villas.[3] There is evidence that the firm also had a location at Währinger Straße 33, not far from Hans Glas's office at Währinger Straße 12.[4] In addition, there was a registered branch in Czechoslovakia that bore the name "Ing. W. Custer & Co., Ges.m.b.H., Prag II., Na Florenci 19."[5] It is not clear whether this was an active project office, an independent subsidiary, or a representation office.

Prior to the official founding of his company, Custer was already documented in Vienna as a building foreman: In May 1924, in the *Amtsblatt der Stadt Wien* (the official gazette of the City of Vienna), he was named as the responsible construction supervisor for the erection of a storehouse for the Bunzl & Biach company at Handelskai 138–140.[6] Bunzl & Biach was a prominent Viennese industrial firm whose co-owner, Ludwig Lajos Bunzl (1857–1928), was the father of Anna Rezek, née Bunzl.[7] This connection to Anna Rezek, who was later to commission the building of a home for the Rezek family, would seem to suggest that Walter Custer had professional ties to the Bunzl and Rezek families early on. In a 1936 issue of the magazine *Österreichische Kunst*, Walter Custer is mentioned as the principal building contractor in connection with the construc-

1 See *Schweizerische Bauzeitung*, 75, no. 43, Oct. 26, 1957, 691.
2 See ibid.
3 See advertisement for "Ing. W. Custer & Co.," 1930s, passed down in private documents.
4 See Branchenverzeichnis Wien (n.d.): entry for Walter Custer under Währinger Straße 33.
5 Compass 1932; see also: ZEDHIA/Compass Industry.
6 See *Amtsblatt der Stadt Wien*, no. 38, May 10, 1924, column 7.
7 See Caroline Wohlgemuth's essay "The Rezek Family: Expulsion and Flight from Vienna" in this volume.

tion of the Villa Rezek at Wilbrandtgasse 37.[8] It is not known whether he was contracted with the overall construction of the house and employed the other involved firms as subcontractors, or whether his contribution was limited to the reinforced-concrete elements and master-builder work.

Both Walter Custer and Philipp Rezek were members of Vienna's Freemason lodge "Zukunft." While Rezek was admitted to the lodge in 1928 and withdrew again in 1934, Custer was referred to in a political appraisal by the Nazi party in 1941 as a "past Freemason" who was married to a "half-Jewess," but at the same time was listed as a "supporting member of the SS." The file has this to say: "His demeanor is reserved and rather self-aggrandizing in the Jewish way, although he is of Aryan descent ... his wife is a first-degree part-Jew. ... It is in any event remarkable that a former Freemason married to a half-Jewess pays dues to the SS as a supporting member."[9]

In the *Amtsblatt der Stadt Wien* from June 14, 1947, Custer is listed as a construction supervisor in connection with a demolition project in Vienna's Meidling district, with his address given as Rathausstraße 19, in Vienna's first district.[10] This address is also mentioned in 1953 in the context of a property issue in the twenty-second district.[11]

Walter Custer died in Vienna on August 14, 1957. An obituary in the *Schweizerische Bauzeitung*, which paid tribute to his training, his earlier activities, and his company in Vienna, also referred to him as a co-founder of the Swiss Chamber of Commerce in Vienna and as a member of that city's Swiss Colony.[12]

There is no evidence of Walter Custer leaving behind a personal or professional estate. A family relationship with Walter Werner Custer (1909–1992), a prominent Swiss architect of a later generation, also cannot be confirmed.[13]

8 See *Österreichische Kunst*, 7, 1936, no. 2, 12f.
9 NSDAP Vienna District Administration, Personnel Department, Main Office for Political Assessments, letter from June 17, 1941; quoted in Marcus G. Patka, *Österreichische Freimaurer im Nationalsozialismus. Treue und Verrat* (Böhlau, 2010), 83.
10 See *Amtsblatt der Stadt Wien*, no. 38, June 14, 1974, column 15.
11 See *Amtsblatt der Stadt Wien*, no. 84, October 21, 1953, column 150.
12 See *Schweizerische Bauzeitung*, 1957, 691.
13 Research in ETH archives and obituaries yield no indication of a family connection.

Maximilian Eisenköck

A Tour Through the Villa Rezek: Rooms, Passageways, Perspectives

Visitors enter the Villa Rezek via the main entrance on the north side of the property on Wilbrandtgasse. Eight steps take one up into a small vestibule[A] that leads into the entrance hall,[B] with linoleum flooring. This functional entrance area included a cloakroom that can be closed off with a curtain, a built-in cabinet, and a lavatory for guests. To the left is the open staircase, which connects all of the house's levels with each other, except for the basement level. Five steps lead from here down to the main hall[C] of the ground floor, where one for the first time gains an impression of the house's spaciousness.

Main hall and living area

Beneath the stairs was a built-in seating niche that was available not only to the family but also to the patients waiting for a medical consultation at the Villa Rezek. The hall opened into the spacious living area: a large, open space[G] measuring some seventy square meters and divided into a dining room, living room, and glassed-in conservatory.[F] All areas face the garden. Through large sash sliding windows, the entire ribbon window can be opened. The living room can thus be easily transformed into a loggia. Curtains could be drawn to shield the dining room, living room, and main hall from each other visually.

Dining area and kitchen

From the dining room, a passageway led into the butler's pantry,[H] which was separated from the kitchen directly next to it by a central, modern piece of kitchen furniture[I] equipped with several pass-throughs.

Work spaces

Adjacent to the main hall was the library,[D] which is intentionally located on the house's north side, as the consistent light creates ideal conditions for working. Next to the library was a laboratory[E] and a small corner niche where Anna Rezek's desk stood.

First upper level and private living spaces

The first upper level was reserved for the private living spaces and bedrooms of the four-member family. On the south side were two colorfully furnished children's rooms,[K–L] each with access to a projecting, spacious terrace—a central element of the overall architectural concept, which is to connect the inside and outside spaces in a harmonious manner.

Opposite these rooms, on the north side, was the nanny's room.[Q] In the immediate vicinity is the laundry chute, through which the clothing could be transported directly to the laundry room in the basement—a detail that underscores the well-thought-out, functional organization of the house.

Anna and Philipp Rezek's bedroom[M] was located on the southwest corner of this level. From here, one could access a dressing room[N] with lemon-yellow built-in cabinets and an integrated dressing table, as well as a bathroom[O] featuring not only a bathtub but also an unusually designed ring shower.

Attic level and guest rooms

The most extensive modifications during the building phase in 1933–34 concerned the attic level. Originally, only a guest room and an attic space were planned for this level. In the course of the construction in 1933, however, the room arrangement was expanded: Instead of one room, two separate guest rooms were installed.

The west-facing, somewhat larger room[S] is equipped with its own bathroom,[T] including a toilet, and has a south-facing terrace with a covered seating area and an outdoor shower. The east-facing room[U] had its own washstand and opens to a terrace on the east side of the house.

The additional roof-covered areas on the south side in the original plan were reduced during the execution of construction work, and the electric dumbwaiter, which initially was to extend up to the attic level, now ended on the first upper level. On the other hand, an open metal stairway was added, which leads directly from the terrace to the uppermost rooftop area, passing a small covered area. From here, one has an impressive panorama view of Vienna—and is secured only by a low railing that continues the house's open character all the way to the very top level.

Basement level

The basement level could be accessed only via the internal servants' stairway—a typical characteristic of traditional household organization that reflects the clear separation between living and working areas.

From the landing, one proceeded first into a storage room, from which one can access the ancillary and utility rooms located on a lower level. On the south side, the property's steep slope made it possible to install a small self-contained apartment for the caretaker, consisting of a living area and a separate toilet. On the south side, there was also the central laundry room and a spacious drying and ironing room with direct access to the garden. Via the laundry chute mentioned above, the laundry was transported from the upper levels directly to this work area, another example of the house's consistently well-conceived functional logic.

The north side of the villa's basement housed the fur chamber for storing temperature-sensitive clothing items and the heating room with an oil tank, while on the east side there was an equipment room for storage and workshop purposes. The original plan of 1932–33 also provided for a wading pool south of the house in the garden, but it was presumably never realized.

As with the entire building, the basement level also follows a clear, functional arrangement: short distances, a precise separation of work and living areas, and technical features that were quite progressive for that time. At the same time, in its social structure, the house is still bound to the traditional model of a middle-class household with several employees, but executed in the rational, reduced formal language of architectural modernism.

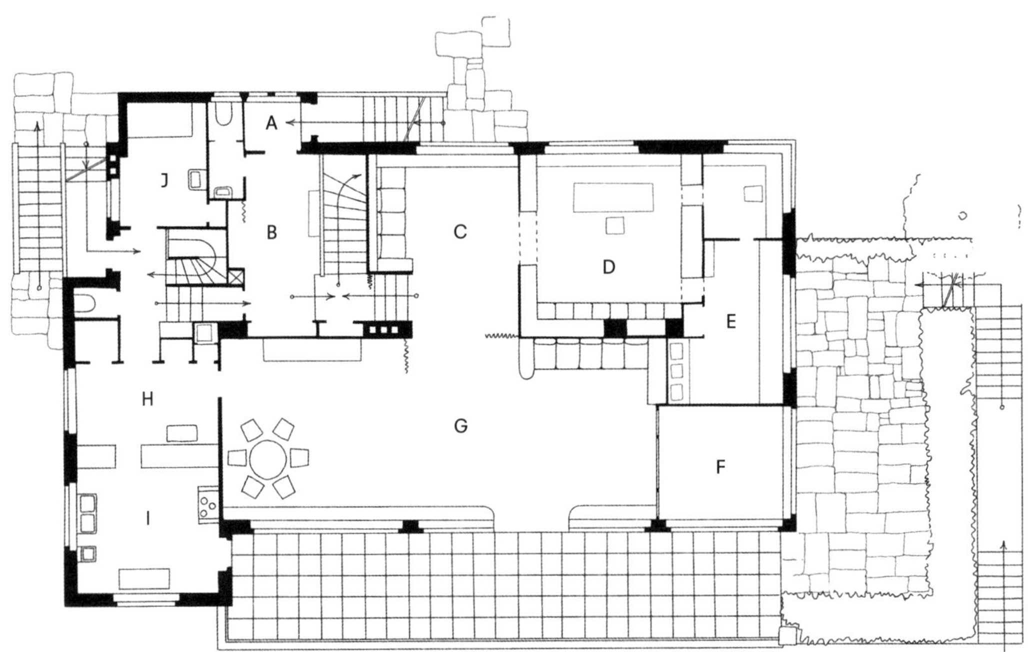

Ground floor

A Vestibule
B Entrance hall
C Main hall
D Library
E Laboratory
F Conservatory
G Dining and living room
H Butler's pantry
I Kitchen
J Domestic staff's room

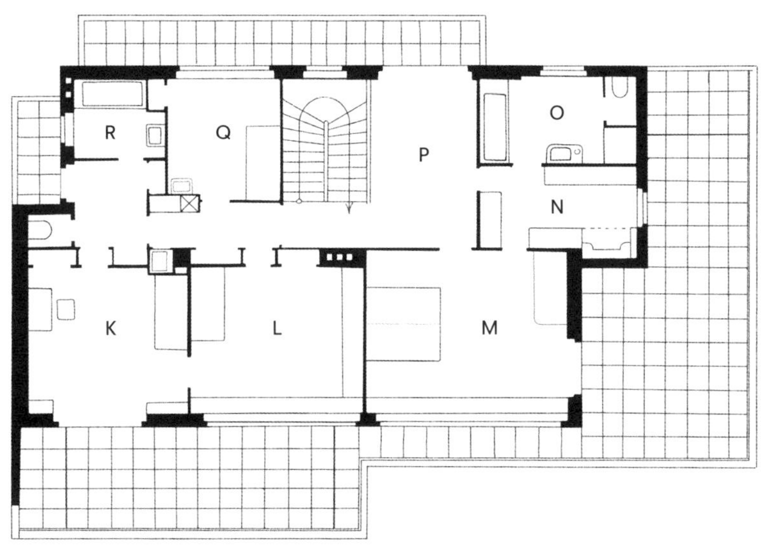

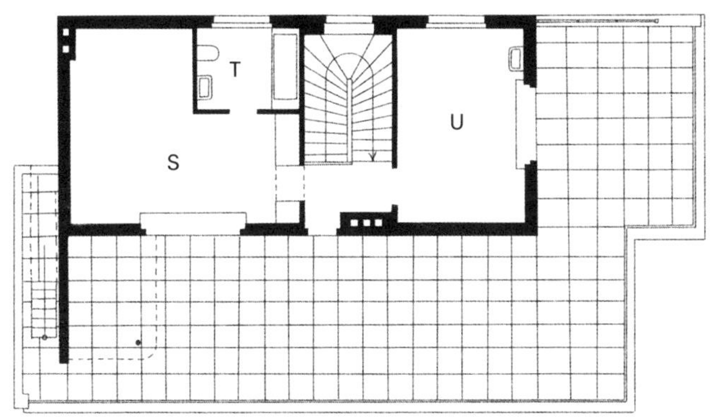

Upper level

0 5 m

K Esther's room
L Susanne's room
M Parents' bedroom
N Dressing room
O Bath
P Upper hall
Q Nanny's room
R Children's bath

Attic level

S Guest room
T Bath
U Guest room

Stefan Oláh

The "Glas House" Today
25 Photographs

37

CLIP STAMP FOLD
TERRASSEN TYP

The Biography of the Villa Rezek: The House Through the Decades, 1932–2025

1932–33
Hans Glas (1892–1969) is commissioned by the physician couple Anna Rezek (1895–1974) and Philipp Rezek (1894–1963) to design a villa for them at Wilbrandtgasse 37 in Pötzleinsdorf. The garden is planned by the landscape architect Albert Esch (1883–1954).

1934
In spring 1934, Anna and Philipp Rezek, along with their daughters Esther (1923–2019) and Susanne (1926–2016)—eleven and eight years old, respectively, at the time—move into the villa.

1938
After Austria's *Anschluss* with Nazi Germany, the entire Rezek family is forced to flee from Vienna to escape the Nazis. Philipp Rezek initially flees to Paris in May 1938. He then boards a ship in Le Havre and on July 5, 1938, arrives in New York City. From there, he flies on to Miami, where he takes a position as a pathologist at Jackson Memorial Hospital. In October 1938, Anna Rezek, the two daughters, and Anna's mother-in-law, Gisella Rezek, flee first to London and then board a ship for New York City, where they arrive on November 23, 1938. From there, they travel on to Miami.

1939
In July 1939, the Villa Rezek is Aryanized and the Rezeks are robbed of their entire assets. Adolf Gustav Oswald Hermsen, chairman of the Hanf-, Jute-, und Textilindustrie AG, acquires the villa for a price significantly lower than its actual value at the time and becomes the new owner. Hermsen and his wife move into the villa in November 1939.

1945
Through a decree from August 20, 1945, the Villa Rezek is confiscated by the Military Government of Austria and henceforth serves as quarters for American generals.

1949
At the order of the Restitution Commission from March 10, 1949, restitution proceedings are initiated.

1952–53
On the basis of a legally binding partial decision by the Restitution Commission from January 31, 1952, the ownership of the villa is returned to Anna and Philipp Rezek, with each receiving half of the ownership. In further oral negotiations before the Restitution Commission on October 14, 1953, the two parties arrive at a settlement: While the ownership of their house is restored to them, the Rezeks agree to make a "compensation payment" to the "Aryanizer" Oswald Hermsen of 81,000 schillings.

1954
On June 2, 1954, Anna and Philipp Rezek sell the Villa Rezek to Amalie and Corrado Bardi.

1971
After the death of her husband, Corrado Bardi, and her son, Amalie Bardi decides to sell the house. The Zoloff company is listed in the land register as the new owner.

1974
Friedrich and Leopoldine Lugmair purchase the Villa Rezek.

1995
The Engelhorn family acquires the house and undertakes a renovation. Among other things, the ocher-yellow façade is repainted white. Despite numerous adaptations over the decades, the Villa Rezek's basic original structure remains largely intact.

2008
On March 28, 2008, the house is sold to the Gosilo Beteiligungsverwaltungs GmbH, an investment management company. Less than two months later, on May 26, 2008, a permit drawing is submitted in which the removal of interior walls on the ground floor and on the top upper level is requested. On June 9, 2008, the city building authorities approve the request. On October 10 of that year, additional plans for an extensive remodeling project are submitted, including the construction of a new and larger garage, the installation of a covered swimming pool and an elevator, and a complete alteration of the interior room arrangement. Although a permit is granted for the renovation project, it is never realized.

2010
On October 14, 2010, the Villa Rezek is listed as a historic monument.

2011–2018
The Villa Rezek is again put up for sale. After another change of ownership in 2013, additional partitioning walls are removed on all levels; no record of this is to be found in the files of the municipal building authority. Plans for a modified but similarly extensive building project are submitted on March 30, 2015, and approved on April 22, 2016, by the city building authorities as well as by the Austrian National Heritage Agency (Bundesdenkmalamt). This building project is also never realized.

2019–2025
In 2019, the Villa Rezek was sold to the present owner, the A.K.L. Stiftung. Despite the high degree of destruction, the foundation initiates the restoration of the villa to its original condition of 1933. The interior rooms, the interior furnishings, and the furniture of the house are reconstructed and restored to their original state. The renovation work was completed in 2025. Since that time, the house has been periodically opened to the public. The house has been included in the worldwide network Iconic Houses since 2025.

Hans Glas: Stages in the Life of an Architect

1892
On September 11, 1892, Hans Glas is born in Vienna into a Jewish family.

1911–1912
Studies machine engineering at Vienna's Technische Hochschule.

1912–1915
Studies in the school of architecture at Vienna's Technische Hochschule.
Attends the private Bauschule operated by Adolf Loos (1870–1933).

1915–1918
Hans Glas is forced to interrupt his studies because he is called up for military duty in World War I.

1918–1919
Continues his studies in the school of architecture at Vienna's Technische Hochschule.

1919–1920
Returns to Adolf Loos's private Bauschule.

As of 1921
Works in the office of the Jewish architect Arnold Hatschek (1865–1931), including assisting in the planning of the villa at Cottagegasse 90–92 in Döbling for Robert (1869–1928) and Bertha (1877–1942) Wortmann, 1190 Vienna.

23. March 1922
Marriage to Olga Taussig (1896–1937).

1928–1929
Attends the school of architecture at Vienna's Technische Hochschule as an audit student.

1928–1929
Plans a housing complex for the City of Vienna at Handelskai 210, Leopoldstadt, 1020 Vienna.

1930
Passes the civil engineering exam on January 15. Arnold Karplus (1877–1943) the architect of the Villa Krasny on the Hohe Warte, is a member of the examination board.

1931/32
Construction of a villa for the industrialist Adolf Münch (1880–1941), president of the Trifailer Kohlenwerks-Aktiengesellschaft coal company, and his wife, Elizabeth Maria Treichel Münch (1879–?), in Belgrade.
Designs workers' quarters for the coal company, commissioned by Adolf Münch and his brother Julius Münch (1873–1932) in Boljevac (today in Serbia).

1932/33
Designs the villa for the physician couple Anna (1895–1974) and Philipp Rezek (1894–1963) at Wilbrandtgasse 37 in Pötzleinsdorf, 1180 Vienna.

1937
Plans a multifamily home at Pfarrwiesengasse 22 in Döbling, 1190 Vienna.

1937
Plans an apartment building for Rudolf Zeitschke and Berty Glass at Štítného ulice 1 / Wolkerova, Olomouc (today in the Czech Republic).

1938
Designs a villa for Věra and Ladislav Szathmáry at Pod Žvahovem 8 in Prague.
Flees Vienna to escape the Nazis in July 1938, traveling to British India via Genoa. On July 23, 1938, Hand Glas sails on the *Conte Biancomano* from Genoa to Naples, through the Suez Canal, and on to Bombay (since 1995 Mumbai). He arrives in Calcutta on August 1, 1938.

1938–1959
In exile, Hans Glas is able to successfully continue his career as an architect. In 1943, as an architect for Hindusthan Co-operative Insurance Society Ltd, he designs the Hindusthan Building on Calcutta's Central Avenue and plans numerous villa projects in the city.

1959
Return to Europe. Hans Glas settles in Switzerland.

1969
Hans Glas dies in Lugano, Switzerland, on January 28, 1969.

Brief Biographies

Felix Augenfeld

1893 Vienna – 1984 New York City

Felix Augenfeld was born in Vienna on January 10, 1893, into a Jewish family. He began studying architecture in 1910 at Vienna's Technische Hochschule and in 1912 became one of the first students at Adolf Loos's private Bauschule. In 1914, Augenfeld was drafted into the military. He was held in Italy as a prisoner of war and was thus not able to finish his studies until 1920. In 1922, he and Karl Hofmann opened an architecture office together in Döbling. Their clients included Sigmund Freud, Anna Freud, Hans Weigel, Gina Kaus, Maria Strauss-Likarz, and the City of Vienna. They designed interiors, furniture, apartments, and houses in Vienna and Brno, as well as stage sets for Max Reinhardt. After the *Anschluss* in 1938, Augenfeld fled to London and in 1939 emigrated to New York City, where in 1941 he opened an architecture office on 66th Street in Manhattan. He designed furniture for Thonet Brothers New York and furnished the La Reine Candy Shop in Manhattan for the candy producer Wilhelm Heller, who had also fled Vienna to escape the Nazis. From 1945 to 1950, he worked as a furniture designer for the American furniture manufacturer Henredon. Augenfeld realized numerous beach and weekend homes. In 1958, he built the Buttinger Library, a private residence and library near Central Park, for Joseph Buttinger and his wife, Muriel Gardiner-Buttinger, a psychoanalyst and close friend of the Freud family who had known Augenfeld from Vienna. In 1966, Augenfeld wed the designer Anna Epstein-Gutmann. Felix Augenfeld never returned to Vienna. He died in New York City on July 21, 1984.

Rudolf Baumfeld

1903 Vienna – 1988 Los Angeles

Rudolf Baumfeld was born in Vienna on December 31, 1903, into a Jewish family. After attending the State Trade School (Staatsgewerbeschule), he studied architecture at the Technische Hochschule and at the Academy of Fine Arts in Vienna. As a student, he worked for architects including Ernst Lichtblau and realized his first independent projects, such as the renovation of the Berger & Fischer bookstore on the Kohlmarkt in the first district (1931). In 1932, he and Norbert Schlesinger opened a joint architecture office, which existed until 1937. Baumfeld furnished twelve shops for the Julius Meinl grocery chain and worked as a consultant for the municipal housing project of the City of Vienna. In 1938, Baumfeld fled Vienna to escape the Nazis, traveling first to Czechoslovakia and then on to Italy. In 1940, he emigrated to the US. In 1943, he began working in the architecture office of Victor Gruen (formerly Grünbaum) in Los Angeles, which specialized in the construction of large indoor shopping centers. Gruen, who had fled from Vienna to New York City in 1938, is regarded as the inventor of the shopping mall. Baumfeld became his partner in 1949. Rudolf Baumfeld died in Los Angeles on February 20, 1988.

Otto Breuer

1897 Vienna – 1938 Vienna

Otto Breuer was born in Vienna on July 26, 1897, into a Jewish family. He studied architecture at Vienna's Technische Hochschule and attended Adolf Loos's private Bauschule. In 1919, he went to Weimar to attend the Bauhaus for a semester. In the 1920s, Breuer founded a home-furnishings business in Vienna and together with the architect Albert Linschütz designed interiors and furniture. For the Werkbundsiedlung housing project in Hietzing, he planned a duplex, Nos. 59 and 60. After the *Anschluss* in March 1938, his business and his entire assets in Vienna were confiscated by the Nazis. Otto Breuer attempted to take his own life in the night of the November pogroms on November 9, 1938, but was unsuccessful. Only a few days later, he hanged himself at the Sanatorium Purkersdorf.

Ella Briggs

1880 Vienna – 1977 London

Ella Briggs was born as Ella Baumfeld in Vienna on March 5, 1880, into a Jewish family. As a young girl, she attended Albert Seligman's private painting school and from 1901 to 1906 studied painting with Koloman Moser at Vienna's Arts and Crafts School. After completing her studies, she moved to New York City, where she worked as a furniture designer. There, she married Walter Briggs, a journalist and Austrian military attaché in the US. They had no children and divorced after five years. Ella Briggs moved back to Vienna, where she worked as an interior architect and furniture designer for the Sigmund Jaray furniture company and for the architects Alfred Keller and Karl Holey. Subsequently, Briggs attended the State Trade School (Staatsgewerbeschule) in Salzburg. From 1918, she studied at the Technische Hochschule in Munich. In 1920, at the age of forty, she completed her studies in architecture. In 1921, she became the first female member of the Austrian Association of Engineers and Architects. Briggs then went back to the US to work for the Kahn & Gregory construction company. In the mid-1920s, she returned to Vienna and for the City of Vienna designed the Pestalozzi-Hof in Döbling (1925). She and Margarete Schütte-Lihotzky were the only women to be awarded contracts for municipal housing projects in Red Vienna. At the end of the 1920s, Briggs moved to Berlin and continued working on social housing projects there. In 1935, after the Nazis had come to power in Germany, she returned to Vienna and in 1936 emigrated to London. After World War II, she worked on a reconstruction program operated by the British government. In 1947 she obtained British citizenship. Ella Briggs died in London on June 20, 1977.

Friedl Dicker

1898 Vienna – 1944 Auschwitz

Friedericke "Friedl" Dicker was born in Vienna on July 30, 1898, into a Jewish family. Dicker's mother died when Friedl was only four years old. From 1905 to 1907, she attended a private drawing class for children taught by Alfred Roller. From 1912 to 1914, she attended Vienna's Higher Institution for Graphic Education and Research and from 1915 to 1916 studied textile arts with Rosalia Rothansl at the Arts and Crafts School. From 1916 to 1919, Dicker attended Johannes Itten's private art school in Vienna. There, she met Anny Wottitz (later Anny Moller-Wottitz) and Franz Singer. When Itten went to Weimar in 1919 to teach at the Bauhaus, Dicker, Wottitz, and Singer followed him. Dicker was regarded as one of the most talented students at the Bauhaus. After completing their studies at the Bauhaus, Dicker and Singer founded the Werkstätten Bildender Kunst in Berlin, specializing in crafts and the design of stage sets for the theater. In 1925, Dicker moved back to Vienna and opened a design studio at Wasserburggasse 2 in the ninth district, which Singer joined in 1926. In their studio work, Dicker was responsible for interior design, furniture, and fabrics, and Singer for architecture. Together, Dicker and Singer designed a great deal of innovative furniture and interiors and planned shops, a Montessori kindergarten, and a tennis clubhouse. Dicker and Singer also designed a garden house (1931) and some of the furnishings for the Moller House, built by Adolf Loos in 1927–28 (construction supervision: Jacques Groag) for Anny Moller-Wottitz and Hans Moller at Starkfriedgasse 19 in Pötzleinsdorf. Dicker and Singer's collaboration, however, was marked by private conflicts; in 1931, Dicker opened her own studio in Vienna, became involved in art education, and taught drawing classes. In 1931, she became a member of the Communist Party. After her studio was searched in 1934, she was arrested. After her release, she fled to Prague, where her aunt, Adela Brandeis, lived. In 1936, she married her youngest cousin, Pavel Brandeis, in Prague. Dicker continued to work as a designer and interior architect, collaborating with Karola Bloch and Greta Bauer-Fröhlich, a former Bauhaus student, as well as with Frieda Stork, Franz Singer's sister. She also gave drawing lessons and devoted herself to psychological work with children. In summer 1938, she and her husband moved to the small Czech city of Hronov, near the Polish border. On December 16, 1942, the couple was deported to the Theresienstadt concentration camp. Pavel Brandeis worked as a carpenter and Dicker as a caretaker in one of the girls' homes in Theresienstadt and taught secret drawing classes for the imprisoned children. On October 6, 1944, Pavel Brandeis was deported to Auschwitz. Dicker volunteered to be transported to Auschwitz as well in order to be with him. Before leaving Theresienstadt, she gave Raja Engländerová, one of her students, two suitcases containing some 4,500 drawings done by the children. On October 9, 1944, Friedl Dicker was murdered in Auschwitz. Her husband, Pavel Brandeis, survived the Holocaust. After the war, the drawings created under her guidance by some 660 children from Theresienstadt were shown at exhibitions all over the world and today are preserved in Prague's Jewish Museum.

Albert Esch
1883 Lednice – 1954 Vienna

Albert Esch was born in the Southern Moravian town of Lednice (now in the Czech Republic) on April 2, 1883, as the son of a director of court gardens for the Principality of Liechtenstein. After studying in England, Belgium, and France, he settled in Vienna and devoted himself to the planning of private gardens and parks. In the interwar period, Esch designed gardens for houses planned by prominent Viennese architects like Josef Frank, Felix Augenfeld, and Karl Hofmann. In 1920, Esch designed small gardens for the houses in a workers' colony that Frank had planned for the Bunzl & Biach company in the Lower Austrian town of Ortmann, near Pernitz. The client was Hugo Bunzl, Anna Rezek's first cousin. In 1933, Esch designed a terraced garden for the Rezek family's new house at Wilbrandtgasse 37. He planned gardens in Belgrade, Brno, and Croatia, as well. Esch also taught at the horticulture school for girls, founded in 1912 by Yella Hertzka at Kaasgraben 19 in Döbling. His modern approach to design made Esch a key figure in contemporary landscape architecture. For decades, he championed the recognition of horticulture as an academic discipline. Esch died in Vienna on September 26, 1954.

Martin Eisler
1913 Vienna – 1977 Brasília

Martin Eisler was born in Vienna on October 27, 1913, into a Jewish family. His father, Max Eisler, was at the time a prominent art historian in Vienna. From 1931 to 1934, Martin Eisler studied architecture with Oskar Strnad at the Arts and Crafts School. In March 1938, he fled from Vienna to Argentina to escape the Nazis. After months on the run, he arrived penniless in Buenos Aires and immediately began working as a furniture designer. In 1955, he and the Italian furniture designer Carlo Hauner founded the Forma company (today known as Interieur Forma) in Brasília, which became synonymous with modern Brazilian furniture design. In cooperation with Brazilian architect Oscar Niemeyer, Eisler outfitted numerous buildings with modern furniture. Among his best-known designs are the Reversível and Costela chairs, which were awarded the Compasso d'Oro, a design prize established by Gio Ponti. Eisler married Rosl Wolf, whose entire family had fled from Germany to Buenos Aires to escape Nazi persecution. Martin Eisler never returned to Vienna. He died in Brasília on April 21, 1977.

Max Eisler
1881 Boskovice – 1937 Vienna

Max Eisler was born in the Moravian town of Boskovice (now in the Czech Republic) on March 17, 1881, into a Jewish family. He studied art history in Vienna, Leiden, and Utrecht. In addition to teaching art history, Eisler was also a founding member of the Austrian Werkbund. Eisler, a close friend of Josef Frank and Oskar Strnad, published numerous essays on modern architecture and is regarded as the intellectual mentor of the *Wiener Wohnkultur* of the interwar period. In 1936, Eisler published an article in the English magazine *The Studio* about the Villa Rezek, "A Viennese house in the district of cottage," in which he praised the furnishings of the visionary house as an outstanding example of good taste in Vienna. Eisler died in Vienna on December 8, 1937.

Paul Engelmann

1891 Olomouc – 1965 Tel Aviv

Paul Engelmann was born in Olomouc (now in the Czech Republic) on June 14, 1891, into a Jewish family. In 1910, he began studying at Vienna's Technische Hochschule but dropped out after the first year. In addition to architecture, he was interested in literature and philosophy. In Vienna, Engelmann met Karl Kraus and became his private secretary. Engelmann became known in Vienna in 1911 for his poem praising the Goldman & Salatsch Building ("Looshaus") at Michaelerplatz 3, which was severely criticized by the Viennese. Engelmann's poem was published in Karl Kraus's magazine *Die Fackel*. From 1912, he attended Adolf Loos's private Bauschule as one of the school's first students. In the interwar period, Engelmann designed interiors and furniture in Olomouc and Vienna. Between 1926 and 1928, in collaboration with Ludwig Wittgenstein and Jacques Groag, he realized the Wittgenstein House on Kundmanngasse in the third district. In 1934, Engelmann emigrated to Tel Aviv, working there as a furniture designer for clients such as the furniture shop The Cultivated Home. Engelmann furnished the King David Hotel and the Press Club in Jerusalem. In the young state of Israel, he planned single-family homes in the spirit of his teacher and mentor Adolf Loos. In addition, he wrote articles about urban planning and architecture and published biographical essays on Adolf Loos, Ludwig Wittgenstein, and Karl Kraus. Engelmann died in Tel Aviv on February 5, 1965.

Josef Frank

1885 Baden bei Wien – 1967 Stockholm

Josef Frank was born in Baden bei Wien on July 15, 1885, into a Jewish family. His father, Ignaz Isak Frank, a textile dealer, was from Hungary; his mother, Jenny Frank, née Feilendorf, was a native Viennese. Frank grew up with an older brother, Philipp, and two younger siblings, Hedwig and Rudolf. In 1903, Frank began studying architecture at Vienna's Technische Hochschule. After completing his studies, Frank moved to Berlin and worked there in the architecture office of Bruno Möhring. In Berlin, he met the Swedish musician Anna Sebenius; they married in 1912 and moved to Vienna. In 1912, Frank co-founded the Austrian Werkbund. In 1913, he began working in the joint office of Oskar Strnad and Oskar Wlach. In 1915, during World War I, Frank was called up to the Balkan front and served as a reserve lieutenant. After the war, Frank became involved in the social housing projects of the City of Vienna. From 1919 to 1925, he taught structural theory at the Arts and Crafts School. In the 1920s, along with Adolf Loos, Otto Neurath, and Margarete Schütte-Lihotzky, he became involved in the Austrian Verband für Siedlungs- und Kleingartenwesen, a centralized association of the Austrian settlement movement. In 1925, Frank and Wlach founded the Haus & Garten home furnishings company. As artistic director, Frank designed furniture, fabrics, lamps, and rugs and planned interiors, houses, and gardens. In 1927, he was the only Austrian architect to be invited by Mies van der Rohe to design a duplex for the Weißenhofsiedlung housing project in Stuttgart. This commission was followed shortly thereafter by two prestigious projects in Vienna: the design of the interior furnishings, furniture, and garden of the Krasny House on the Hohe Warte (1927–28) and the planning of the Villa Beer in Hietzing (1929–30). In 1932, Frank oversaw the construction of the Werkbundsiedlung housing project in Hietzing. At the end of 1933, Anna and Josef Frank emigrated to Stockholm, although Frank continued to travel to Vienna frequently until 1938. On July 15, 1935, Frank celebrated his fiftieth birthday in Vienna with friends, including Soma Morgenstern, Walter Sobotka, Felix Augenfeld, Jacques Groag, Karl Hofmann, Otto Breuer, Jacqueline Groag, and Oskar Strnad's widow, Mathilde Strnad. In Stockholm, a very creative collaboration began with the Swedish firm Svenskt Tenn, a partnership that was to continue until Frank's death. Furniture and fabrics based on Frank's designs are still produced today by Svenskt Tenn. Wlach continued operating Haus & Garten in Vienna until its Aryanization in spring 1938. In August 1938, Frank officially moved his residence to Stockholm, although Frank continued to travel to Vienna frequently until 1938, and in 1939 became a Swedish citizen. In December 1941, the Jewish couple emigrated to New York City. In spring 1942, Frank began teaching architecture and design at the New School for Social Research in Manhattan as part of the University in Exile program. In exile, Frank continued designing fabrics for Svenskt Tenn as well as for the American home furnishings company F. Schumacher & Co. Josef and Anna Frank returned to Sweden in 1947. In 1949, Frank submitted several proposals for the redesign of Vienna's Stephansplatz, but they were not given any consideration. In 1965, the Austrian Gesellschaft für Architektur (Architectural Society) in Vienna mounted an exhibition devoted to Frank, and he was awarded the Grand Austrian State Prize for architecture. Anna and Josef Frank never had children. Josef Frank died in Stockholm on January 8, 1967. His elder brother, the philosopher Philipp Frank—a close friend of Albert Einstein—lived in New York beginning in 1938 and never returned to Vienna. Frank's younger sister, Hedwig Tedesko, survived the Holocaust in exile in Switzerland. His younger brother, Rudolf Frank, was murdered in a concentration camp in 1944.

Ernst Freud

1892 Vienna – 1970 London

Ernst Freud was born in Vienna, at Berggasse 19, on April 6, 1892, as the fourth of six children. His father was Sigmund Freud, the world-famous Viennese physician and founder of psychoanalysis. Ernst Freud, who initially wanted to be a painter, studied architecture from 1911 to 1913 at Vienna's Technische Hochschule and also attended Adolf Loos's private Bauschule. In 1913, he moved to Munich to continue his studies at the Technische Hochschule there. He served as a soldier in World War I and completed his studies in 1919. In Munich, Freud met Lucie Brasch. They wed in May 1920, moved to Berlin, and had three sons: Stefan Gabriel, Lucian Michael, and Clemens Rafael. Freud worked at first for the architect Alexander Baerwald, a staunch Zionist who planned houses in Palestine as well as in Europe. As an independent architect, Freud designed interiors, consulting offices for psychoanalysts, and houses in Berlin. Together with Karl Hofmann and Felix Augenfeld, he remodeled the weekend home of his sister Anna Freud in Lower Austria. After the Nazis came to power in Germany, Ernst Freud and his family emigrated to London at the end of 1933. With the help of international organizations, Sigmund Freud, along with his wife and his daughter Anna, emigrated to London on June 4, 1938. Ernst Freud had found and renovated a house for his parents in Hampstead, Maresfield Gardens, today the Freud Museum. Ernst and Lucie Freud and their children were granted British citizenship at the end of August 1939. Sigmund Freud died in London on September 23, 1939. His sisters Rosa, Marie, Adolfine, and Pauline, were murdered in concentration camps. Ernst and Lucie Freud never returned to Vienna. Beginning in the 1960s, Ernst Freud devoted himself to editing and publishing his father's correspondence. Ernst Freud died in London on April 7, 1970. His son Lucian Freud became an important painter of the twentieth century.

Karl Bernhard Gärber
1870 Vienna – 1926 Vienna
Karl Bernhard Gärber was born in Vienna on August 13, 1870, into a Jewish family and completed his studies in architecture at Vienna's Technische Hochschule. In about 1900, he established a joint architecture office with Arnold Hatschek, which endured until shortly after World War I. Their office was originally located on Salvatorgasse in the first district; in 1913, it was moved to Währinger Straße 12/Türkenstraße 1 in the ninth district, into a residential and office building that had been built by Hatschek and Gärber in 1910. Hans Glas had his architecture studio at this address—later residing in the building as well—from the beginning of his career until 1938. Karl Gärber took his own life on July 4, 1926.

Jacques Groag
1892 Olomouc – 1962 London
Jacques Groag was born in Olomouc (now in the Czech Republic) on February 5, 1892, into a Jewish family. He began studying at the Technische Hochschule in Vienna in 1909 and also attended Adolf Loos's private Bauschule. After World War I, he completed his studies in architecture; on June 25, 1919, he passed the second state examination for civil engineering. In 1926, Groag opened his own architecture office and realized a remarkable number of important projects in Vienna and in what is today the Czech Republic. In 1927–28, he oversaw the construction of the Moller House at Starkfriedgasse 19 in Pötzleinsdorf, which Adolf Loos had planned for Anny Moller-Wottitz and Hans Moller. In collaboration with Ludwig Wittgenstein and Paul Engelmann, he realized the Wittgenstein House (1925–28) at Kundmanngasse 19 in the third district. He planned two houses in the Werkbundsiedlung housing project in Hietzing. In 1937, he married Hilde Blumberger (later known as Jacqueline Groag). After the *Anschluss* in 1938, the Groags fled from Vienna to Prague and in 1939 on to London. Jacques Groag worked as an interior architect and furniture designer, while his wife was active as a fabric, rug, and wallpaper designer. Jacques Groag also worked for the British government's Utility Furniture Programme, which after World War II supported the series production of inexpensive furniture. He died in London on January 28, 1962.

Jacqueline Groag
1903 Prague – 1986 London
Jacqueline Groag was born as Hilde Pick in Prague on April 16, 1903, into a Jewish family. In 1926, she began studying with Franz Čižek at the Arts and Crafts School in Vienna, and from 1927 to 1929, she studied architecture with Josef Hoffmann. After completing her studies and following the death of her first husband, Karl Ludwig Blumberger, she worked as a designer for the Wiener Werkstätte. As Hilde Blumberger or Hilde Bloomberg, she became an internationally sought-after fabric designer. At the beginning of the 1930s, she moved to Paris and designed fabrics for Coco Chanel, Jeanne Lanvin, and Elsa Schiaparelli. In 1937, she married Jacques Groag. In 1938, the Groags fled from Vienna to Prague and in 1939 via Paris to London. In exile, she changed her name to Jacqueline Groag and opened her own design studio. With her designs, which were influenced by the graphic patterns of the Wiener Werkstätte, she became one of England's most successful fabric designers in the twentieth century and is regarded as a pioneer of modern textile design. In 1984, she was named a Royal Designer for Industry, the highest accolade for designers in Great Britain. Groag remained successful as a designer until a very advanced age. She died in London on January 13, 1986, at the age of eighty-two.

Arnold Hatschek
1865 Györ – 1931 Vienna
Arnold Hatschek was born in Györ (now in Hungary) on May 19, 1865, into a Jewish family. After completing his studies in architecture at Vienna's Technische Hochschule in 1892, he worked for the Fellner & Helmer architecture office. In about 1900, he opened a joint office with the architect Karl Bernhard Gärber. The office was located on Salvatorgasse in the first district; in 1913, it was moved to Währinger Straße 12 / Türkenstraße 1 in the ninth district, into a residential and office building that had been built by Hatschek and Gärber in 1910. Hatschek designed villas, residential and office buildings, and factories, which were frequently featured in architecture magazines. Hans Glas worked for Hatschek beginning in 1921. In 1924, the two of them realized a villa for Bertha and Robert Wortmann at Cottagegasse 90–92 in Döbling. In 1926, Hatschek built a housing complex for the City of Vienna on Chrobakgasse / Wurmsergasse in the fifteenth district. The address Währinger Straße 12/Türkenstraße 1 was also where Hans Glas had his architecture studio from the beginning of his career until 1938. He also lived in this building for a time. Arnold Hatschek died in Vienna on March 1, 1931.

Yella Hertzka

1873 Vienna – 1948 Vienna

Yella Hertzka was born as Yella Fuchs in Vienna on February 4, 1873, into a Jewish family. Her parents were Ferdinand Fuchs and Agnes Fuchs, née Tedesko. Hertzka completed a training course at a horticulture school for women, the Rheinische Obst- und Gartenbauschule für Frauen, in Bad Godesberg, Bonn. On May 20, 1897, she married the publisher Emil Hertzka, later the director of the Viennese music publishing house Universal Edition. Hertzka was involved in international women's rights and was an activist in the peace movement. In 1912, she founded a two-year horticulture school for girls at Kaasgraben 19 in Döbling, where Albert Esch was one of the instructors. Hertzka organized garden parties in the park of her horticulture school, where the guests included Gustav Mahler, Arnold Schoenberg, and Ernst Krenek. After the death of her husband in 1932, she became the primary shareholder and head of the governing board of Universal Edition. In 1938, Hertzka fled to London to escape the Nazis but returned to Vienna in 1945 and became the public administrator of the publishing house. She died in Vienna on November 13, 1948.

Karl Hofmann

1890 Vienna – 1962 Melbourne

Karl Hofmann was born in Vienna on October 3, 1890, into a Jewish family and studied architecture at Vienna's Technische Hochschule. Together with Felix Augenfeld, he founded a successful architecture studio in Döbling in 1922. Their clients included Sigmund Freud, Anna Freud, Hans Weigel, Gina Kaus, Maria Strauss-Likarz, and the City of Vienna. Hofmann and Augenfeld designed interiors, furniture, apartments, and houses in Vienna and Brno and created stage sets for Max Reinhardt. In September 1938, Hofmann and his wife, Gertrude Hofmann, who had studied architecture with Oskar Strnad at the Arts and Crafts School in Vienna, fled to Brno; in 1939, they continued on to Sydney and then finally to Melbourne. In exile, Hofmann planned a number of interiors and designed furniture in collaboration with the Hungarian furniture designer Schulim Krimper, who had also fled from Europe to Melbourne to escape the Nazis. Hofmann died in Melbourne on July 24, 1962.

Hilde Holger

1905 Vienna – 2001 London

Hilde Holger was born as Hilde Sofer in Vienna on October 18, 1905, into a Jewish family. Holger began taking dance lessons at the age of six and later toured through Europe with the ballet group founded by Gertrud Bodenwieser. In the 1920s, she started her own dance group in Vienna and became a famous expressionist dancer under the stage name Hilde Holger. Holger was Hans Glas's lover in the 1930s; the Hilde Holger Archive in London contains numerous love letters between the two. The letters to Holger from Hans Glas, who from August 1938 lived in exile in Calcutta, end in December 1938. In 1939, Hilde Holger fled from Vienna to Bombay to escape the Nazis and there married Dr. Adi Boman-Behram in 1940. She died in London in 2001.

Arnold Karplus

1877 Vitkov – 1943 Caracas

Arnold Karplus was born in Vitkov (today in the Czech Republic) on June 24, 1877, into a Jewish family. After attending the State Trade School (Staatsgewerbeschule) in Opava, he studied architecture at the Technische Hochschule in Vienna and at the German Technical University in Prague, where he graduated in 1903. Karplus moved to Vienna in around 1904 and worked in the architecture office of Alexander Wielemans von Monteforte. Karplus married Elsa Zemanek; they had four children: Hanna, Gerhard, Hans, and Ruth. From 1911 to 1927, Karplus was building director of Vienna's Baugesellschaft (building society). In 1927–28, Karplus designed a modern villa for Agathe and Otto Krasny on the Hohe Warte in Döbling. Josef Frank and Oskar Wlach, and their company Haus & Garten, were responsible for the interior design, furnishings, and the garden landscaping. In 1928–29, Karplus realized a public housing project for Red Vienna in Döbling, the "Dr. Friedrich-Dittes-Hof." When Hans Glas passed the civil engineering exam in Vienna on January 15, 1930, Karplus was a member of the examination board. From 1933 to 1938, the Karplus family lived in the Steiner House at St.-Veit-Gasse 10 in Hietzing, which Adolf Loos had planned in 1910 for the painter Lilly Steiner and her husband, Hugo Steiner. In 1934, Karplus's son, Gerhard Karplus, also an architect, began working in his father's architecture office. In about 1934, the two of them renovated the Palais Kranz on Liechtensteinstraße in the ninth district. In 1937–38, they planned a modern apartment building at Modenapark 14. Karplus's office was located at Josefstädter Straße 75 in the eighth district. In March 1939, Elsa and Arnold Karplus fled from Vienna to New York City to escape Nazi persecution. Arnold Karplus died in Caracas, Venezuela, on October 17, 1943, at the age of sixty-six.

Gerhard Karplus

1909 Vienna – 1995 New York City

Gerhard Karplus was born in Vienna on December 19, 1909, to Elsa and Arnold Karplus. He studied architecture at Vienna's Technische Hochschule from 1927 to 1933. In 1934, he began working in his father's architecture office. Together, they realized several projects in keeping with the philosophy of Viennese Modernism. Gerhard Karplus was an avid skier and competed as a ski racer for the Jewish sport club Hakoah. On August, 25, 1938, he fled from Vienna to escape Nazi persecution, first to Prague and from there via Zurich and London to New York City. Karplus was able to successfully continue his architectural career in exile, working for firms such as the renowned architecture office Mayer & Whittlesey. Gerhard Karplus's sister, Ruth Karplus (later Ruth Lotte Rogers-Altmann), fled to New York City as well and became a successful designer and painter there. His younger brother, Hans Karplus, emigrated to South America. Gerhard Karplus died in New York City on February 27, 1995.

Heinrich (Henry) Kulka
Litovel 1900 – 1971 Auckland

Heinrich Kulka was born in the Moravian town of Litovel (now in the Czech Republic) on March 29, 1900, into a Jewish family. From 1918 to 1923, he studied architecture at Vienna's Technische Hochschule and also attended Adolf Loos's private Bauschule. Kulka worked as a draftsman and as an assistant to Adolf Loos in the latter's Vienna workshop and later in Paris, where his projects included furnishing the shop of the men's clothier Knize on the Champs-Élysées. As an equal partner in the business, Kulka managed the Vienna office beginning in 1928 and was instrumental in the planning of Loos's houses Nos. 49 to 52 in the Werkbundsiedlung housing project in Hietzing. After the *Anschluss* in 1938, Kulka fled with his wife, Hilde Kulka, née Beran, and their children Elizabeth and Richard to Czechoslovakia, where his wife had relatives. In 1939, the Kulkas emigrated to Great Britain and then moved to New Zealand in 1940. There, Kulka worked for the Fletcher Construction Company, one of the country's largest building firms. Kulka was able to successfully continue his career and in New Zealand became a sought-after architect and interior designer. He died in Auckland on May 7, 1971.

Ernst Lichtblau
1883 Vienna – 1963 Vienna

Ernst Lichtblau was born in Vienna on June 24, 1883, into a Jewish family. After attending the State Trade School (Staatsgewerbeschule) in Vienna, Lichtblau studied architecture with Otto Wagner at Vienna's Academy of Fine Arts from 1902 to 1905. From 1910 to 1920, he worked on a freelance basis for the Wiener Werkstätte and Josef Hoffmann. As of 1924, Ernst Lichtblau was active as an independent architect and planned several buildings in Vienna, including the house at Wattmanngasse 29 in Hietzing, which became known as the "Chocolate House." In 1925, he founded the Ernst Lichtblau Werkstätte Ges.m.b.H and created design products for everyday use. Ernst Lichtblau was involved in several social housing projects for the City of Vienna. In 1929, he became director of the newly founded BEST, the Beratungsstelle für Inneneinrichtung des österreichischen Verbandes für Wohnungsreform (Advisory Board for Interior Decoration of the Austrian Association of Reformed Housing), located in the Karl-Marx-Hof. For the Werkbundsiedlung housing project in Hietzing, he planned the houses Nos. 41 and 42 and furnished three other houses (Nos. 2, 22, and 63) designed by other architects. Under extremely difficult circumstances, Lichtblau fled from Vienna on August 21, 1939 to escape the Nazis, first to London and then on to New York City. He initially worked as a design consultant for Macy's department store in Manhattan. On July 4, 1945, Ernst Lichtblau was granted American citizenship. In 1945, he began teaching textile design at the Cooper Union School of Art in Manhattan. In fall 1947, he became a lecturer at the Rhode Island School of Design, in Providence, Rhode Island, and later a professor for interior architecture there. In the mid-1950s, he was named dean of the school's Faculty of Architecture. He was one of the few expelled architects who came back to Vienna, returning in 1962. He was commissioned by the City of Vienna to plan a school on Grundsteingasse, in the sixteenth district. Ernst Lichtblau died in Vienna on January 8, 1963, at the age of seventy-nine.

Albert Linschütz
1900 Vienna – 1932 Vienna

Albert Linschütz was born in Vienna on March 11, 1900, into a Jewish family. From 1917 to 1922, he studied architecture at Vienna's Technische Hochschule. In the 1920s, he and Otto Breuer jointly operated a home-furnishings business in Vienna. Linschütz designed houses, apartments, interiors, and furniture. Linschütz designed, for example, the interior and furniture for the Salmannsdorf home of the renowned psychologist Alfred Adler as well as for his country home. Linschütz furnished the apartment of Anna and Philipp Rezek at Grillparzerstraße 14 in the first district, where the couple resided until they moved into the Villa Rezek in spring 1934. Bearing the note "Wohnung Dr. Rezek," photographs of the interior furnishings and furniture appeared in 1929 in the German architecture magazine *Moderne Bauformen*. The Rezek family apparently took several walnut armchairs and stools, a mahogany sideboard, wingback chairs, the parents' bed, a chaise longue, lamps, and curtains with them when they moved into the modern villa. Near the end of the 1920s, Linschütz made a name for himself in Vienna as an opponent of the construction of the city's first high-rise building, on Herrengasse, calling for protests against the planned structure. Linschütz found a supporter in Josef Frank, who also expressed concerns with regard to the city's landscape. In 1929, he married Margarete Bondi. Albert Linschütz died in Vienna in 1932 at the age of only thirty-two.

Walter Loos
1905 Vienna – 1974 Buenos Aires

Walter Loos was born in Vienna on January 12, 1905, as the son of a furniture dealer. From 1921, he studied with Rudolf Larisch and Franz Čižek at the Arts and Crafts School in Vienna and from 1923 to 1925 studied architecture there with Josef Hoffmann, also attending Josef Frank's lectures on structural theory. At that school, he met his future wife, Fridl Steininger, who studied textile art with Rosalia Rothansl and architecture with Josef Hoffmann. In the 1930/31 academic year, Loos was enrolled as an audit student at Vienna's Technische Hochschule. In the mid-1920s, he lived in Paris and worked in the studio of Adolf Loos, with whom he was not related. After his return to Vienna, he became an independent architect and furniture designer, collaborating with prominent architects such as Jacques Groag and Walter Sobotka. In the Werkbundsiedlung housing project in Hietzing, he realized houses Nos. 24 and 26. From 1932 to 1934, Walter Loos designed a cube-shaped house at Kaasgraben 24 in Döbling for the composer Alexander Zemlinsky. As staunch opponents of National Socialism, Fridl Steininger and Walter Loos emigrated to London in March 1938, moving to New York City a year later. There, Loos worked as a designer for Rena Rosenthal. In 1939, Fridl Steininger and Walter Loos married and in 1940 moved to Buenos Aires. Loos continued to be successful as a furniture designer and interior designer, while Fridl Loos operated a well-known fashion salon. Walter Loos planned holiday homes, hotels, and offices. Walter and Fridl Loos returned to Austria only a single time after World War II. Walter Loos died in Buenos Aires on March 11, 1974.

Viktor Lurje
1883 Vienna – 1944 Jaipur

Viktor Lurje was born in Vienna on July 28, 1883, into a Jewish family. From 1902 to 1906, he studied architecture at Vienna's Technische Hochschule. After completing his studies, he became a freelance designer and created craft objects, posters, fabrics, and furniture, specializing in inlay work. After World War I, he worked for the Vienna ceramics firm Brüder Schwadron, the Wiener Werkstätte, and as an assistant to Josef Hoffmann at the Arts and Crafts School. In the 1920s, Lurje became increasingly active in Germany, working for companies including the Deutsche Werkstätte and furnishing museums and hotels. In 1930, he realized a housing project for the City of Vienna at Pilgerimgasse 4–6 in the fifteenth district. In 1938, Lurje and his wife, Leopoldine Lurje, fled from Vienna to escape the Nazis, first to Shanghai and later to India. In around 1944, he furnished a palace of the maharaja in Jodhpur. Lurje died in that city on October 5, 1944.

Franz (Francis) Gino Mayer
1891 Vienna – 1971 New York

Franz Gino Mayer was born in Vienna on May 8, 1891, into a Jewish family. Mayer studied machine engineering at Vienna's Technische Hochschule, interrupted his studies in World War I, and completed them in 1919. In 1927, he became a member of Vienna's photographers' guild and in 1935 passed the master's examination. Mayer photographed numerous modern buildings in Vienna in the 1930s, including those designed by Karl Hofmann and Felix Augenfeld, and the Werkbundsiedlung housing project in Hietzing. In about 1935, he created an extensive photographic documentation of the Villa Rezek that was featured in Austrian and international architecture magazines. After the *Anschluss* with Nazi Germany in 1938, Mayer was forced to close his office in Vienna. In December of that year, he fled with his family via Belgium and France to the US. As Francis Mayer, he became a successful art photographer in New York City, working for universities and the Metropolitan Museum. Mayer died in Manhattan on April 16, 1971. The *New York Times* called him a "professional photographer of art masterpieces." He was buried at Vienna's Döbling Cemetery on July 14, 1971.

Hermann Nikolaus
1877 Transylvania – 1954 Vienna

Hermann Nikolaus was born in Transylvania (now in Romania) in 1877 and completed training in engineering. In about 1905, he settled in Vienna, where he soon specialized in window construction. In 1910, he applied for a patent in Austria for a sliding sash window he designed, subsequently registering his patent in France, Great Britain, and the US as well. In Vienna, the "Patentschiebefenster System Nikolaus" was distributed by the prominent home-furnishings shop Portois & Fix. In his workshop at Cumberlandstraße 49 in the fourteenth district, Nikolaus manufactured not only window systems but also wooden roller shutters and furniture. His constructions were used in buildings such as the Villa Rezek, the tuberculosis pavilion in Lainz, the restaurant on Vienna's Kahlenberg, the Hotel Imperial, and the headquarters of the Austrian Broadcasting Corporation on Argentinierstraße. Hermann Nikolaus died in Vienna in 1954.

Anna Plischke (Lang)
1895 Vienna – 1983 Vienna

Anna Plischke was born as Anna Schwitzer in Vienna on July 20, 1895, into a Jewish family. In 1913/14, she attended Rosalia Rothansl's textile class at the Arts and Crafts School in Vienna. Subsequently, she trained as a horticulturist in the Rothschild Gardens on the Hohe Warte in Döbling. Her first marriage was to the industrialist Robert Lang. In 1935 she wed the architect Ernst Plischke. Together, they developed a new concept of an outdoor living area as a seamless connection between the indoor and outdoor space. In 1939, to escape persecution at the hands of the Nazis, the couple fled from Vienna to Wellington, New Zealand. While Ernst Plischke worked as an architect there, Anna Plischke designed gardens characterized by natural forms, shrubs, and a distinctive creative style. With her 1951 essay "A Garden for Pleasure," she formulated her concepts for garden design in a theoretical manner as well. In 1963, the couple returned to Vienna, where Anna Plischke died on April 8, 1983.

Ernst Plischke
1903 Klosterneuburg – 1992 Vienna

Ernst Plischke was born in Klosterneuburg, near Vienna, on June 26, 1903. From 1919 to 1923, he studied architecture with Oskar Strnad at Vienna's Arts and Crafts School and from 1923 to 1926 at the Academy of Fine Arts. Plischke worked in the office of Peter Behrens and then with Josef Frank. In 1928, he designed an apartment for the ceramic artist Lucie Rie. In 1930, Plischke participated in the Werkbundsiedlung housing project in Hietzing, planning the rowhouses Nos. 35 and 36. The Gamerith House (1933–34) on the Attersee, built for Grete and Walter Gamerith, is regarded as his most important work in Austria. In 1935, he married the landscape architect Anna Lang. In 1939, the couple fled from Vienna to Wellington, New Zealand, where Plischke had a successful career as an architect and designer. Beginning in 1940, he worked as an urban planner for the Department of Housing in Wellington. In 1948, he and the architect Cedric Harold Firth opened a joint architecture office, Plischke & Firth. In 1963, Plischke and his wife returned to Vienna, where he became a professor for architecture at the Academy of Fine Arts and later the rector of that institution. Ernst Plischke died in Vienna on May 23, 1992.

Bruno Pollak

1902 Tyśmienica – 1975 London

Bruno Pollak was born in the Galician city of Tyśmienica (today in Poland) on September 30, 1902, into a Jewish family. While Pollak was still in school, the family moved to Vienna. He attended the Akademisches Gymnasium there, from which he graduated in 1920. He enrolled at Vienna's Technische Hochschule in 1921 and continued studying there, with interruptions, until 1931. He was granted Austrian citizenship in 1924. In 1927, Pollak began working as a furniture designer in Friedl Dicker and Franz Singer's studio in Vienna. Pollak became known for his stacking armchairs made of nickel-plated tubular steel, which were available in various models and produced by the Vienna steel-furniture manufacturer Josef & Leopold Quittner. Historic photographs show a Pollak-designed tubular steel cantilevered chair, painted white and featuring iron mesh lining, on the terrace of the Villa Rezek. Pollak also had his own business, called BP Stühle u. Tische, registered at the address of Dicker and Singer's studio, Wasserburggasse 2 in the ninth district. In February 1929, Pollak applied for a patent for the stackability of his chairs— through the nesting of one into another horizontally—under his own name in Austria and subsequently also in Denmark, France, Great Britain, Germany, Switzerland, and the US. In 1934, the British furniture company Practical Equipment Ltd. (PEL) acquired the rights from Pollak to series-produce his chair. In the mid-1930s, Pollak emigrated to England and never returned to Austria following World War II. He died in London in 1975.

Elizabeth Scheu Close

1912 Vienna – 2011 Minneapolis

Elisabeth "Lisl" (later Elizabeth) Scheu was born in Vienna on June 4, 1912, to the writer and publisher Helene Scheu-Riesz and the attorney Gustav Scheu. She grew up in the Scheu house at Larochegasse 3 in Hietzing, which Adolf Loos had planned for his parents in 1912–13. Already as a schoolgirl, Scheu wanted to become an architect. She began studying architecture at the Technische Hochschule in Vienna in 1930 but discontinued her studies after two years due to the misogynist atmosphere at the school and the palpable antisemitism she felt in Vienna. She emigrated to the US and completed a master's degree in architecture at the Massachusetts Institute of Technology (MIT) in Boston. In 1938, she and her fellow student and later husband Winston Close opened Close & Scheu Architects, which focused on modern architecture, and Scheu became one of the first successful female architects in the US. Elizabeth Scheu Close died in Minneapolis on November 29, 2011; she was nearly one hundred years old.

Franz Singer

1896 Vienna – 1954 Berlin

Franz Singer was born in Vienna on February 8, 1896, into a Jewish family. Beginning in 1917, he attended Johannes Itten's private art school, where he met Friedl Dicker. When Itten went to Weimar in 1919 to teach at the newly founded Bauhaus, Franz Singer and Friedl Dicker followed him, and Singer studied there until 1923. In 1926, Singer returned to Vienna and joined Dicker's design studio at Wasserburggasse 2 in the ninth district. Despite the economically difficult times, the studio was very successful. Singer and Dicker designed furniture, interiors, business premises, and houses. They furnished, for example a Montessori kindergarten and developed multifunctional furniture for small spaces. From 1934, Singer resided primarily in London but continued to work for the studio in Vienna from his home in Great Britain. In 1934, Singer also began serving as a consultant for the home furnishings companies John Lewis and Peter Jones in London. Following the *Anschluss* in 1938, Singer remained in London, where he continued to work as an architect and furniture designer, specializing in children's furniture and toys, and was involved in social housing projects. After the war, Franz Singer spent several years in Salzburg but never returned to Vienna. He died in Berlin on October 5, 1954.

Walter Sobotka

1888 Vienna – 1972 New York City

Walter Sobotka was born in Vienna on July 1, 1888, into a Jewish family. After studying architecture at the Technische Hochschule in Vienna, Sobotka was active as a freelance architect and furniture designer from 1923, furnishing numerous apartments and houses and planning two housing complexes for the City of Vienna. In 1919, he married Gisela Schönau, and in 1925, their daughter Ruth was born. In 1925, Sobotka briefly worked for Josef Frank and Oskar Wlach's home-furnishings company Haus & Garten. He designed the houses Nos. 29 and 30 for the Werkbundsiedlung housing project in Hietzing. In July 1938, Sobotka fled with his family from Vienna to New York City, where he worked as a furniture designer for Thonet Brothers New York. In 1941 he began teaching at the Carnegie Institute of Technology in Pittsburgh, first as a teaching assistant for architecture, textiles, and applied arts and from 1946 as a professor for interior architecture. In addition to his teaching activities, he continued to work as a furniture designer, interior architect, and set designer. In the 1950s, Sobotka, in partnership with Erich Boltenstern, attempted to reestablish himself as an architect in Vienna. The bureaucracy of the Austrian authorities, however, which Sobotka found deeply offensive, hindered the resumption of his career in Austria, as his "foreign" architecture license was not recognized there. Sobotka died in New York City on May 8, 1972.

Oskar Strnad

1879 Vienna – 1935 Bad Aussee

Oskar Strnad was born in Vienna on October 26, 1879, into a Jewish family. From 1900 to 1903, he studied architecture at Vienna's Technische Hochschule. On July, 6, 1906, Strnad married Mathilde Zipper, a craftswoman from Vienna. He embarked on a career as a freelance architect, interior architect, and furniture designer in Vienna and along with Oskar Wlach founded an architecture office that Josef Frank joined as well in 1913. It was in these years that Oskar Strnad realized his most important projects: the house for Oskar Hock and the villa for the writer Jakob Wassermann, both in Döbling. In 1909, Strnad started teaching general formal theory and from 1914 architecture at the Arts and Crafts School in Vienna. He designed the houses Nos. 13 and 14 for the Werkbundsiedlung housing project in Hietzing. Strnad was also an internationally sought-after set designer and created innumerable stage sets for Vienna's Volkstheater and Staatsoper, for the Salzburg Festival, and for stages in New York City and Moscow, often working closely with Max Reinhardt. Strnad died in Bad Aussee on September 3, 1935, at the age of fifty-six.

Helmut von Wagner-Freynsheim
1889 Vienna – 1968 Bregenz
Helmut von Wagner-Freynsheim was born in Vienna on January 25, 1889, as the son of a railway executive and the grandson of the art historian Carl Lützow. He studied architecture in Darmstadt and Vienna and was one of the first students at Adolf Loos's private Bauschule. Beginning in the 1920s, he realized numerous single-family homes in Vienna, the houses Nos. 69 and 70 in the Werkbundsiedlung housing project in Hietzing, and housing complexes. In 1930 he moved to Kitzbühel, where he designed modern villas. In addition to his architectural activities, Wagner-Freynsheim was also a successful watercolorist. He died in Bregenz on February 16, 1968

Ernst Wiesner
1890 Malacky – 1971 Liverpool
Ernst Wiesner was born in Malacky (now in the Slovak Republic) on January 21, 1890, into a Jewish family. From 1909 to 1911, he studied architecture at Vienna's Technische Hochschule and from 1910 to 1913 at the Academy of Fine Arts in Vienna. He subsequently worked as a freelance architect in Brno and designed numerous houses. His villas in Brno reveal the influence of Adolf Loos. His Villa Haas, which he realized at Lipová 43 in Brno in 1929–30, also displays distinct similarities to Hans Glas's Villa Rezek. In 1939, Wiesner emigrated to Great Britain, where he taught architecture at the University of Oxford and later at the University of Liverpool. Ernst Wiesner died on July 15, 1971, in Liverpool.

Oskar Wlach
1881 Vienna – 1963 New York City
Oskar Wlach was born in Vienna on April 18, 1881, into a Jewish family. He studied architecture at the Technische Hochschule from 1889 to 1903. After completing his studies, he became a freelance architect and opened an office together with Oskar Strnad, which Josef Frank joined as well in 1913. During World War I, he was drafted and stationed in Istanbul, where he planned several residential buildings. Although the joint office had closed down during the war, the three young architects continued to work together occasionally. Wlach married the Viennese painter and craftswoman Klari Krausz; the couple had no children. In 1925, Wlach and Frank founded a home-furnishings business in which the two architects were equal partners: Haus & Garten. Wlach was the business manager and Frank the artistic director. Wlach designed a great deal of furniture and interior décor, but he was always overshadowed by Frank. He designed, for example, the houses Nos. 31 and 32 for the Werkbundsiedlung housing project in Hietzing. After Frank emigrated to Sweden at the end of 1933, Wlach continued to run the business in Vienna until 1938. After the *Anschluss* in March 1938, Haus & Garten was Aryanized and taken over by Julius Theodor Kalmar and his brother Josef Kalmar as "Aryanizers." In November 1938, Oskar and Klari Wlach fled via Switzerland and Great Britain to New York City, where they arrived on May 1, 1939. Wlach had great difficulty adjusting to life in exile. He became a licensed architect in the US in 1940 but was not able to establish himself professionally. At the beginning of the 1950s, he applied for the restitution of Haus & Garten in Vienna but was unsuccessful. Oskar Wlach died, impoverished, in 1963 in a New York City nursing home. He was eighty-two.

Anny Wottitz-Moller
1900 Vienna – 1945 Haifa
Anny Wottitz was born in Vienna on May 19, 1900. Together with Friedl Dicker, she attended Johannes Itten's private art school in Vienna and from 1919 studied at the Bauhaus in Weimar. There, she completed training in bookbinding with Otto Dorfner and from 1922 also periodically managed the bookbinding shop. After stays in Berlin, she returned to Vienna and again collaborated with Dicker. In 1924, she married the textile manufacturer Hans Moller. In 1927–28, Adolf Loos designed a modern villa for the Mollers at Starkfriedgasse 19 in Pötzleinsdorf. In 1938, Anny Wottitz emigrated with her daughter, Judith, to England and later to Haifa, Israel, where she died on July 30, 1945.

Liane Zimbler
1892 Přerov – 1987 Los Angeles
Liane Zimbler was born as Juliane Angela Fischer in Přerov (now in the Czech Republic) on May 31, 1892, into a Jewish family. She worked as an illustrator and fashion designer for clients such as the well-known fashion salon of Emilie Flöge, Gustav Klimt's life companion. Zimbler initially had no formal training as an architect. From 1916, she worked as a furniture designer for the Carl Bamberger AG company and from 1918 for the Rosenberger architecture office in Vienna. She married the Viennese attorney Otto Zimbler. In 1924, she became an independent architect and furniture designer, opening her own studio at Schleifmühlgasse 5 in the fourth district. Only in the 1930/31 academic year did she enroll as an audit student at Vienna's Technische Hochschule—at the age of thirty-eight. On February 21, 1938, three weeks before the *Anschluss*, Zimbler became the first woman in Austria to pass the civil engineering examination. At the beginning of April of that year, she fled with her family from Vienna via London to the US to escape Nazi persecution. After five months, the Zimblers finally reached New York City on September 10, 1938, and then continued on to Los Angeles. Zimbler began working as a designer for Anita Toor, a prominent interior architect in Los Angeles, whose studio she took over in 1941.

She specialized in remodeling houses and apartments, designing interiors, and furnishing shops in Los Angeles. While she served as a role model for many female architects in the US, she fell into oblivion in Austria. Zimbler died in Los Angeles on November 11, 1987.

Index of Names

Bibliography

Adunka, Evelyn. *Max Eisler. Wiener Kunsthistoriker und Publizist zwischen orthodoxer Lebenspraxis, sozialem Engagement und wissenschaftlicher Exzellenz.* Hentrich & Hentrich, 2018.

Arnbom, Marie-Theres. *Die Villen von Pötzleinsdorf. Wenn Häuser Geschichten erzählen.* Almathea, 2020.

Boeckl, Matthias, ed. *Visionäre & Vertriebene. Österreichische Spuren in der modernen Architektur.* Exhibition catalog. Ernst & Sohn, 1995.

Boltenstern, Erich. *Wiener Möbel in Lichtbildern und maßgeblichen Rissen.* Julius Hoffmann Verlag, 1935.

Breuer, Otto. "Das redliche Bemühen." *Innendekoration*, 1927, 171–172.

Cavallar, Claudia, and Sebastian Hackenschmidt. "Cover Versions." In *Josef Frank: Against Design.* Edited by Christoph Thun-Hohenstein, Hermann Czech, and Sebastian Hackenschmidt. Exhibition catalog. Austrian Museum of Applied Arts, 2015.

Chakrabarti, Kaustav. *European Jewish Immigrants in India Between the Two World Wars.* Priyashilpa Prakashan, 2008.

Das Gupta, Prodosh. *My Sculpture.* Oxford Book & Stationery Co., 1955.

Döcker, Richard. *Terrassentyp, Krankenhaus, Erholungsheim, Hotel, Bürohaus, Einfamilienhaus, Siedlungshaus, Miethaus und die Stadt.* Akademischer Verlag Fritz Wedekind & Co., 1929.

Eisler, Max. "A Viennese house in the district of cottage." *The Studio*, 11, 1936, 43–47.

Eisler, Max. "Werkstätten 'Haus & Garten' in Wien." *Innendekoration*, October 1930, 403–406.

Eisler, Max. "Das Wiener Möbel gestern und heute." In *Wiener Möbel in Lichtbildern und maßgeblichen Rissen.* Edited by Erich Boltenstern. Julius Hoffmann Verlag, 1935.

Eisler, Max. *Oskar Strnad.* Gerlach und Wiedling, 1936.

Eisler, Max. "Schutz der Landschaft vor der Architektur." *profil, Österreichische Monatsschrift für bildende Kunst.* Zentralvereinigung der Architekten Österreichs, June 1, 1933.

Eisler, Max. "Peter Behrens: Landhaus einer Dame im Taunus." *Moderne Bauformen*, 36, 1932, 117-132.

Esch, Albert, and Albert Camillo Baumgartner. *Der Garten von heute. Sein Aufbau und seine Ausgestaltung.* Winkler-Verlag, 1933.

Farges, Patrick. "Exil in Kanada – ein Exil der 'kleinen Leute'?." In *Alltag im Exil.* Edited by Daniel Azuelos. Königshausen & Neumann, 2011.

Frank, Josef. "Das neuzeitliche Landhaus" (1919). In *Josef Frank 1885–1967.* Edited by Johannes Spalt and Hermann Czech. Hochschule für angewandte Kunst in Wien, 1981.

Frank, Josef. "Der Gschnas fürs G'müt und der Gschnas als Problem" (1927). In *Josef Frank. Schriften*, vol. 1. Edited by Tano Bojankin, Christopher Long, and Iris Meder. Löcker, 2012.

Frank, Josef. "Die Großstadtwohnung unserer Zeit" (1927). In Spalt and Czech, 1981.

Frank, Josef. "Die Moderne Einrichtung des Wohnhauses" (1927). In *Spalt and Czech*, 1981.

Frank, Josef. "Fassade und Interieur" (1928). In Spalt and Czech, 1981.

Frank, Josef. "Vom neuen Stil" (1927). In Spalt and Czech, 1981.

Gaugusch, Georg. *Wer einmal war – das jüdische Großbürgertum Wiens 1800–1938, S–T.* Amalthea Verlag, 2023.

Glas, Hans. "Die Eigenwohnung im Zweifamilienhaus als Beispiel für die Anwendung des Wohnbauförderungsgesetzes." *Zeitschrift des Österreichischen Ingenieur- und Architektenvereins* [Vienna], 1929, nos. 45/46, 455–456.

Glas, Hans. "Einfamilienhaus Direktor M., Beograd." *Architektur und Bautechnik* [Vienna], special issue "Dein Heim," vol. 20, nos. 5/6, March 12, 1933, 23–26.

Grimme, Karl Maria. *Gärten von Albert Esch.* Michael Winkler, 1931.

Hanisch, Ruth. "Die unsichtbare Raumkunst des Felix Augenfeld." In *Visionäre & Vertriebene. Österreichische Spuren in der modernen Architektur.* Edited by Matthias Boeckl. Exhibition catalog. Ernst & Sohn, 1995.

Hövelmann, Katharina. *Bauhaus in Wien? Möbeldesign, Innenraumgestaltung und Architektur der Wiener Ateliergemeinschaft von Friedl Dicker und Franz Singer.* Brill, 2021.

Hofmann, Else (presumably). "Eine neue Villa von Arch. Z.-V.-Ing. Hans Glas." *Österreichische Kunst*, 7, 1936, no. 2, 1936, 12–13.

Hofmann, Else (presumably). "Ein neues Haus in Döbling von Arch. Hans Glas." *Österreichische Kunst*, vol. 8, 1937, no. 11, 24.

Hubenstorf, Michael. "Österreichische Ärzte-Emigration." In *Vertriebene Vernunft II. Emigration und Exil österreichischer Wissenschaft 1930–1940.* Edited by Friedrich Stadler. LIT Verlag, 2004.

Krippner, Ulrike, Sabine Plenk, and Valerie Ludescher. *Garten der Villa Beer, Wenzgasse 12, 1130 Wien, Anlagengeschichte und Empfehlungen für eine denkmalgerechte Sanierung.* BOKU University, Department für Raum, Landschaft und Infrastruktur, Institut für Landschaftsarchitektur, i. A. der Villa Beer Foundation. Vienna, 2023.

Le Corbusier. *Vers une architecture.* Les Editions G. Cres et Cie, 1923. Chapter title: "Les yeux qui ne voient pas – Les paquebots." English edition: *Towards a New Architecture.* Translated by Frederick Etchells. J. Rodker, 1931. Chapter title: "Eyes Which Do Not See: Liners."

Maderthaner, Wolfgang. "Von der Zeit um 1860 bis zum Jahr 1945." In *Wien. Geschichte einer Stadt*, vol. 3: *Von 1790 bis zur Gegenwart.* Edited by Peter Csendes and Ferdinand Opll. Böhlau, 2006.

Matzer, Ulrike. "Das beauftragende Ehepaar Philipp und Anna Rezek." In *Villa Rezek, Conservation Management Plan.* SIMB-Verlag, 2023.

Meder, Iris, ed. *Josef Frank. Eine Moderne der Unordnung.* Anton Prustet, 2008.

Meder, Iris. "Der Garten bestimmt den Innenraum." In Thun-Hohenstein, Czech, and Hackenschmidt, 2015.

Meder, Iris. "Josef Frank, Max Eisler and Austrian Architectural Criticism." In Thun-Hohenstein, Czech, and Hackenschmidt, 2015.

Melinz, Gerhard, and Gerald Hödl. "'Jüdisches' Liegenschaftseigentum in Wien zwischen Arisierungsstrategien und Rückstellungsverfahren." In *Veröffentlichungen der Österreichischen Historikerkommission. Vermögensentzug während der NS-Zeit sowie Rückstellungen und Entschädigungen seit 1945 in Österreich*, vol. 13. Böhlau, 2004.

Miche, Wilhelm. "Raum und Bewusstsein." *Innendekoration* [Darmstadt]. October, 1931, 376–387.

Musleah, Ezekiel N. *On the Banks of the Ganga: The Sojourn of Jews in Calcutta.* Christopher Publishing House, 1975.

Neurath, Otto. "Die internationale Werkbund-siedlung als Ausstellung." *Die Form*, 1932. Reprinted in Iris Meder (ed.). *Josef Frank. Eine Moderne der Unordnung.* Anton Prustet, 2008.

Newfield, Dora. "Mr. Strauss Comes to Town." *Victory Magazine* V (1943), February, n. p.

Oberhuber, Oswald, Gabriele Koller, and Gloria Withalm. *Die Vertreibung des Geistigen aus Österreich. Zur Kulturpolitik des Nationalsozialismus.* Edited by Zentralsparkasse und Kommerzialbank Wien and Hochschule für angewandte Kunst in Wien. Hochschule für angewandte Kunst, 1985.

Österreichische Nationalbibliothek, ed. *Handbuch österreichischer Autorinnen und Autoren jüdischer Herkunft*, vol. 1. De Gruyter, 2002.

Ott-Wodni, Marlene. *Josef Frank 1885–1967, Raumgestaltung und Möbeldesign.* Böhlau, 2015.

Ottilinger, Eva B., ed. *Wohnen zwischen den Kriegen. Wiener Möbel 1914–1941.* Böhlau, 2009.

Prokop, Ursula. "Josef Frank und der kleine Kreis um Oskar Strnad und Viktor Lurje." In Thun-Hohenstein, Czech, and Hackenschmidt, 2015.

Prokop, Ursula. *Zum jüdischen Erbe in der Wiener Architektur. Der Beitrag jüdischer ArchitektInnen am Wiener Baugeschehen 1868–1938.* Böhlau, 2016.

Rainer, Michael. "Das Gebäude und sein Zustand." In *Villa Rezek, Conservation Management Plan.* SIMB-Verlag, 2023.

Röder, Werner, and Herbert A. Strauss, eds. *Biographisches Handbuch der deutschsprachigen Emigration nach 1933–1945.* De Gruyter Saur, 1999.

Roubicek, George. In *Wir und Österreich. 15 Stimmen.* Edited and published by the Federal Ministry for European and International Affairs and the Jewish Community of Vienna. Vienna, 2023.

Rukschcio, Burkhardt, and Roland Schachel. *Adolf Loos. Leben und Werk.* Second edition. Residenz Verlag, 1987.

Schrom, Georg, and Stefanie Trauttmansdorff. *Franz Singer, Friedl Dicker. 2 x Bauhaus in Wien.* Exhibition catalog. Hochschule für angewandte Kunst – Österreichische Gesellschaft für Architektur Vienna, 1988.

Schröter, Michael, ed. Sigmund Freud, *Unterdeß halten wir zusammen. Briefe an die Kinder.* Second edition. Aufbau, 2011.

Shapira, Elana, ed. *Design Dialogue: Jews, Culture and Viennese Modernism.* Böhlau, 2018.

Shapira, Elana. "Sinn und Sinnlichkeit. Der Architekt Josef Frank und seine jüdische Klientel." In Thun-Hohenstein, Czech, and Hackenschmidt, 2015.

Spalt, Johannes, and Hermann Czech, eds. *Josef Frank 1885–1967.* Exhibition catalog. Hochschule für angewandte Kunst in Wien, 1981.

Stadler, Friedrich (ed). *Vertriebene Vernunft II. Emigration und Exil österreichischer Wissenschaft 1930–1940.* LIT Verlag, 2004.

Strauss, Herbert A., and Werner Röder, eds. *International Biographical Dictionary of Central European Emigrés 1933–1945*, vol. II, part 2: *L–Z, The Arts, Sciences, and Literature.* Research Foundation for Jewish Immigration, Inc., 1983.

Strnad, Oskar. "Mit Freude Wohnen, 1932." In *Neues Wohnen, Wiener Innenraumgestaltung 1918–1938*. Exhibition catalog. Austrian Museum of Applied Arts, 1980.

Swami Agehananda Bharati (Leopold Fischer). *The Ochre Robe*. George Allen & Unwin, 1961.

Thun-Hohenstein, Christoph, Hermann Czech, and Sebastian Hackenschmidt, eds. *Josef Frank. Against Design*. Exhibition catalog. Austrian Museum of Applied Arts, 2015.

Uhlír, Jiri. "Thonet 1900–1938: Innovation und Krise." In *Bugholz, vielschichtig. Thonet und das moderne Möbeldesign*. Edited by Sebastian Hackenschmidt und Wolfgang Thillmann. Birkenhäuser, 2020.

Weibel, Peter, and Friedrich Stadler, eds. *Vertreibung der Vernunft. The cultural exodus from Austria*. Springer, 1993.

Welzig, Maria. *Josef Frank (1885–1967). Das architektonische Werk*. Böhlau,1998.

Witt-Dörring, Christian. *Wiener Innenraumgestaltung 1918–1938*. Exhibition catalog. Austrian Museum of Applied Arts, 1980.

Zimmermann, H. K. "Ein Landsitz am Taunus, erbaut von Professor Peter Behrens, Berlin." *Deutsche Kunst und Dekoration*, 70, 1932, 32–39.

Zweig, Stefan. *"Worte haben keine Macht mehr." Essays zu Politik und Zeitgeschehen 1916–1941*. Edited by Stephan Resch. Sonderzahl, 2019.

Online sources

https://alex.onb.ac.at/cgi-content/alex?apm=0&aid=dra&datum=19380004&seite=00000414&zoom=2 (accessed July 20, 2025)

https://anno.onb.ac.at/cgi-content/anno?aid=kvz&datum=19340418 (accessed July 20, 2025)

https://apis.acdh.oeaw.ac.at/person/30048 (accessed Aug. 8, 2025)

https://www.archinfo.sk/diskusia/blog/pamiatky-historia/otto-a-karl-kohnovi-praha-pariz-ekvador.html (accessed May 19, 2025)

https://www.architektenlexikon.at/de/12.htm (accessed July 27, 2025)

https://archive.metromod.net/viewer.p/69/2951/object/5138-11945051 (accessed July 1, 2025)

https://archive.org/details/in.ernet.dli.2015.277486/page/n235/mode/1up (accessed July 3, 2025)

https://boku.ac.at/fileadmin/data/H03000/H85000/H85200/TOPSTORY___Aktuelles/2025/Institutsprofil/Beer_Anlagengeschichte_BOKU_ILA_11-12-2023.pdf (accessed Aug. 8, 2025)

https://books.google.at/books?id=ONFOAQAAMAAJ&pg=PP1&source=gbs_selected_pages&cad=1#v=onepage&q&f=false (accessed May 5, 2025)

http://www.calcutta1940s.org/Frames.html (accessed Apr. 1, 2025)

https://collections.library.vanderbilt.edu/repositories/2/archival_objects/92678 (accessed July 30, 2025)

https://collections.library.vanderbilt.edu/repositories/2/archival_objects/92678 (accessed July 30, 2025)

www.czechfriends.net/newsletter/from-previous-newsletters/people-places (accessed June 7, 2025)

https://www.dasrotewien.at/seite/architekten-des-roten-wien--5 (accessed Aug. 1, 2025)

http://david.juden.at/2008/76/15_meder.htm (accessed May 1, 2024)

https://digipres.cjh.org/delivery/DeliveryManagerServlet?dps_pid=IE8917300 (accessed May 25, 2025)

https://elib.uni-stuttgart.de/handle/11682/5256 (accessed Apr. 20, 2025)

https://en.banglapedia.org/index.php/Sarkar,_Nalini_Ranjan (accessed Apr. 1, 2025)

https://gedenkbuch.univie.ac.at/person/philipp-rezek (accessed July 30, 2025)

https://gedenkbuch.univie.ac.at/person/anna-rezek-bunzl (accessed July 30, 2025)

https://www.heritagetimes.in/nalini-ranjan-sarkar-the-real-father-of-iit/ (accessed Apr. 20, 2025)

http://www.hochhausherrengasse.at/wp-content/uploads/2016/12/Wien-Museum_Hochhaus-Herrengasse.pdf (accessed Apr. 20, 2024)

https://hiko.univie.ac.at/PDF/13.pdf (accessed July 20, 2025)

https://in.worldorgs.com/catalog/kolkata/insurance-agency/hindustan-building-lic (accessed Mar. 25, 2025)

https://licindia.in/history (accessed May 1, 2025)

https://finanzbildung.oenb.at/docroot/waehrungsrechner/#/ (accessed July 20, 2025)

https://magazin.wienmuseum.at/die-kakteenmode-der-zwischenkriegszeit (accessed Apr. 30, 2025)

https://metromod.net/2019/04/04/hilde-holger/ (accessed Apr. 1, 2025)

http://ns-quellen.at/gesetz_anzeigen_detail.php?gesetz_id=29310&action=B_Read (accessed July 20, 2025) https://www.oeaw.ac.at/ikw/shoah-in-waehring (accessed July 30, 2025)

https://www.oeaw.ac.at/ikw/shoah-in-waehring/ausschluesse/juedische-aerzte-und-aerztinnen-in-waehring (accessed Aug, 10, 2025)

https://www.oeaw.ac.at/ikw/shoah-in-waehring/arisierungen-in-waehring (accessed July 20, 2025)

https://www.universaledition.com/News/Zum-75.-Todestag-von-Yella-Hertzka-Vielseitige-Netzwerkerin-Musikverlegerin-und-Kaempferin-fuer-Gleichberechtigung-Frieden-und-Freiheit/ (accessed Aug. 8, 2025)

https://ub.meduniwien.ac.at/blog/?p=33417 (accessed July 1, 2025)

https://www.ub.uni-heidelberg.de/helios/digi/digilit.html (accessed May 13, 2025)

https://www.voglhofer.at/_rtf-voglhofer/CMS_fg4e735474df264_orig_1187.pdf (accessed May 1, 2024)

https://www.wien.gv.at/kultur/kulturgut/architektur/gebaeudedaten.html (accessed May 19, 2025)

Archives

Architecture Collection in the Archive of the Albertina, Vienna
Archive of Austrian Landscape Architecture at BOKU University, Vienna
Archive of Georg Schrom, Vienna
Archive of the Jewish Community of Vienna
Archive of the Museum of Applied Arts, Vienna
Archive of the Technische Universität, Vienna
Archive of the Wien Museum
Archive of Wiener Wohnen
Archives of the Rezek family, USA
Archives of Vanderbilt University, Nashville
Austrian National Library
Austrian State Archives
Collection and Archive of the University of Applied Arts Vienna
Family archives of the Bunzl and Weinberger families, Vienna
Friedrich Achleitner Archive, Architekturzentrum Wien
Heidelberg historic literature, Heidelberg University
Hilde Holger Archive, Primavera Boman-Behram, London
Historic Land Register of the City of Vienna
Municipal and Provincial Archives of Vienna
The Federal Archives, Berlin

Image Credits

© Adolf Loos Archive/Albertina, Vienna: p. 11 A; Scheu House/photographer: unknown; p. 11 B–D; plans: Adolf Loos; p. 12 G; Moller House/ photographer: unknown; p. 12 H; plans: Adolf Loos; p. 75 F–G; photographer: Martin Gerlach Junior; p. 75 H

© Archive of the Jewish Community of Vienna: pp. 120, 121

© Archive of Maximilian Eisenköck: p. 48 Q; Dr. Rezek Apartment, published in *Moderne Bauformen* 1929, no. 10; p. 92 D; photo of Münch House, published in *Architektur und Bautechnik* [Vienna], special issue "Dein Heim," 20, nos. 5/6, 1933; p. 93 G; article by Max Eisler, published in *The Studio*, 11, 1936; p. 93 H; photo of house on Pfarrwiesengasse, published in *Österreichische Kunst*, 7, 1936, vol. 2, 1936; pp. 138, 139

© Archive of Stefan Voglhofer: p. 86 A; photographer: unknown

© Archive Villa Beer/photographer: Julius Scherb: pp. 12 I–J, 38 C–D; Villa Beer, published in *Innendekoration* November 1931

© Austrian National Library: p. 38 E; magazine *Die Bühne*, 1929

© Das Gupta, Prodosh: p. 108 F, published in *Das Gupta Prodosh, Sculptures and Drawings*, Virendra Kumar Jain, New Delhi 2008

© Döcker, Richard: p. 14 M–N; published in *Terrassentyp, Krankenhaus, Erholungsheim, Hotel, Bürohaus, Einfamilienhaus, Siedlungshaus, Miethaus und die Stadt*, Stuttgart, 1929

© Family Archives of the Rezek, Mendelsohn, and Lindau families, USA: pp. 92 F, 116 A–C, 117 D–F

© Glas, Hans/Municipal and Provincial Archives of Vienna: p. 89 C–D

© Glas, Hans/Municipal and Provincial Archives of Vienna/Municipal Building Inspection for the District of Währing (MA 37): pp. 22–25

© Gray, Eileen/National Museum of Ireland: p. 21 S

© Heidelberg historic literature, Heidelberg University: p. 30 C; photograph of Santos House, published in *Deutsche Kunst und Dekoration* 1931; (https://doi.org/10.11588/diglit.7203#0128); p. 41 F; design: Albert Linschütz, published in *Moderne Bauformen* 1928 (https://doi.org/10.11588/diglit.48540)

© Hilde Holger Archive/Primavera Boman-Behram: pp. 87, 95 I; photographer: Anton Josef Trczka ("Antios"); pp. 112, 113

© House of Arts, Brno/Dům umění: p. 83 K; Villa Haas, published in *Forum*, 1934

© LArchiv, Archive of Austrian Landscape Architecture at BOKU University, Vienna: pp. 28, 32, 33; Sammlung Albert Esch, Sig. AE-1933-1-F1

© MAK: p. 67 A

© MAK/photographer: Franz Gino Mayer (Francis G. Mayer): p. 63 R–T

© MAK/photographer: Julius Scherb: pp. 12 E–F, 20 Q–R, 38 A–B; Krasny House, published in *Innendekoration*, November 1930

© Mayer, Franz Gino (Francis G. Mayer): Photo on cover and spine; pp. 9, 10, 16, 17, 19, 29, 35, 49, 50, 51, 53, 54, 56, 57, 60, 61, 62, 63; published in *The Studio*, 11, 1936

© Oláh, Stefan: pp. 141–171

© *profil, Monatszeitschrift für bildende Kunst*: p. 71 E; Roubicek House, published in *profil*, May 1935, vol. 5

© Singer, Franz and Friedl Dicker/Collection of Georg Schrom: pp. 42 H–I, 76 I–J

© Strum & Sogl/Municipal and Provincial Archives of Vienna/Municipal Building Inspection for the District of Währing (MA 37): p. 70 B–C

© Thonet: p. 41 G

© Vanderbilt University/Philipp Rezek Papers: pp. 123, 132, 133; https:// collections.library.vanderbilt.edu/repositories/2/archival_objects/92678

© Waddell, Clyde: pp. 97 A, 105 C, 107 D–E, 110 G, published in *Clyde Waddell photograph album of Calcutta*, 1945 (University of Pennsylvania, Rare Book & Manuscript Library: Ms. Coll. 802), https://openn.library.upenn.edu/Data/0002/html/mscoll802.html

© Wien Museum/photographer: Martin Gerlach Junior: pp. 13 K–L, 27 A–B, 43 J–M, 45 N–P

© Wikipedia Commons: p. 100 B; https://commons.wikimedia.org/wiki/File:Nalini_Ranjan_Sarker_Portrait.jpg

© WStLA/photographer: Martin Gerlach: p. 89 B

About the Editors

Caroline Wohlgemuth is active as an author, curator, and lecturer. She studied law and arts management in Vienna and London. In the course of her studies at the University of Applied Arts Vienna, she explored the architecture and design of interwar Vienna and the expulsion of Jewish architects and designers in 1938, publishing the results of her research in her book *Mid-Century Modern: Visionary Furniture Design from Vienna*. The book was published in both German and English and is sold all over the world. In the Villa Rezek, she curated an exhibition devoted to the history of the house and to the story of the architect Hans Glas and the Rezek family.

Maximilian Eisenköck is a freelance architect in Vienna. His architectural activities are focused not only on the design of extraordinary new buildings but also on the preservation and renovation of structures from the twentieth century, including the Villa Rezek, built in Vienna in 1933.

Stefan Oláh is a photographer based in Vienna and at the Attersee. He designs and photographs picture series for various art, cultural, and scientific institutions. In addition, he devotes himself to the depiction of various architectural, cultural, and living spaces at the interface of art, design, architecture, and contemporary history.

Additional authors

Margit Franz qualified as a university lecturer in 2019 at the Karl-Franzens-Universität in Graz in the field of contemporary history with her book *Gateway India: Deutschsprachiges Exil in Indien zwischen britischer Kolonialherrschaft Maharadschas und Gandhi*. She devoted a chapter of this book to Hans Glas. Margit Franz is a freelance author, curator, historian, and development and peace researcher based in Eastern Styria and Western Canada.

Maria Welzig is an art historian based in Vienna, with her research focus on modernist architecture.

Acknowledgments

My special thanks go to the following people, without whose tremendous help and support this book could not have been written:

Kinga Liechtenstein for checking all of the content in the German and English versions
Catharina Rosenauer for her assistance with research and writing the brief biographies
Ela Angerer
Noah Mendelson, Karen Lindau, Margot Lindau, and Eve Lehmann, the grandchildren of Anna and Philipp Rezek
Peter Weinberger and the late Kitty Bunzl, grandniece of Anna Rezek
Sabine Loitfellner, formerly of the Archive of the Jewish Community of Vienna
Wolf-Erich Eckstein
Primavera Boman-Behram, Hilde Holger Archive, London
Matthias Boeckl, University of Applied Arts Vienna
Markus Kristan
Paulus Ebner, Archive of the Technische Universität Vienna
Thomas Matyk, MAK Museum of Applied Arts Vienna
Lothar Trierenberg, Villa Beer, Vienna
Marie-Theres Arnbom
Katharina Daimer
and the Vienna Jewish Choir.

My very special thanks go to Erwin Wurm for many interesting conversations about the art and architecture of the 1920s and 1930s, as well as about Anna and Sigmund Freud, and to my dear children, Claire, Konrad and Leopold.

Imprint

Editors
Caroline Wohlgemuth
Maximilian Eisenköck
Stefan Oláh

Concept
Caroline Wohlgemuth

Translation, copy editing, and proofreading
Douglas Deitemyer

Graphic Design
Willi Schmid

Lithography
malkasten

Printing
Gugler Medien GmbH, Melk / Donau, Austria

Park Books AG
Niederdorfstrasse 54
8001 Zurich
Switzerland
www.park-books.com
T +41 44 262 16 62
E info@park-books.com

Product safety
Responsible person pursuant to EU Regulation 2023/988 (GPSR):
GVA Gemeinsame Verlagsauslieferung Göttingen GmbH & Co. KG
Post Box 2021
37010 Göttingen
Germany
T +49 551 384 200 0
E info@gva-verlage.de

Park Books is being supported by the Federal Office of Culture with a general subsidy for the years 2026–2028.

ISBN 978-3-03860-446-4
German edition: ISBN 978-3-03860-445-7

With the kind support of

Bundesministerium
Wohnen, Kunst, Kultur,
Medien und Sport

ZukunftsFonds
der Republik Österreich